P9-EMP-785

NOTHING
JUST GIVE ME THE BALL AND GET OUT OF THE WAY
BUT
NET

NOTHING BUT NET

JUST GIVE ME THE BALL AND GET OUT OF THE WAY

BILL WALTON

with GENE WOJCIECHOWSKI

Foreword by Coach John Wooden

NEW YORK

Copyright © 1994 Bill Walton and Gene Wojciechowski

All rights reserved. No part of this book may be used or
reproduced in any manner whatsoever without written
permission of the Publisher. Printed in the United States of
America. For information address Hyperion, 114 Fifth Avenue,
New York, New York 10011.

Library of Congress Cataloging-in-Publication Data

Walton, Bill
Nothing but net : just give me the ball and get out of the way /
Bill Walton with Gene Wojciechowski;
foreword by coach John Wooden.
—1st ed.
p. cm.
ISBN 1-56282-793-6
1. Walton, Bill. 2. Basketball players—United States—
Biography. I. Wojciechowski, Gene. II. Title.
GV884.W3A3 1994
796.323′092—dc20
[B]   93-23505
                                                              CIP

First Edition
10 9 8 7 6 5 4 3 2 1

The author gratefully acknowledges permission to use the following song lyrics:

Maggie's Farm by Bob Dylan © 1965 Warner Brothers, Inc.; © renewed 1993
Special Rider Music. All rights reserved. Used by permission.

The following lyrics © Ice Nine Publishing Company, Inc:

Throwing Stones, Weir/Barlow; *I Need a Miracle,* Weir/Barlow; *Ship of Fools,*
Garcia/Hunter; *Truckin',* Garcia/Hunter/Weir/Lesh; *Casey Jones,* Garcia/
Hunter; *Ramble On Rose,* Garcia/Hunter; *Franklin's Tower,* Garcia/Hunter/
Kreutzmann; *When Push Comes to Shove,* Garcia/Hunter; *Uncle John's Band,*
Garcia/Hunter; *Touch of Gray,* Garcia/Hunter.

Acknowledgments

The author and coauthor would like to thank the following people for their time, assistance and patience: John Bassett, Carl Bassewitz, Bill Bennett, Dale Brown, Carla Byrnes, Rick Carlisle, Wilt Chamberlain, Johnny Davis, Betsy Ertmann, Emilie Hickey, Steve Herz, Lionel Hollins, Steve Jones, Arthur Kaminsky, Harvey Kubernik, Greg Lee, Maurice Lucas, Terry Lyons, T. L. Mann, Lori Matsuoka, Brian McIntyre, Janet Pawson, Ram Rod, Josh Rosenfeld, Bill Ruiz, Bill Russell, Bob Ryan, Alan Sanders, Wally Scales, Dan Shaughnessy, Craig Sherman, Earl Strom, Jeff Twiss, the entire Vandeweghe family, particularly Ernie and Gary, Ted Walton, Gloria Walton, Bruce Walton, Bob Webb, Leslie Wells, Joe Wojciechowski, John Wooden, Dave Zuccaro.

To my family—my Mom and Dad, my brothers and sister.

To my children—Adam, Nathan, Luke and Chris.

And to Lori—

Thank you for your patience and thank you for your support.

This note's for you.

Foreword

Since Bill Walton was one of the most intelligent and inquisitive basketball players with whom I ever had the pleasure of working, it is not surprising that he decided to relate on paper his thoughts about the game he loved so much.

As a player, Bill was one of the greatest who ever performed at his position at every level of competition—high school, college and professional. There are many true students of the sport who consider him to be the very finest when all aspects of the game are taken into consideration.

Furthermore, it wasn't merely the quick and proper execution of the fundamentals that made him so great. It also was his ever-boyish enthusiasm for the game that triggered his desire to work to become the best, plus his consideration for his teammates, which made him such an unselfish team player. All of these qualities stimulated those with whom he played to make the effort to become the best of which they were capable. This in turn led to championship teams at every level because basketball truly is a team game.

This book undoubtedly will substantiate the fact that Bill Walton truly is a unique, one-of-a-kind and very special individual.

John Wooden
April 14, 1993

NOTHING
JUST GIVE ME THE BALL AND GET OUT OF THE WAY
BUT
NET

Introduction

I've been lucky. I played for John Wooden at UCLA. I played for Lenny Wilkens and, later, Jack Ramsay at Portland. Red Auerbach brought me to Boston, where I was coached by K. C. Jones. All five men are members of the Naismith Memorial Basketball Hall of Fame and all five have had a profound influence on my life.

But easily one of the greatest pieces of advice I ever received came from my first coach, Rocky Graciano, who coached our team at Blessed Sacrament Elementary School in San Diego. The advice was given inside a rest room at St. Augustine High School.

I was in seventh grade at the time and our team was getting ready to play in one of the local Catholic league championship games. I was a key player for our team, and as tip-off approached, I was edgy. The whole idea of leading a team and playing for a league title terrified me. My stomach was in knots.

Rocky, who had watched me grow up, knew something was wrong. He immediately noticed that I wasn't in any hurry to leave the rest room.

"You're nervous, aren't you?" he said.

"I'm *real* nervous."

"Bill," he said, "you've got to learn to love these moments because this is what sports is all about, playing for the championship. You're going to play in a lot of these championship games before you're through, and you have to look forward to each one as if it's the greatest opportunity and the greatest moment in your life. You've got to train your-

1

self to rise to the occasion of a championship level of performance."

I've kept that theme close to my heart ever since.

Rocky was right. I ended up playing for three championships at Helix High School, three at UCLA, one at Portland and one at Boston. Never once did I forget Rocky's words. The lure of championships became the reason I played, the reason I endured injuries, the reason I envied any player who got to feel the sweet sting of champagne in his eyes during a title celebration. I know that feeling and there is nothing to match that singular moment of triumph and accomplishment. It was the reason for my existence.

I've always loved basketball because of its simplicity. The ball is perfectly round, so you can control it (unless, of course, you're playing on the parquet of Boston Garden). You play inside; the weather doesn't affect a thing. The game is reduced to you, an opponent, a ball, a basket. That's it. There are no external forces. It is the only game I know that allows you to come remotely close to sports perfection in your performance.

You start out with ten players and everyone thinks they have equal claim to the ball. As the game goes on, the better players begin to assert themselves and take control. The other guys start falling by the wayside, becoming less and less important as each minute goes by. Finally, it comes down to one player versus another player. A winner. A loser.

I miss being one of those players. Basketball was both my refuge and my escape. Because of the game, I was able to accomplish a lot in life despite my shyness and my stuttering. I was able to get a college education. I was able to play for some of the greatest basketball minds who ever pondered and meditated on the game, and to play with some of the greatest stars ever to grace the court with their presence.

I made money, but that was never the point. Everybody makes money. Stockbrokers make it. Game show hosts do too. Money isn't why you play.

Basketball is different. Not everyone can be one of the players on which the outcome of the game rests. I had my moments and my memories, and I wouldn't trade any of them—not even for all the Grateful Dead shows in the world.

Rocky told me to treat each championship as the greatest experience and opportunity in my life. I did.

After being part of the Boston Celtics winning the 1986 NBA Finals, I took part in a celebration that still thrills me whenever I think about it.

We had beaten the Houston Rockets in six games. The next day we reported to downtown Boston for the championship victory parade. None of us had bothered to go to bed. It was such an electric moment that sleep didn't matter. Winning . . . accomplishing had become our adrenaline.

We showed up on time. When you don't go to bed, you're usually early to morning events.

We took our places atop a flatbed truck that would take us slowly through the streets of Boston. It was bedlam that day. Fans tried climbing aboard, but the police would pull them off the truck and throw and shove them back into the crowd. Then they would do it all over again. People were cheering, yelling . . . essentially going crazy.

Every so often, someone from the crowd would throw us some cans of beer, which we gratefully accepted. It wouldn't have been polite or safe to throw them back.

One time I caught a beer, popped it open and happily toasted the guy who tossed it up to the truck. Just about then, Jan Volk, the Celtics' executive vice president and general manager, made his way across the flatbed and delivered a brief, but stern lecture.

"Uh, Bill, I don't think this is appropriate behavior," he said.

"Jan, this is what we *live* for. This is what *I* live for."

"Well, I still don't think you should be drinking in public."

"Jan," I said, "leave me alone."

That was for you, Rocky. This book is for everyone else.

CHAPTER 1

"Minor surgery is what they do to somebody else."
—Bill Walton, 1981

It was, in its own gray, bleak, dreary way, the most perfect day I had had in months. The date was February 12, 1990. The sound of the Grateful Dead poured out of the speakers in my garage, filling the space with energy and noise and a sort of brilliant musical creativity that made my workout easier yet. All afternoon I had been pumping iron in my weight room. Soaked in sweat, exhausted but exhilarated by the weight-lifting session, I let my mind wander, dizzy with possibilities.

In early February 1990, Kareem Abdul-Jabbar's and my jersey numbers had been retired during a special halftime ceremony at Pauley Pavilion. We remain the only two UCLA men to have their basketball numbers retired.

Yet nearly three years had passed since I last played professional basketball. Three years—it might as well have been a lifetime. My feet had betrayed me again, requiring more surgery. But I was consumed by a single thought: to play again. The kind of comeback every doctor—and you'd need an entire Rolodex to keep track of all the ones I've seen—had said was foolish, dangerous, virtually impossible.

What some of them didn't understand was that I needed the game. I craved it. I loved it. It was my passion. Why else would I have subjected myself to thirty surgeries during the course of my playing career? It wasn't for money; an NBA paycheck meant nothing to me. Some played for silver, I played for life.

The game dominated my every thought. I was obsessed and driven with the need to return to the basketball court. That's why I was in the weight room that day and nearly every day before it for the previous fifteen years.

Done with the workout, I closed the garage door and began to make the short walk, maybe twenty yards or so, to the Jacuzzi and pool area of the house. I was fired up. The comeback was going to happen. I was on track.

As I walked, a pain, worse than usual, surged through my right leg. With each step the pain grew progressively worse.

I made it across the driveway and to the pool's edge, but then the pain became too great. I couldn't take another step. I ordered my foot to move forward, but it had taken on a life of its own. I was only a few yards away from the Jacuzzi, but I couldn't put the foot on the pavement one more time. I couldn't take it. There was just too much pain.

With tears streaming down my cheeks, jaws grinding in a horrible grimace, I gingerly dropped to my hands and knees and crawled toward the pool house, where a phone was located. I was embarrassed by the pain's overpowering grip on me.

I eventually reached the pool house, called a friend who lived nearby, and asked him to come and find me my crutches. When he arrived, I struggled up and made my way into the house, where I immediately called Dr. Tony Daly. Dr. Daly, one of the few doctors I trust, also serves as the team physican for the Los Angeles Clippers and has treated me for years.

I was accustomed to pain. A professional athlete learns to expect it and cope with it. But this was different. This was accumulated pain with no new injury, the kind that just won't go away. The mere thought of my foot touching the floor was almost too much to take.

Dr. Daly listened to my brief description of the afternoon's events, and without hesitation told me to come in.

Never before did I dread a visit to him as much as this one. Shortly after my arrival, I was wheeled to the X-ray room. Not long after that, Dr. Daly presented me the chilling diagnosis.

"There's nothing left," he said. "There's no chance. There's no hope."

My foot and ankle, Dr. Daly explained, were partially dislocated and the bones were disintegrating because they were grinding into each other. The talus bone, which joins with the ends of the fibula, tibia and calcaneus to form the ankle joint, had slipped. It had actually moved out of the joint. In laymen's terms, the leg bone was almost ready to slide off its base and rip through my skin.

No hope. I had heard those words before, ignored them and gone on to play basketball, much to the dismay of the doctors who had examined and treated my damaged feet. This would be the same, I tried telling myself. I would play again.

"Bill, you need an ankle fusion," Dr. Daly said.

For several years, Dr. Daly and Dr. F. William Wagner, my two orthopedic surgeons, had strongly suggested I undergo the ankle-fusion procedure. Each time I dismissed their comments. I was in denial. I refused to believe that my life as a player was truly in jeopardy.

In fact, almost a year had passed since Dr. Wagner had told me I had two options: ankle fusion (his recommendation) or ankle-cord lengthening. He knew my troubled feet better than almost anyone. If not for Dr. Wagner, in conjunction with Dr. Daly, I wouldn't have been able to make a last run with the Boston Celtics and be part of that 1986 NBA championship team.

However, this time there was nothing left to fix. I had stalled for almost a year, but I would have to have the ankle-fusion surgery.

Because of a previous commitment I had made to the people at the San Diego Hall of Champions, the operation would have to wait at least five more weeks. My hometown Hall of Fame had been kind enough to select me as its newest member. I didn't think it would be acceptable to skip the induction ceremonies. I had told them weeks earlier I would attend, accept the award and make a speech.

This was the city I had been born and raised in, the city where I learned to play basketball, the city where I live. Yet I would have to suffer what I considered to be the ultimate indignity by showing up at my own induction ceremony wearing coat, tie and ankle cast . . . on crutches.

Of course, the downside to all this was the five-week delay in the surgery. It is one thing to have surgery; it is quite another to spend each of those thirty-five days wondering what is going to happen to the rest of your life. Every night I would lie in bed filled with the terror of what was about to happen. The finality of my decision was beginning to hit me. Once those four large steel bolts were threaded through my right ankle, I would never be able to play basketball again. Ever.

I would never be able to hike again. Or play basketball with my four sons. Or run. Or even walk fast. The simplest, most elementary physical acts, movements that most of us take for granted, would forever be altered in my life. It was the longest few weeks of my life.

The Hall of Fame awards dinner went well enough. My friend and former UCLA teammate Jamaal Wilkes delivered an eloquent introduction, which was followed by my short acceptance speech. I was distracted, because my surgery awaited the next day.

Operating rooms were nothing new to me. Sadly, I had spent more than my share under a surgeon's knife. Legs. Hands. Ankles. Feet. Hardly a part of my body hadn't felt the slice of a scalpel.

But that day at Presbyterian Intercommunity Hospital in Whittier was different. For the first time in my adult life, I was so afraid of what was going to take place on that operating table. I was afraid for my future. What if it didn't work? What if the pain didn't go away?

Sleep was out of the question. It felt as if twelve members of the Jabbar family reunion were stabbing my right foot and ankle with fire-kissed swords, while holding a blowtorch to the same area. Jabbar and his relatives never grew tired, and the blowtorch never seemed to run out of fuel.

The attendants came to my hospital room early in the morning. I was placed on a gurney for the trip to the operating room. That's when I was overwhelmed by the moment, by the finality of it all.

My career had included individual and team success. But it had also included many more instances of injury, frustration, disappointment and pain. As I lay helplessly on my back, the hospital hallway lights flashing past, I was overcome by sadness, humiliation, and a sense of defeat. My talents seemed wasted. I had had so much opportunity, so much potential, and yet I accomplished so little.

As they wheeled me closer to the operating room, it all became clear how helpless and how hapless I was. My life had become a great wasteland of failure. It was an utterly depressing realization.

I had played on two national championship teams at UCLA and been part of two NBA championships, one with the Portland Trail Blazers, the other with the Celtics. I had been raised by two loving, caring parents, Ted and Gloria Walton, and been coached by the likes of John Wooden, Lenny Wilkens, Jack Ramsay, Red Auerbach and K. C. Jones, among others. I had seen the world. But nothing prepared me for what was about to take place on this operating table.

I was so sad that I started crying. I couldn't stop; the tears kept rolling down my cheeks. A few minutes later Dr. Daly came over to check on me. As he approached, I tried to suppress my emotions. It was useless. I just couldn't keep it together.

"Bill, what's wrong?" Dr. Daly said.

"I'm really, really scared," I said.

By then, some of the other operating-room personnel had noticed me crying. I was embarrassed by the emotional display, but what could I do? I was strapped to a gurney with nowhere to go.

Dr. Daly found a towel for me, which I immediately used to cover my face, to cover my failures, my tears.

"It's going to be okay, Bill," he said. "When we're through, you're not going to believe how good it's going to be."

A nurse came over and gave me an injection of something. It was supposed to make me sleep, but I didn't want to close my eyes. I didn't want to submit. I didn't want it to end. But I had no choice.

That day, I started over.

"Strawberry Fields Forever"
—John Lennon

Twenty-five years ago I sat at a patio table at the Stanford golf course and country club with Coach Howard Dallmar and two other high school basketball recruits, a guard from Los Angeles, Greg Lee, and a forward from Santa Barbara, Keith Wilkes. I can close my eyes and remember everything about that breakfast meeting, right down to the fresh strawberries that were served.

Our weekend recruiting trip (my very first) was almost done and Dallmar was busy making one last emotional sales pitch before we were driven to the airport. The pressure applied during the entire visit had been unrelenting. Everywhere we went—and this was the first time Lee, Wilkes and I had ever been together—there was a Stanford chaperon. Here we were, three of the top high school players in the country, and we couldn' get a moment to ourselves to talk about ball. Instead, we had to smile a lot and look interested whenever Dallmar, who was a nice enough guy, offered more reasons why we ought to sign with Stanford.

Shortly before we were finished with breakfast, Dallmar excused himself to go to the rest room. As he disappeared from view, we immediately leaned in and then lowered our voices, so no one at the adjoining tables could hear.

"Hey, look," we said, "we've got to forget about this. We should just all go to UCLA and play together."

And that's exactly what happened. Three signatures later, UCLA got Lee, Wilkes and me, one of the easiest signees of all time.

In return, we got John Wooden, the first and only person to be inducted into the Basketball Hall of Fame as a player and as a coach. We made out like bandits.

Believe it or not, as early as sixth grade, I started thinking about playing at UCLA. This was no coincidence either. That's the year, 1963, I first met John Wooden, the man who would ultimately teach me almost everything I know about basketball and, in the process, teach me about life.

Back in 1963, John Wooden had yet to win the first of his ten NCAA championships, but that hardly mattered. All the coaches in San Diego were well aware of the former Purdue All-American. A lot of them were already utilizing his offensive and defensive philosophies and applying them to their own teams.

It just so happened that my parents, who weren't athletes and had little to do with my playing career, let me attend a basketball clinic at the University of San Diego one day. Rocky Graciano was the guy who made the arrangements and encouraged me to go.

One of the featured speakers was Coach Wooden. Even though I was only in sixth grade, I already loved everything about the sport. And when John Wooden talked about it that day, the concepts and teachings seemed to come alive. I was in absolute awe of this man who treated the game with such reverence and respect.

It wasn't until 1965 that I actually watched a Bruins game on television. In fact, it was the first time I ever saw a basketball game, pro or college, on television.

The Bruins were playing Michigan in the NCAA championships at Portland. They were incredible. Michigan had a powerful team, led by Coach David Strack and a starting lineup that included Cazzie Russell and John Thompson in the backcourt, Bill Buntin at center and Oliver Darden and captain Larry Tregoning as forwards. The Wolverines were a big, powerful, muscular team whose sheer size often intimidated opponents.

In contrast, UCLA featured skinny, scrawny guys—much like me—who based their game on ball movement, teamwork and quickness. It was a style epitomized by the play of Bruins guard Gail Goodrich, who set an NCAA record by scoring 42 points in the championship game. As UCLA put the finishing touches on a 91–80 victory and its second championship in as many years, I said to myself, "That's what I want to do. That's where I want to play."

Two years later, as a sophomore at Helix High School, I received my very first letter from a college recruiter. The recruiter was Denny Crum, and he was an assistant on Coach Wooden's UCLA staff. I couldn't believe it. UCLA was interested in me.

There was nothing fancy about the letter. It said something like "We heard you were a good basketball player and we wanted to introduce ourselves. We also wanted to make sure you're taking the proper academic courses required for admission to UCLA."

Soon thereafter, I started to follow the Bruins with a passion. When I was sixteen, I saw Lew Alcindor play his last game at Pauley Pavilion. The place was packed for the finals of the NCAA West Regional, and the atmosphere was electric.

Alcindor scored 17 points in that game and UCLA easily

defeated Santa Clara, 90–52, to advance to the Final Four. But it wasn't just Alcindor and the victory that impressed me. It was the energy, and the way the Bruins played and conducted themselves. The crowd was surging, the band was jamming, the cheerleaders were dancing. I was sold.

By my senior season at Helix, every major college in the country was trying to sign me to a letter of intent. I was 6′ 11″ and had moved from forward to center following the graduation of my older brother Bruce. It was an exciting time, but also one in which I saw human nature at its best and worst.

Some of those recruiters had no shame, to say nothing of morals or ethics. They would promise you anything and everything. I quickly eliminated those schools from any consideration. In fact, I soon became convinced there was only one program and one coach for me: UCLA and John Wooden.

Denny Crum is the person who insisted that Coach Wooden, who rarely scouted prospective players, fly down to San Diego and watch me play. Coach Wooden agreed to make a rare exception and attended one of our Helix games. At a later date, he came to our house for dinner.

Coach Wooden's recruiting speech was short, to the point and like none of the others I had heard. He didn't believe in trying to convince somebody to come to UCLA. He only wanted players who wished to be there in the first place.

"I'm not here to tell you how great you're going to be," he said. "That's going to be up to you. You know about our program and you know we'd like to offer you a scholarship. If you accept it, I think it will be good for you. If you come to UCLA, you'll play center and you'll play with good players."

I've always respected John Wooden because he never promised a thing. That evening or ever. He didn't guarantee me a starting position. He didn't say he was going to build the offense around me. Everything would have to be earned, exactly the way I wanted it.

Of course, Coach Wooden had built his program to the point where he could afford to be choosy. He could basically say to the best high school players, "I want you, you, you, you and you." And we would say, "Sure. Where do we sign?" But I also believe that John Wooden would have made the same speech to me that night even if he weren't at UCLA. He wasn't interested in playing silly mind games. Either you wanted to be part of his team or you didn't. In his twenty-seven years at UCLA, he only visited twelve recruits' homes.

Anyway, I wasn't the type of player who always wanted to get the ball and score and win the game. That wasn't my style of play. I could do it on a limited basis, but I liked to see the ball move around and see the team win. I didn't want to be in a situation where I was going to be taking 25, 30 shots a game. With Coach Wooden's system and the talent he had assembled at UCLA, I didn't think that would be the case.

John Wooden wasn't the only person Crum convinced to come watch me play. One time he invited Greg Lee to join him for a Helix game. This wasn't unusual. Crum, who was recruiting six or seven guys at the time for UCLA's Class of '74, would always arrange for us to see the other players UCLA was trying to sign.

I don't recall much about the win, but Greg said I scored something like 50 points, had 30 rebounds and never took a jump shot. He said I basically let everyone else on the team shoot and I would score my points on tip-ins and putbacks. That sounds about right.

During the game, Crum told Greg, "Everyone's talking about this left-handed guy named Tom McMillen, but Bill's in another world." McMillen, who would later sign with Maryland, was considered the nation's top recruit.

When it came time to make a final decision, there wasn't much of a choice. There was UCLA and everyone else. Second place was nowhere.

I chose UCLA because of John Wooden and several other factors: the players already on the roster, the players coming in, the legacy of Alcindor, the NCAA championships, the academic reputation of UCLA, the beauty of Pauley Pavilion and the proximity of the campus to San Diego. I talked to some other schools, but when it came right down it, they never had a chance. I wanted to play for John Wooden at UCLA. And I wanted to win.

Summer couldn't end fast enough for me. As much as I loved my parents, I couldn't wait to leave home and get away. I wanted to be on my own, to live life without someone looking over my shoulder. Little did I realize that by becoming a member of Coach Wooden's team, I was actually going to be under more supervision than I was at home. In essence, he replaced my parents.

From the very moment each player arrived on campus, Coach Wooden made sure we understood what was expected of us. He did a fantastic job of creating a mood of championship behavior. He simply said that we were there to get an education and to win NCAA titles. Nothing less would be acceptable to him, the fans, the school and, most importantly, to us.

John Wooden considered it a privilege to coach at UCLA. To that end, he was determined to build and maintain a championship program capable of withstanding the test of time. He made a complete and total commitment to the school and he demanded that his players do the same. That was typical of him. Never did he ask his players to do something unless he had done it himself.

The NCAA didn't allow practice to begin until October 15, which just happened to be the day after Coach Wooden's birthday. Actually, that makes all the sense in the world:

John Wooden's birthday: October 14 . . . the official start of the basketball season: October 15. Perfect.

One of the greatest things that Coach Wooden taught us—and he taught us so much—was how to learn. The learning process is an acquired skill. On my very first day as a freshman player at UCLA, Coach Wooden walked into the locker room, pulled up a stool, sat down and told us exactly how he wanted us to put on our socks, how to lace our shoes, how to put on those shoes, how to tuck our jerseys in, how to tie the drawstrings in our pants, how to dry our hair after practice. He showed us how to warm up, how to shoot a jump shot, how to eat properly, how to organize our day, how and when to sleep. No detail was too small.

As freshmen, we were ready to kick butt and show how cool we were. But instead of giving us the ball and pointing us toward the court, Coach Wooden knew it was more important to first teach the most basic of skills. A solid, indestructible foundation.

My entire game-day routine—in fact, my entire life routine—was taught to me by John Wooden. It was simple: Eat a meal 4½ hours before a game. Go to bed immediately after eating. Keep the room entirely quiet—no radio, TV, phone or stereo. Wake up 2½ hours before the game and go directly to the arena. Play the game. Be off your feet by midnight, no matter what.

John Wooden was expert in having his players emotionally and physically ready to play. He used to tell us that it was more important to sleep well two nights before a game than the night before. He said sleep was a cumulative thing, and there was no way the body could recharge itself with only one night's worth of rest. "You've got to build up to an event," he said. Who knows if any of it was true, but I believed him.

The purpose of all this was to show us the importance of starting with the basics, of mastering those basics and then moving on to the next level. After all, once you learn how to teach yourself something, you can do anything.

Freshmen were ineligible for the varsity team in my college years. We had our own team and our own season. During that six-week practice period, we worked on everything. Not a second was wasted.

We were required to be on the floor at precisely 3 p.m., with practice beginning at 3:30. For the next two hours (1½ hours during the conference season) Coach Wooden would prowl the sidelines like a caged tiger. And if we didn't perform to his satisfaction or if we screwed around too much, he would tell the managers to return the balls to the racks, turn off the gym lights, order us off the court and lock the doors. That was his punishment, to deny us the chance to perform, to play, to learn.

He taught us every facet of the game: the press offense, the press defense, inbounding the ball, zones, man-to-man defense, fast breaks . . . you name it, we did it. We didn't have any plays, not a single one. Coach Wooden simply wanted us to come up the floor, get in our basic positions, build triangles and get the ball to the best players. There was no real mystery to the system. It was easy: let the best players make the plays. He was able to develop good players into much better players.

John Wooden didn't complicate things. His idea of coaching a game wasn't to have the star player acting as a decoy. He wanted the star player to have the ball. And nobody, except Red Auerbach of the Celtics, knew how to put a team together as well as John Wooden. Finding that proper mix of players is probably more important than actually coaching a team. Coach Wooden would recruit a top player, assess that player's strengths and weaknesses, and then find other players who complemented those strengths and who compensated for those weaknesses.

This is a man who is tireless in his devotion to promoting the game. He wasn't one of those coaches who sat around restaurants shooting the breeze with boosters or trying to make deals so he could earn more money. Even now, he's out there teaching basketball, promoting basketball. He loves the game. He lives the game. He dreams about the game.

You would never find a more meticulously organized coach than John Wooden. He kept a file of every practice schedule and assorted notations for each of his twenty-seven seasons at UCLA. If it were, say, November 10, 1973, and Coach Wooden wanted to go back and see what he had done in practice a year earlier, all he had to do was pluck a card from his file. He was always examining his own methods, always trying to refine and improve the way he taught the game.

Our practice sessions were his own private laboratory of basketball. And throughout my entire freshman season, I thought I was the guinea pig in one of his grand experiments.

Imagine my surprise when Coach Wooden instructed me to play the high post and stay there while we ran his offense. He wanted me to run his high-post attack, which is the exact opposite of what I wanted to do. If you're a center in a high-post offense, all you do is pass the ball and set screens for other guys. Hey, I was all for teamwork, but I also wanted to shoot once in a while or, as my teammates will attest, all the time. When you're 6′ 11″ and you're playing against all these stiffs eighteen feet away from the basket, you start wondering "When is it going to be my turn?"

Coach Wooden would have none of my complaints. He wanted me right where he put me. I thought it was a mistake, and I told him so. I was still a teenager. I thought everything adults told me was a mistake.

"Hey, Coach, this is not what I had in mind when I came here," I said. "I want to get under the basket and get some opportunities."

"I know that, Bill," he said, "I know that. But all that comes later. It comes after you learn how to play away from the basket."

I didn't believe it at the time, but it turned out that playing the high post that entire freshman season was the best thing in the world for me. It allowed me to develop skills that I would need as I moved up to each new level of competition. I became more versatile, which is the key to success in basketball and life. Had I not learned how to play away from the basket, my game would have stagnated. I wasn't a great or even a good perimeter player, but the time spent at the high post taught me footwork, positioning and different moves that I would use countless times during my career. Later, when I found myself matched against the tallest players in the game, Kareem Abdul-Jabbar, or Artis Gilmore, or Ralph Sampson, I could step out to the perimeter, forcing them to come guard me. More times than not, that opened up a passing lane for another player to score.

John Wooden was so intense during those practices. He never stopped moving, never stopped chattering away. Up and down the court he would pace, always barking out his pet little phrases.

"Be quick, but don't hurry."

"I don't want turnovers, but if we're going to have turnovers, I want them of commission, not of omission."

"Never mistake activity for achievement."

"Keep the head directly over the midpoint between the two feet."

"Failing to prepare is preparing to fail."

"Flexibility is the key to stability."

"That's not your shot. You're not looking for your teammates."

"When everybody thinks alike, nobody thinks."

"Goodness gracious sakes alive, Bill. How many times do I have to tell you: Don't outlet the ball down the middle of the court!"

On and on and on it went, to the point where those sayings became part of your life. You have to understand that John Wooden wasn't simply teaching basketball. To him, basketball was a microcosm of life itself, which is why our practices became psychological training sessions and philosophy sessions. If you asked him for advice, he would always say, "I don't give advice, I give opinions."

Some people hated to practice. Not me. I needed the work, the constant repetition. Every day I woke up with a sense of anticipation because I knew John Wooden already was working on the details of that afternoon's session. I'd ride my bike over to his office and constantly bug him.

"Hey, Coach, what are we going to do today? How can I get more shots? Why isn't this guy playing more? Why are we doing this?"

He probably got tired of the same questions, but I couldn't help it. Because of the talent we had, our practices were almost always more interesting and competitive than the actual games we played during the season.

Swen Nater was the best center I ever faced in college and he was our second-stringer at UCLA. In fact, our entire second team could have started most anywhere else in the country.

The minute practice ended, Coach Wooden became as calm and composed as a minister. It was a most amazing personality transformation. Before practice, he would be as calm as could be. During games, perfectly calm. After the games, a sweeheart. But during practice? A hurricane!

I dug it. I was a self-motivated player who never needed much prodding. When John Wooden got fired up, I was right there with him. I loved to feel his energy and passion for the game. Every day in the gym he would create an environment of competition. When you walked onto the floor in that UCLA uniform, you were competing against an ideal, an abstract standard of excellence defined by John Wooden. The actual opponents mattered little. It was the ideal that mattered most.

Looking back on my years at UCLA, 1970–74, I feel so lucky to have played for John Wooden at the peak of his career. He was such a great student of the game, as well as such a great teacher. But he wasn't perfect. Like all of us, he made mistakes along the way. Not many, but a few.

John Wooden has often said that when he first started coaching, he had lots of rules and few suggestions. As time went on, he had fewer rules and lots of suggestions. I played for him in four of his last five seasons at UCLA, and I can assure you, there were some rules that never became suggestions.

In 1972, as part of an on-campus anti-Vietnam War protest, I helped barricade the UCLA administration building. As some of my teammates helped out, I commandeered a UCLA golf cart and drove to the building's front door.

Later, I participated in another antiwar protest which took place off campus, this time on Wilshire Boulevard. The Los Angeles police weren't quite as understanding as UCLA's security force and at one point they started clubbing some of the protesters. For whatever reason, they didn't hit me, but they did arrest me for unlawful assembly and disturbing the peace. I just kept yelling, "The whole world is watching!"

Coach Wooden wasn't too pleased. I'm sure it disappointed him, but at least he made the effort to understand my motives and intentions. I thought the war was wrong. Still do.

Coach Wooden was also against the war. And while he defended my right to protest, he felt very strongly that my actions as a protester shouldn't violate the rights of others.

It was during one of our many discussions on the subject of individualism and society (our talks weren't limited to basketball) that John Wooden wondered if I might accomplish more by writing letters to my elected officials.

In 1974, rather than writing to my congressman or even my senator, I decided to go straight to the top, to President Richard Nixon. So one day, while begging John Wooden for more shots during a meeting at his office, I took a few sheets of stationery and a few envelopes with the Bruins letterhead, which had "UCLA Basketball" at the top, followed by "NCAA Champions" and a listing of all the championship seasons. Then I wrote a letter to Nixon and listed some of the well-known atrocities of his administration. At the end of the letter, I thanked him for his time and requested that he immediately resign.

Abbie Hoffman once said, "Sacred cows make the best hamburger."

That done, I signed it and asked other members of the team to do the same. They all agreed. I then went to see John Wooden.

"Coach," I said, "we've got this letter here and we'd love for you to be part of it. Would you mind signing this, please?"

"Sure, Bill, let me take a look at it," he said.

He took the letter and started reading. As his eyes scanned each line you could see the change in his demeanor. His hands gripped the paper a little tighter and his knuckles eventually went white. He was literally shaking with anger when he reached the end of the letter.

"How could you do this?" he said, looking at me like a parent who had been betrayed by his son.

"Well, you told me to write letters, so I did."

"Bill," he said, the frustration in his voice so evident, "you've just got so much to learn."

That was obvious, but we went ahead and sent the letter anyway to Nixon. He did resign later that year. I'd like to think it was our letter that did it.

There were other Wooden rules you didn't dare defy, such as his team dress code and grooming requirements. Coach Wooden was a stickler for neat appearances. He and I never did agree on his rules regarding hair length.

In the introductory letter he sent each of us before every season, we were forbidden to wear a mustache, beard or goatee and our sideburns could be no longer than the top of the lobes of the ear. Our hair, read the letter, was to be of "reasonable length, with the coaches being the judges as to what is reasonable length."

I was tired of looking like an Army draftee on his way to Vietnam. I wanted to make my own decisions.

I showed up for Picture Day the first day of my senior season and was immediately kicked out of Pauley Pavilion. Coach Wooden took one look at me and said, "Bill, your hair's too long." I thought my hair was okay—in fact, I had just gotten it cut—but Wooden didn't think so. I got on my bike, rode down to Westwood and got it cut again.

Coach Wooden was willing to listen to an argument—up to a point. After that, the conversation would come to an abrupt end.

Me: "Coach, I've thought about it for a long time and I think I should be allowed to grow my hair as long as I want."

Coach Wooden: "I'm sorry, Bill, but you know how I feel on the subject."

Me: "But, Coach, I don't think it's fair that we can't decide for ourselves what the proper hair length is."

Coach Wooden: "You feel strongly about this, do you?"

Me: "Yes, very strongly."

Coach Wooden: "Well, Bill, I feel strongly about this particular rule too. So we're going to miss you, but it was nice having you here."

End of discussion.

Even today, I'm still haunted by that rule on hair length. In 1992, I appeared with John Wooden on Roy Firestone's *Up Close* show. I've been a guest on Roy's show dozens of times, but this was different. This was with John Wooden.

Self-conscious as I was about the prospect of our first-ever appearance together on live TV, I asked the makeup artist to pull out the scissors and give me a quick buzz. I wore a coat and tie for the show, my new uniform. John Wooden arrived at the studio wearing a sweater and a golf shirt. It was a funny role reversal. It even produced a halfhearted on-air apology from John Wooden about his casual dress.

I also wasn't a big fan of John Wooden's rule against criticizing a teammate. I was always tough on my teammates. I was tougher on myself. I didn't expect crummy players to be good, or good players to be great, but I did expect them to play to their absolute potential, to try their hardest, to be committed. Anything less and I usually went wild.

It wasn't unusual for me to run by the bench during a game and yell at Coach Wooden as I moved upcourt, "Get me some rebounders in here." I wanted to win. I was a bit overbearing at times.

I flat out told teammates they better not miss a shot. Heck, I can miss just as well as they can. I told them they weren't hustling enough, that they weren't dedicated enough, that they didn't care enough about the game.

Coach Wooden regularly warned me to curtail the criticism. I wasn't much for diplomacy. That's when he said he'd cut me from the team if I continued to blast my teammates. Now that got my attention. I toned it down . . . just enough.

The worst language I ever heard John Wooden use was the word "crap." He said it on the court in a team meeting and we literally fell on the ground laughing in disbelief.

The angriest I ever saw him was during a road trip at the 1974 NCAA West Regional in Tucson, Arizona. We had beaten Dayton in triple overtime earlier that night and now a few of us were relaxing in the hotel Jacuzzi. It was pretty late and we were still fired up from the victory. I mean, you just couldn't come back to your room after a game like that, get into bed and fall asleep. The adrenaline was still flashing through your veins.

I had on a pair of shorts, but the elastic waistband was shot and they kept slipping down a little. Rather than keep tugging at the shorts, I just took them off. I figured, what's the harm? It was very late and nobody would be the wiser.

Yes, well, just about that time, one of our assistant coaches, Gary Cunningham, came walking by.

"Bill, your shorts," said one of my teammates.

"Don't worry," I said. "He'll understand."

Cunningham acted as if he never saw us. But a little while later, the hotel night manager came out and said, "Hey, you guys have got to keep your shorts on."

The hotel manager was peeved. He called Coach Wooden and complained about our behavior. That's all Coach Wooden had to hear. He bolted out of his room, still wearing his nightgown and stocking cap, and marched directly to the Jacuzzi.

"Go to your rooms immediately!" he said.

Needless to say, there were no postgame Jacuzzi stops the rest of the tournament.

It is probably just as well that John Wooden never heard what we yelled to Denny Crum shortly before a 1972 Final Four semifinal game at the Sports Arena in Los Angeles.

Crum, in only his first year as Louisville's head coach, had led the Cardinals to a 23–3 regular season record. Three tournament games later, he faced his old coach, John Wooden.

Florida State and North Carolina played in the first game. As that game dragged on, we found ourselves in the same holding area as the Louisville players. Crum was standing there with his team, so we started yelling, "Hey, Coach Crum! Hey, Denny, what are you doing with that team? Why don't you come over and join a real team?"

We were kidding, of course. Crum had recruited us and brought us together at UCLA. We loved the guy. But he bailed out on us and went to Louisville. None of us from Southern California had ever even heard of Louisville.

Crum knew we were joking with him, but his players didn't. You should have seen their faces. They were shocked at the way we were talking to their coach. They were even more shocked when we beat them by 19 points.

It was tough for John Wooden to stay mad at us for too long. Basically we were good guys. We liked to have fun and play ball. That's what we enjoyed.

Every opening night of every season I played at UCLA, Coach Wooden would come into the locker room before tip-off and talk about his expectations for us that year.

The first time I heard the speech I was awestruck. I watched as he slowly paced the room, the whole time telling us how we needed to act like champions and to perform like champions. Then he stopped and glanced at the floor, as if he had noticed something out of place. We naturally followed his gaze and there it was, a penny sitting on its edge against the locker room wall.

Coach Wooden picked up the coin and held it up for all to see.

"Men," he said, "this penny means good luck."

He then inserted the coin into the slit of his penny loafers.

We went 30–0 that season and beat Florida State in the championship game.

The next year we assembled in the locker room for our opening-night game against Wisconsin. As was his habit,

Coach Wooden began explaining his goals for us and sure enough, near speech's end, he stopped and spied another penny on the ground.

"Men," he said, "this penny means good luck."

We went 30–0 that season and beat Memphis State in the NCAA title game.

The third season we sat in the locker room and listened once again to the same speech. We knew it by heart. We also knew by this time that Coach Wooden had instructed one of his assistant coaches to place a penny on the floor before Wooden entered the dressing room. I mean, c'mon, we weren't that stupid.

Nothing was coincidence for John Wooden. He planned for everything and considered every possibility, even good fortune. The penny trick just happened to be one of his favorites.

I wasn't so mesmerized by the speech this time. Instead, I watched as Coach Wooden began to smoothly search for that penny against the wall. Problem was, he couldn't find it. He scanned the floor for his beloved coin, but it was nowhere to be found. That's because I had picked it up and put it in my pocket shortly before he made his entrance that night.

"Coach," I said, "we're a great basketball team. We don't need luck. We know what to do."

As it turned out, we didn't. That was the season we went 26–4 and lost in the semifinals to North Carolina State. We learned many valuable lessons, one of them obviously being that you never discount luck and you never fool with John Wooden's special penny.

John Wooden was always talking about great expectations. He never would let you settle for being average or being near the top. Given the talent we had and the principles he taught, John Wooden considered undefeated seasons and national championships the only acceptable results. That was something that was driven into us from the very first day we arrived at UCLA.

Actually, that's one of the reasons I've been somewhat critical of the current coaching staff at UCLA. I sometimes think Coach Jim Harrick is content to settle for less than the accepted UCLA standard of basketball excellence. I don't think that just getting to the NCAA tournament, or, as was the case in 1991–92, advancing to the West Regional final and losing to Indiana by 27 points, is having a good season. Nor do I think finishing 22–11 and blowing a double-digit lead to an underachieving Michigan team in the second round of the 1992–93 NCAA tournament is something to be proud of. It might be all right for some. That's not the way we learned to play this game.

I'm biased, of course. But in the case of UCLA, or Kentucky, or North Carolina, or Indiana, or Kansas—historically, the truly great basketball programs—the standards of acceptability are and should be much higher. Kentucky, despite NCAA probation and sanctions, has been able to seriously challenge for a championship. Indiana is always there. Kansas won a title in 1988 under Larry Brown and, after a brief stay on NCAA probation, has been back to the Final Four twice under Roy Williams. Dean Smith just led his Tar Heels to a second national title in twelve years, despite his unusual penchant for substituting bench players in the game at critical junctures.

And UCLA? The Bruins haven't reached the Final Four since 1980. That eats at me. What a disgrace.

By the time I made the varisty, UCLA had won five consecutive national champsionships and seven of eight overall. The fans expected us to win. The media expected us to win. The coaches expected us to win. We expected to win. We loved the pressure. We wanted it that way. John Wooden would say, "Winners are prepared for whatever obstacles they face."

I wish Harrick the best at UCLA. When I was inducted into the Basketball Hall of Fame in May 1993, Harrick flew all the way to Springfield, Massachuetts, to offer his congratulations. I appreciated the gesture.

Nonetheless, I'm still not sure his teams are always prepared for those inevitable obstacles.

I take full responsibility for our four losses and the failure to win the 1973–74 championship. Of the three UCLA teams I played on, that one was definitely the most talented. To lose to North Carolina State in the semifinals was a terrible embarrassment for us, one that I have never gotten over.

My most vivid basketball memories are of the defeats:

January 19, 1974—Notre Dame 71, UCLA 70. (We blew an 11-point lead in the last 3:32, which ended our 88-game winning streak.)

February 15, 1974—Oregon State 61, UCLA 57.

February 16, 1974—Oregon 56, UCLA 51 (the infamous "Lost Weekend").

March 23, 1974—North Carolina State 80, UCLA 77.

I was devastated, destroyed and crushed after each loss. I couldn't sleep. Coach Wooden would tell us to stay calm, to balance our emotions, but I couldn't do it. I'd replay the game in my mind a million times. I still do, always wondering what I could have done better.

No game has caused me to lose as much sleep as the loss to North Carolina State. If I could have one week back in my life, the week we played North Carolina State would be it. At that point, we were a team in disarray.

Ten games into the regular season, I cracked two bones in my back against Washington State at Pullman. It happened when I was submarined on a lob pass to the basket. I missed two weeks of action and when I returned (against

Notre Dame) I had to wear a corset with steel rods inserted into the contraption to help support and protect my back. My game stunk and so did we.

Against Dayton in the West Regional semifinals, we needed three overtimes and luck to beat the Flyers. We blew a 17-point lead and would have lost the game if Dayton Coach Don Donoher hadn't called a timeout moments before Donald Smith sank a jumper for the Flyers. After that, we beat San Francisco to advance to the Final Four, but there were problems.

Earlier in the year, we had played North Carolina State in St. Louis and defeated them by 18 points. We knew it wasn't going to be so easy this time.

In my three seasons on the varsity, John Wooden never talked about an opposing player, except one: David Thompson. As it turned out, perhaps we should have talked about him more.

Coach Wooden wasn't much on scouting opposing teams. If, for example, we were playing, say, Washington, he would come into the locker room and say, "Okay, we're playing Washington tonight. From what I remember reading in the paper, they seem to have several fine players. From what I remember about a game we had against them last season, this player was left-handed. Now, Bill, you take him."

Then he'd make a few other comments and sometimes stop at midsentence.

"You know, forget about it. Just go play your game. If you play your game, we'll be fine. Don't worry about them."

And that was it. There were no film sessions, no big chalk talks, no strategy, no scouting breakdowns. He didn't want us to tighten up. So vague was the information about our opponents, that we used to have to send ball boys out for game programs. We at least wanted to know who played on the other team.

None of this concerned John Wooden. He knew he had

done his job. Now it was time for us to do ours. He was more concerned about that ideal opponent and about us not beating ourselves.

There was such a simplicity to his work. He not only taught you how to play the game; he taught you how to win. He only asked that we not beat ourselves.

Before almost every game we played, Coach Wooden told us, "Sometimes you're going to play and the other team will beat you because it's better. That happens. Just make sure that when you walk out of this building tonight, you can hold your head up high, knowing that you gave it your very best and that you didn't beat yourself. Now let's get going."

That's usually all it took. We'd come charging out of the locker room roaring, "Let's kill 'em!"

Meanwhile, the opposing coach would be busy diagramming these intricate little plays in hopes of beating us. "Now, team, this is what they're going to do here . . . And here's what they like to do here . . . And Walton likes to shoot this shot . . . And watch out for their press . . ."

Hey, it didn't matter. We were going to do what we'd been taught to do. The opposing coach could draw all the plays he wanted, we didn't care.

We should have won that game against North Carolina State. I'm not making excuses—they won the game fair and square—but we committed the ultimate basketball sin: We beat ourselves.

With less than 11 minutes left to play, we had an 11-point lead and then went dead. North Carolina State coach Norm Sloan instructed his team to use the four-corners offense (there was no shot clock back then) and we lost our concentration, our composure and our lead. The game moved to overtime and a second one after that.

With two minutes left in the second overtime, we were up by seven points, which should have been more than enough to win that day. Instead, they cut the lead to four and went on to score 11 unanswered points in the 80–77 victory.

North Carolina State had one great player—Thompson— and when you have that, you always have a chance to win. His emergence changed the way the game was played. He certainly changed our won-loss record that year. Thompson scored 28 points and had 10 rebounds against us in the semifinal.

Still, for the UCLA team to lose that game, or any game, was quite embarrassing. I always prided myself on being a champion, but there we were, chumps. I thought we were vastly superior to everyone we played. That may sound arrogant, but that's how I felt. And when I think back on that game, all I can see are so many of my easy short shots just rolling off the rim.

As usual, John Wooden was right. Blowing the game as we had, beating ourselves, was the worst kind of defeat to endure.

After the disheartening loss to North Carolina State, we still had to play Kansas in the Final Four consolation game. I didn't want to have anything to do with a game for losers, so I said I was out. So did some of the other seniors on the team. I told Coach Wooden that he should let the second-teamers play the entire game against Kansas. We would sit on the bench and root for the subs. They deserved a chance to play too.

Somehow a reporter learned of our planned boycott and started asking Coach Wooden about it. That's when Coach Wooden asked us to reconsider.

"Hey, I don't like the consolation game either," he said. "But look at it like this: There are a lot of fans out there who want to see you play. They came here based on who was going to play for UCLA. You really shouldn't cheat those fans. You starters, I promise I won't play you much."

And he didn't. I played only 20 minutes and attempted

just three shots. Wilkes played 20 minutes, Dave Meyers played 14 and Lee and Tommy Curtis played four minutes apiece. We beat Kansas by 17 points—as if anyone cared.

Afterward, I stood in the locker room and said, "The only good thing about any of this is that I'm never cutting my hair again."

John Wooden heard me and just shook his head.

As for the other losses that year, I am still in a fog. The Lost Weekend was a nightmare. And Notre Dame—well, every time I see Digger Phelps he reminds me of January 19, 1974, a very dark day in my life and in the history of UCLA basketball. That darn Digger Phelps, he got such extreme pleasure out of ruining my life.

Of all the college teams I played against, Notre Dame was the one I wanted to beat the most. They beat the UCLA varsity when I was a freshman and I was determined not to let it happen again.

At the time, Notre Dame was an all-guys school. We used to tease their players all the time, reminding them that they went to a school that didn't have women.

I loved playing against the Irish, especially at their gym, the 11,418-seat Joyce Athletic & Convocation Center. The people were crazy there. They were so loud, so intense, so desperate to see UCLA lose. One of my goals during big road games was to do something, anything, that would shut that crowd up. Victories were usually enough.

Notre Dame crowds were tough. They used to heat up nickels with cigarette lighters and then throw them at us.

The fans at Oregon were also a mean bunch. One time I fell out of bounds and into the Oregon home crowd. One guy got up from his seat in the first row and started kicking me. Turns out that the guy was an assistant coach for one of the other sports at Oregon.

They fired him.

When it comes to my career at UCLA, the game that everyone always wants to talk about is the victory against Memphis State in the 1973 NCAA championship. I made 21 of 22 field goal attempts and finished with 44 points, which broke Goodrich's NCAA record set in 1965.

John Wooden is constantly bugged about that night and he'll tell you it wasn't my best game either. In fact, he'll say that under the circumstances, Goodrich's 42 points against Michigan were more notable. My teammates and I played at least a half dozen better games than the one against Memphis State that March 26 night at the St. Louis Arena.

What a strange Final Four that was. During our semifinal victory against Bob Knight's Indiana team, UCLA athletic director J. D. Morgan, who always sat next to John Wooden on the bench, asked me what was wrong. I told him I was playing terrible because I was so tired.

"I can't get any sleep," I said. "I've got a terrible hotel room. I've got to try to sleep in a bed that's way too short, and there's always the sound of trucks running past the hotel on the expressway."

Morgan told me to take his hotel suite and he'd come over and stay at my place for the night. I couldn't believe my luck, especially when I saw that Morgan's room had a king-size bed and, best of all, peace and quiet.

Everything was fine until about 3 A.M., when I heard somebody trying to get into the room. I was so scared I thought my heart was going to burst. Then, just as I was settling down, the phone rang. I didn't know what to do. I answered it, but there was no one on the other end.

A few minutes after that, someone started knocking hard on the door. As I dialed Morgan's number at my old hotel, someone started yelling, "Police! Open the door now!"

I finally was connected to my/Morgan's room and he told

me to do as the police said. So I opened the door and waiting for me was some sort of special forces police unit.

Apparently a member of the hotel staff saw Morgan leave with his luggage and figured the room was now vacant. That's when they sold it to the guy who would later try to unsuccessfully open the door. He reported it to the hotel staff, which immediately contacted the police.

I was taken downstairs to the lobby and told to wait. All I had was a gym bag and several textbooks. At about 4 a.m., after the police had contacted Morgan and the situation had been explained, an assistant hotel manager asked if I would follow him to the elevator. He kept apologizing for the whole incident and said the hotel would try to make amends. He wasn't kidding.

We got in the elevator and up it went. And up. And up. It didn't stop until we reached the penthouse. What a place: telephones and televisions in every room . . . five bathrooms . . . ornate floral arrangements . . . a food spread that made our training table look embarrassing by comparison . . . chandeliers.

Two thoughts crossed my mind:

1. Where's the bed?
2. We already had the place for the team party when we beat Memphis State.

Our game against the Tigers was the first time an NCAA championship was played on a Monday night and in prime time (whatever that meant to a twenty-year-old). The place held 19,301 and every seat was filled. It was such an electric setting, absolutely perfect for basketball.

Memphis State had a good team. Gene Bartow, who would eventually be the first to succeed Coach Wooden at UCLA, was the Tigers' coach, and his lineup included Larry Finch and Larry Kenon. Memphis State had defeated Providence,

98–85, partly on the performances of Kenon and Ron Robinson, and partly because the Friars' star, Marvin Barnes, only played 11 minutes because of a dislocated knee.

With about four minutes left in the first half, I had three fouls. This was the biggest game of the season and I was two whistles away from fouling out.

So many times Coach Wooden had talked about the importance of balance. It was something he stressed constantly. "You're out of balance," he would say.

I usually thought he was referring to my personal life.

But against Memphis State, I was out of synch. I was so intense, so focused that I almost let the emotions of the moment overwhelm my abilities. With those three fouls, John Wooden had no choice but to take me out of the game. At halftime, the score was tied, 39–39.

The second half was a different story. Bartow kept his team in a zone defense, which allowed Lee and our other guard, Larry Hollyfield, to get me the ball inside. We kept running the same play over and over again, and each time, I'd be open right near the basket. It was almost too easy.

Behind by 10 points with about 11 minutes to play, Memphis State called a timeout. As we sat in the huddle, Lee asked Coach Wooden, "Hey, Coach, how about calling another play so somebody else besides Bill can score."

Wooden looked at him with a puzzled expression.

"Why?" he said.

I picked up my fourth foul shortly after the timeout, but Coach Wooden decided to take a chance and kept me in the game. To protect myself and stay in the game, I basically quit playing defense and concentrated on scoring. It wasn't a fifth foul that caused me to leave the game, but a sprained ankle that I suffered with 2:35 left to go. I didn't realize it at the time, but the first guy to help me toward the UCLA bench was Finch. Finch, now the coach at Memphis State, had a pretty good night himself. He scored 29.

I never looked at scoreboards during a game, other than to find out how much time was left. I figured that if I didn't know the score, I'd always keep pushing myself.

We were up by 15 points and would eventually win, 87–66. Coach Wooden's offense had worked to perfection.

My game wasn't so error-free. Coach Wooden likes to kid me about the one shot I missed. I made plenty of other mistakes as well. I converted only two of five free throws (some the front end of one-and-one situations), allowed my man (Kenon) to score 20 points and committed six turnovers and four fouls. I also was called for four dunking violations. Another time, I accidentally tipped in a basket for Memphis State.

A lot of the credit for UCLA's victory that day should go to Lee and Hollyfield, who combined for 23 assists. I was 10 for 10 in the second half, but only because they fed me the ball where it was almost impossible to miss.

Before the start of every season, Coach Wooden would write down his prediction for our team and then seal it inside one of those official UCLA Basketball envelopes that I borrowed to send to Nixon. The year we beat Memphis State, Coach Wooden had predicted we wouldn't lose a game. He was right. Funny about that guy. He was right about a lot of things.

It was his seventh consecutive NCAA championship and for me my 129th consecutive victory dating back to Helix High.

After the game, someone asked Coach Wooden if I was returning for my senior season. The NBA and ABA were both pressuring me to turn pro, but what the leagues didn't know (but should have) was that I had already made up my mind. Earlier that season, Coach Wooden had asked me if I was coming back to UCLA.

"Are you?" I said.

"Why, yes, Bill. I promised all of you that I'd be there for the completion of your college careers."

"Well, if you're back, I'm back."

The ABA, whose officials I met in my hotel suite in St. Louis, had the most lucrative offer. The league wanted to basically grant me my own franchise in Los Angeles. I could even pick my own teammates from all of the other ABA rosters, with the exception of Julius Erving. Plus, they wanted to pay me a lot of money.

But I didn't want to leave UCLA. I was having the time of my life. Things couldn't have been any better: John Wooden was my coach. We won all the time. And I had yet to be exposed to the crass commercialism and greediness of sport. I thought the whole world was perfect.

I was so naive.

As the meeting progressed, I knew there was no way I was going to accept their offer—millions or no millions, franchise or no franchise. There in my borrowed palatial penthouse suite, I told both the NBA and the ABA, "This is what UCLA has done for me. How could you possibly beat this?"

———

Jabbar and I are the only UCLA men's basketball players whose jersey numbers are retired. But the only banners that hang inside Pauley Pavilion are those of Bruins championship teams, the way it ought to be. One day, though, they might want to make an exception and find a place for a John Wooden banner. He would never approve of such a thing. A man of modesty, he would say that those championship banners are reminder enough of what he helped accomplish.

His record was phenomenal. In twenty-seven years at UCLA, he won 80.8 percent of his games (620–147) and ten national championships. No other UCLA coach has won one.

The most money he made during his tenure was $32,000. He made more than that for filming a single Reebok commercial a year or so ago. We—his former players—always ask him to let us put a financial package together for him so he can buy his mansion on the hill, or whatever. It's the least we can do. But every time he tells us no.

"I'm happy that you guys are successful," he says. "I'm successful in my own mind."

Funny about that guy.

In my wallet is a copy of John Wooden's Pyramid of Success. Not that I need a copy. I know the blocks of the Pyramid by heart. From the bottom left to right they read: Industriousness, Friendship, Loyalty, Cooperation and Enthusiasm. Then the second tier: Self-Control, Alertness, Initiative and Intentness. Then third: Condition, Skill and Team Spirit. Then: Poise and Confidence. Then finally: Competitive Greatness.

Success, which is the ability to reach your full potential, is the result.

This isn't Zen we're talking about here, just commonsense principles that work. The principles are timeless, and they help explain why John Wooden was able to relate to players in four different decades. Greg Lee is fond of saying Coach Wooden motivated players from the Ozzie and Harriet generation to the Woodstock generation. As players changed, so did John Wooden. That's a concept lost on guys such as former University of California coach Lou Campanelli.

Coach Wooden didn't treat everyone the same. He admitted that much in his preseason letters to the players. But he tried to be fair with each player, which is all you can really hope to get. A fair chance.

At UCLA, the second-string guys knew they were going to be abused by the first-teamers. Everything was designed for the first team. We were treated like kings. The second unit, cannon fodder.

But you also knew your position was not guaranteed. If you played well, you remained a king. If you didn't, you were on the bench, from which there was virtually no escape.

Nater and I battled every day at UCLA for three years. He wanted to play so bad. He used the daily practices as his games, his proving ground. We would get into fights all the time, but that was okay.

One time during a game, Coach Wooden decided to move me to forward and insert Nater at the center position. I was ecstatic about the chance. I got to play the perimeter for the first time in years and had no defensive responsibilities. I also got to shoot all the time.

Our offensive structure immediately collapsed. Naturally, Nater got blamed for it and Coach Wooden promptly pulled the poor guy from the game, forever banished to the bench.

Nater recovered. He's now the athletic director and coach at Christian Heritage College in suburban San Diego. His teams are really entertaining and fun to watch.

John Wooden never dwelled on individual success. He has never liked to be called "The Wizard of Westwood," or "The Wiz," or any of those other nicknames we used to diss him with. He finds them distasteful. To him, the title of Coach was honor enough.

Wooden was almost always a complete gentleman, but there were moments when he showed a bit of an excessively competitive personality, the kind of thing that I admired.

We were getting ready to play yet another bunch of stiffs one weekend when Coach Wooden went into his normally sedated pregame speech. This time, there was one additional thought:

"Men, the coach of the other team is bad for the game of

basketball," he said. "Your job is to beat them by so many points that they fire him. Tonight."

We killed them.

That concept has stayed with me throughout my career and I regularly use that motivational tactic on myself when I'm feeling a little sluggish.

John Wooden is eighty-three now, but his mind is as razor-sharp as the day I first saw him when I was in sixth grade. He could still coach a team if he wanted to. It isn't the coaching he misses, it's the teaching.

I call him all the time and tease him about whatever pops into my mind, just like I did twenty-five years ago. I'll leave messages on his answering machine, the kind of messages that will grate on him. He doesn't miss a thing. When we do finally connect, he'll often go right at me.

"Bill, regarding the message you left on December 10: I just don't agree with what you said that day and here's why."

Sometimes I get close to catching him. Once I asked him how far Springfield, Illinois, where Abraham Lincoln once lived, was from Martinsville, Indiana, where Coach Wooden was born and raised. Lincoln is John Wooden's favorite American.

"Oh, about a hundred miles," he said.

"Is that right? By the way, did you and Lincoln ever hang out together?"

"No, we didn't, but—"

Then he caught himself.

"Wait a second, Bill. You know Abraham Lincoln was quite a bit older than I am."

"I know that, Coach. I just wanted to make sure you did."

CHAPTER

3

"Picture a bright blue ball, spinning, spinning
free . . . dizzy with possibilities."
—*Bob Weir*

More than twenty years have passed since the United
States sent twelve overmatched college basketball
players, one taskmaster head coach, and two assistants to
the 1972 Olympic Games. I wish I had been on that team.
I wasn't. Even today some people hold me responsible for
the most embarrassing defeat in U.S. Olympic basketball
history.

I've been blamed for many things in my life, some of them
actually true. But the U.S.A.'s embarrassing 51–50 loss to
the Soviet Union in the gold medal game at Munich wasn't
my doing. I merely became a postdefeat whipping boy, one
in a long line of excuses provided by people who ran what
was then called the U.S. Olympic Basketball Committee.
The committee, along with the Amateur Athletics Union,
shared responsibility of overseeing the sport in this country.
I called them "The Suits."

Never before had a U.S. men's team failed to win the gold

medal. Beginning in 1904, when basketball was first introduced as a demonstration sport at the Games, and through
1968, the United States had always finished first. Seven
Olympics. Seven gold medals.

That was before 1972, when an official from FIBA, the
sport's international governing organization, put several
precious seconds back on the clock in the waning moments
of that U.S.A.–U.S.S.R. game, thus allowing the Soviet
Union to make the disputed winning shot as time expired.

Part of the blame has to be shared by the suits who ran
U.S.A. amateur basketball. In their own bumbling way, the
suits helped contribute to the loss in 1972, as well as the
disappointing bronze medal finish in the 1988 Olympic
Games.

I played basketball for the simple reason that it gave me
joy, that it was fun. One of the few times in my amateur
career that it wasn't fun came in the spring of 1970.

When I was in high school, I often received invitations to
play in various summer leagues and all-star games. But
because of assorted rules that I still don't fully understand,
I wasn't allowed to accept any of the offers.

All that changed after my final game at Helix High, when
I was no longer considered, at least in a technical sense, a
prep player. I was a free agent. I immediately joined a San
Diego AAU team that was coached by a distant uncle of
mine.

This was no ordinary team. Except for me, every player
on the roster was in the Navy. These guys were older,
tougher, street-smart and didn't back down to anybody. I
was young (only seventeen) and skinny, but willing. The
common denominator was that we loved playing ball.

Our team advanced to the playoffs and beat the Los Angeles AAU champion in a vicious and grueling series. That
earned us a spot in the AAU national championships held
that year at the University of South Carolina in Columbia,

where our team was promptly beaten in the first round of the tournament. I had a huge game, but it didn't matter. We lost, so who cares how many points I scored.

Actually, one coach did. His team, which was comprised of players in the Army, would eventually win the AAU title, which meant—and don't ask how any of this worked—he got to coach the U.S. national AAU Armed Forces team in the 1970 World Championships in Yugoslavia.

Shortly after I returned to San Diego, this coach, who will remain unnamed, called. Would I be interested in trying out for his team and a chance to represent my country in the World Championships?

Interested? I was dying to go. I thought it was the greatest thing in the world. My dad, who had served in the Army, didn't. He and my Helix High School principal were adamantly against it, because I'd basically have to drop out of school for four months.

Schoolwork wasn't a concern to me. I had always been a top student. I'd make up the work, I told them. Then I begged and pestered them until they finally allowed me to go. As it turned out, it was probably the best and the worst experience of my life.

Abraham Lincoln once said that everything we learn, we learn from somebody else. And almost everything we learn is what not to do.

The tryout took place at some sort of military installation at Fort Hamilton, New York. Of the twenty-five or so players invited to the tryout, I was the only one who wasn't in the Army. I was seventeen years old, 6' 10½", and weighed 190 pounds. I came from the gentle and gentile suburbs of San Diego. I was naive and innocent, but very excited.

In walked the coach. He looked at us as if we were scum. He treated us that way too.

This coach was the most abusive man I had ever met in my life. Every other word out of his mouth was an expletive.

I had heard cuss words before, but never like this and certainly not in such malicious ways.

"Okay," he said. "There's twenty-five of you guys. Two weeks from now, when I pick this team, you all will still be serving your country. Twelve of you will be going to Yugoslavia, where you'll fly over first-class, spend three full months traveling in beautiful chartered buses, enjoy five-star accommodations, eat wonderful food, see the European sights and return back with a World Championship gold medal.

"The rest of you sorry guys who don't make the team," he said, "I'm going to personally sign your orders for combat duty in Vietnam."

The fight for survival began. We practiced on a terrible court three times a day for three hours at a time. We stayed in barracks and slept in beds so small that I felt I was back in the womb.

Everybody else on the team was in his mid-twenties, but they looked out for me and also seemed to respect the way I played. Of course, by the end of three-a-days, my knees were shot. Hard floors and nine hours of practice do not provide the best workout conditions for a developing teenager.

This coach was a piece of work. He would show up for the start of practice and then leave, letting his assistants take it from there. Every so often, after having a drink in the foyer, he would return to the workout and start yelling at us again. He was cruel too. If a player missed a shot, he would say something like "You're on your way to Nam."

Despite all the horrible things he did—and they were constant—he did teach me the value of playing aggressively, of approaching the game as a physical battle of wills. Survival of the fittest and the strongest.

I made the team, along with Darnell Hilliman, Ken

Washington, Bob Wolfe, Garfield Smith, Jim Williams, Rod McDonald, Brad Luchine, Art Wilmore, Mike Silliman, Tal Brody and Warren Isaacs. I was now a member of the U.S.A. team chosen to travel to Yugoslavia for the basketball World Championships. The other guys? They went to Vietnam.

We should have sent the coach instead.

Before the actual tournament began, we traveled around Italy, Germany and Yugoslavia playing in exhibition games. I didn't know a thing about those countries. I grew up in Southern California. I thought the whole world was really nice and wonderful, sunny, warm and carefree. Then I got over there and I found out different.

Our routine was almost always the same: We'd travel by bus to a town, have lunch, attend a reception, take a nap and play in an evening exhibition.

The biggest problem was that I never played. The coach ignored me. Here I was, the first high school player ever invited to join a national AAU team, and I couldn't get in the game.

One time he approached me during a lunch stop. This was news in itself because he rarely talked to me.

"Bill, the national team of Yugoslavia recently came through this town and recruited all their big guys," he said. "Would you mind helping them out and playing for the other team tonight?"

He must have thought I'd take it as an insult to be asked, but I couldn't say yes fast enough. He even seemed a little surprised by my answer.

I wanted to play and I didn't care what uniform I wore. I hadn't come to Yugoslavia to be a tourist.

That night I met my new temporary coach, who naturally didn't speak a word of English. The local players didn't speak English either, which was fine. I didn't speak a word of Yugoslavian. I was issued this worn-out undersized jersey that barely fit—and I was rail-thin at the time. Then I went out there and had the time of my life.

I can't remember the exact numbers, but I had a huge game, scoring all the points and basically grabbing every rebound. It was wonderful, made even sweeter by the fact that we almost won the game and stuck it to the U.S. coach. The referees, who were Yugoslavian homers, of course, didn't call a single foul on me all night. As soon as I realized I had free rein, I started using every dirty tactic taught to me. I elbowed guys. I stuck my knees out as my ex-teammates drove down the lane. I used every cheap shot you can think of. But no sound of whistles.

The crowd was going nuts. The longer we stayed close to the U.S. team, the crazier it got. And even though I couldn't speak to my Yugoslavian teammates, I could communicate. Basketball has an international language all its own.

By the end of the game, the fans were chanting, "Wal-ton! Wal-ton!" We lost by something like three points, when we probably should have lost by fifty. The crowd stormed the court and actually carried me off on their shoulders. I wish I could have seen the coach's face when that happened.

When I rejoined the U.S. team the next day, I was back on the bench. He didn't say a word to me. Then the World Championships started, and still my warm-up suit never came off.

He came up to me before our game against the Soviet Union.

"Bill, the Russians have some very big, tall guys," he said. "I'm going to need you today, so make sure you're ready."

I was already ready. So I sat right next to him on the bench, just waiting for the chance to battle the Russians. One problem: He never even gave me a first look.

Every time he made a substitution, he looked right past

me. I was so excited about the possibility of playing that I almost said to him, "Put me in! Put me in!" Instead, I kept my mouth shut and waited and hoped. In this situation I didn't have the courage to do what was necessary. I hadn't learned to substitute myself by this point.

I don't think I even played in one game during the World Championships. As for our team, I think we came in fifth.

It didn't matter anymore.

Just before we were scheduled to return to the United States, the coach said that Greece was only two hours away and that their federation was offering us some big money if we would agree to play a couple of exhibition games there. Everybody on the team hated him so much by this time that we voted not to go. We just wanted to get away from him and go home.

When we got to New York, he offered the customary good-byes, telling us how proud he was of us. I was so mad I didn't even want to talk to him. My thoughts were: "Let me out of here. I never want to see you or anyone like you again. Let me go home."

I went home, all right, and spent the next four years playing for John Wooden, who was the exact opposite of this guy.

Two years later, after my sophomore season at UCLA, officials from the U.S. Olympic Basketball Committee asked me if I wanted to try out for the 1972 Olympic team. We had just won the NCAA championship and I was worn down from the long collegiate season. But this was the Olympics, so I said I'd think about it.

Coach Wooden and I sat down and discussed the situation. I told him about my experiences with the Armed Forces team and said I wasn't in any big hurry to jump back into that type of situation. I also said I didn't want to go through another boot-camp tryout session. If they wanted me to live in Army barracks, sleep in tiny beds, eat at mess halls and play in a bunch of meaningless exhibition games, I wasn't interested.

The Suits said they wanted me to drop out of UCLA, play months of basketball in preparation for the ten-day Olympic tournament and be willing to accept whatever accommodations they thought suitable. I negotiated. I told them that if they wanted to choose me for the team, I would be honored to play, but under no circumstances was I going to subject myself to another situation like before. If the U.S. officials didn't think my proposal was proper, I could live with their decision.

Whatever happened, I was going to do things on my terms. It's like Dylan tells us in "Maggie's Farm": *Well I try my best to be just like I am, but everybody wants you to be just like them.*

I wanted some say in my own future. We were basketball players, not slaves, cannon fodder or military grunts. I wanted us to win the gold medal. But there had to be some limits on the demands made.

I needed time to rest, to recharge my batteries. My first responsibility was to Coach Wooden and UCLA. If I didn't take a significant break from the game, I was going to be useless for the following season.

After talking it over with Coach Wooden, I decided to offer the Basketball Committee a compromise. I told them I'd show up two weeks in advance of the Olympic tournament and I'd be in great shape. I'd be fresh, replenished and ready to go. I told them I'd play in the tournament, but then I wanted to go straight home. No barnstorming tours. I asked to be treated like a person, like a human being. I wanted to be treated with dignity and respect. I wanted to be treated like I was accustomed to at UCLA.

The U.S. officials said no.

I wish I had played on that 1972 Olympic team. I wish I

could have played in every game in every situation during my whole life. But under the circumstances, it was best that I didn't play. Had I gone through that incredibly demanding schedule all spring and summer long—the training, the exhibition games, the travel—I wouldn't have been ready for UCLA's next season. The U.S.A. was my country, but UCLA was my team.

After hearing about the conditions of the training camp I feel I made the right choice. Back then, the coaches ruled supreme and it showed. The players were fodder. My UCLA teammate Swen Nater was invited to the camp. So outrageous were the conditions, so demanding and demeaning was Coach Hank Iba, that Swen quit after a week. Basketball is supposed to be fun. The week that Swen described sounded more like agony and punishment.

Twenty years later, everything I had asked the U.S. Olympic Basketball Committee for in 1972—the upgraded accommodations, no tryouts, the respect, the less grueling playing schedule—the Dream Team got. Yet I get blamed and the referees and officials get blamed for that loss to the Russians, for the U.S.A. not winning the gold medal. People saw that I wasn't there and decided it was my fault. If those officials would have had some foresight and had been willing to work with the players, I would have been there. Maybe the U.S.A. would still have lost by some freak last-second call, but I don't think so. I don't think we would have trailed the Russians by eight points with 6:07 remaining in the game. I don't think it would have been close.

If there was hate mail about my decision, I don't remember receiving any. Then again, I don't remember if I read mail in college or, for that matter, if I even got mail in college. I can live with my decision. Obviously the U.S. Basketball Committee officials have to live with theirs.

In the spring of 1973, the Soviet national team was invited to the United States for a rematch tour. Some basketball people still hadn't recovered from the embarrassing finish at the Olympics, nor had they forgiven me for not trying out for the U.S. team. I committed to appear in just two games on the tour, one at the Forum in Los Angeles and one in San Diego.

Former Boston Celtic Hall of Famer Bob Cousy was our coach, and included on the roster were such players as Marvin Barnes, Ernie DiGregorio, Bobby Jones and Greg Lee. There was incredible anticipation for the first game, which was shown on national television. This was going to be payback time. This was going to be a lesson in real basketball. There wouldn't be any FIBA officials adding any seconds to the game clock this time.

When the game started we came out smoking. The ball was hot, it was moving like crazy. We had the Russians spinning around just trying to find the thing. They'd never seen anybody like Ernie D., an extremely creative player who loved to make plays seem a lot more difficult than they actually were.

Eight minutes into the game, we had a big lead. I was playing well, as was everybody on the team. The Russians called a timeout. They had flustered, befuddled looks on their faces, as if they couldn't understand how we were crushing them. After the timeout, we resumed our scoring spree. They couldn't stop us.

Since they couldn't beat us with their skills, they tried the next-best thing. They got physical.

Their tactics were crude, but effective. Every time down court, I would get hit high and low by these 6' 10", 260-pound Russian men. By the fourth hit, I could barely get up off the ground. My knee was swollen, my body bruised. They had done their job.

I limped over to the sidelines. One of the event organizers rushed down to the bench and told Cousy to get me out of there. Out I went, accompanied to the locker room by team physician Dr. Tony Daly. It would be the first of many meetings.

Dr. Daly examined my swollen knee and then said, "I just saw what happened out there and I'm not letting you go back into that game—if you can call it that."

So I sat in the locker room, an ice pack on my knee, and listened to Chick Hearn's call of the game on the radio. With only a few moments left to play in the rout, Chick said that Greg Lee was getting ready to enter the game.

All game long Lee had been waiting for his chance, but Cousy would never put him in. Cousy loved Ernie D. He thought Ernie D. was the greatest, so he played him almost every minute of the game and let him do whatever he wanted. Meanwhile, Lee sat.

Lee and Ernie D. found themselves on the floor at the same time in the game's closing seconds. Lee told Ernie D. to inbound the ball. Ernie D. told Lee to do it. Ernie D., you see, wanted to take the last shot. Actually, I think he wanted to take every shot.

Lee eventually relented and took the ball to make the inbounds pass, faked that pass to Ernie D., and then, much to the amazement of Cousy, the Russians and the Forum crowd, shot the ball from out of bounds and banked it in.

Chick couldn't believe it.

"You know, ladies and gentlemen, I think that may be legal under international rules!"

It wasn't.

That game ended my official international playing career. I was unable to play in the game at San Diego and the tour moved on without me.

In 1979 I did make a triumphant return to the international sports scene, but few noticed.

A team of Greg Lee, Lee's brother, Jon, myself, my brother Andy and Roger Goldingay, a former professional soccer player, went on a cultural and basketball exchange trip to the Galápagos Islands. We were on a boat for about two weeks and then came ashore to put on a few clinics. One of the locals in the town of Puerto Ayora on the island of Santa Cruz told me I was the first professional basketball player to ever visit the islands.

While in Puerto Ayora, the coach of the local team asked if we'd be interested in a game. Sure, we would. You never turned down a chance to play.

At halftime, we were ahead, 79–2. The local team's two points had come on separate free throws. I can't remember the final score, but I'm confident we beat the spread.

I never got another chance to compete for an Olympic medal. Because of the eligibility rules regarding amateur status, 1972 was it for me. Four years later, as the U.S. team was winning another gold medal at the 1976 Summer Games in Montreal, I was with the Portland Trail Blazers. The 1976–77 season was when we won the NBA Finals.

I've always thought it was wrong that professional players weren't allowed to participate in the Olympics. I never bought the argument that the Olympic team should be used as a reward for college players, or that having the pros eligible would deprive the college standouts of an Olympic opportunity. So what? That's the college player's problem. These are supposed to be the world championships of basketball. You send your best team. The Olympics isn't about giving a chance to people who aren't the best. It's about sending people who deserve to be there because of their talents, not because they happen to be still in college.

The United States has always been very, very reluctant to send the pros to the Olympics. It is obvious to me that the people who run the Olympics in this country and internationally were not willing to give up their power, their control to the athletes. The Suits made the decisions that mattered. In the 1992 Olympics, Michael Jordan, Magic

Johnson, Larry Bird and Charles Barkley were the ones calling the shots, the way it should be.

Change comes very slowly in the world, particularly in amateur athletics, where the decision-makers often have their own self-interest at heart, rather than the athletes'. Also, it's rare when a person voluntarily relinquishes power, even if it's obvious that power is being misused.

The rest of the world has wanted the U.S.A. to send its best NBA players to the Olympics for years. Our own basketball federation fought the move. It wasn't worried about anything, except protecting its turf, turf that it had selfishly hoarded for more than fifty years. By allowing NBA players admission to the Olympics, something was going to give, mainly the power of these U.S.A. basketball officials.

In today's Olympic basketball programs, the NBA is king. The powers that be are Commissioner David Stern, Barkley and the rest of the players. The minute the decision was made to allow the best players in the world to play—the elite of the NBA—the balance of power changed forever. Decisions are now based on the players' needs. Or the players will just say no to the Olympics, as they should. Great players don't have to tolerate the craziness of the Suits who are just trying to mindlessly exercise their power. Great players don't have time for that. They want to play ball.

I would have happily played in the Olympics had there been a Dream Team situation during my career. But at least the change was eventually made. The Olympics have become the ultimate reward for the ultimate players.

Still, there was potential for disaster at the 1992 Summer Games. There was no way that team was going to lose to anyone, but there was a chance the Dream Team concept could have flopped. Had those players not been treated with respect, had there not been changes in the way we prepared for the Olympics, those NBA stars would have stayed home.

The Olympics should be for the best athletes. The better

the athletes involved, the better the Games. But when you don't have powerful international sports figures such as Jordan, Magic, Barkley and Malone willing to stand up and say no to the Suits and no to the officials, then the quality of play and the ultimate enjoyment of the fans suffers.

Had the players' demands not been met, the United States would have ended up sending more college players to Barcelona and gotten beat. Most people have no idea how wide the gap is between professional players and players who play part-time. Most people also have no idea how much smaller the gap is between the U.S. college players and the European professional stars who are Olympic regulars.

The talent on the Dream Team, compared to the other teams in Barcelona, was incredible. When you're one of the best players in the world, like Jordan and Magic and Bird, there's only one or two or maybe three players who can give you a competitive match. There wasn't a single guy on any of those other teams—not Croatia, Lithuania, the Unified Team, Brazil . . . anybody—who could have ever even made the Dream Team. Also, don't put much stock in the Dream Team's "loss" to the college all-stars at the "training camp" at La Jolla, California. The La Jolla camp was a big party. The college all-stars, otherwise known as the U.S.A. Select Team, played well that day, but in the Olympic tournament, they wouldn't have had a chance. The gap between the best players in the NBA and the best players in college is as wide as the Grand Canyon.

The scrimmage "victory" by the Select Team was deceiving. C'mon, do you really think the scrimmage would have been close had the Dream Team been entirely focused? The first string always loses in practice. They know they're going to play. There's no way Montross, then a junior at North Carolina, is better than David Robinson or Patrick Ewing. Maybe Duke's Bobby Hurley did have limited success against John Stockton and a few others, but he did zilch against Jordan, who was nicknamed "the Glove" for the way he stops other players.

There is absolutely no way the best team in the NCAA could even dream of beating the worst team in the NBA. If you put North Carolina, the 1993 NCAA champion, against the 1992–93 Dallas Mavericks, the losingest team in the NBA, the Mavericks would win every game. The Tar Heels wouldn't have a chance.

The skill-level gap between the top people in a profession—and I don't care what the profession is—vs. everyone else is immense. You're talking about men vs. boys.

A few years ago, when Jerry Tarkanian's team at UNLV was beating everyone by big spreads, some people started suggesting that the Runnin' Rebels were good enough to compete on the NBA level. Not a chance. NBA players are so much more mature, physically and mentally. You're talking about taking twenty-one-year-old men (or younger) and asking them to beat a team of professionals. UNLV, as good a team as it was, wouldn't have come close. Larry Johnson and Stacey Augmon have become solid NBA players, but Greg Anthony isn't anything special. Anderson Hunt and George Ackles didn't even make the first cut.

There are possible exceptions. Maybe, just maybe, some of the greatest college teams of all time might have been able to beat some of the worst teams in the history of the NBA. I'm talking about a college team with a classically dominant player, such as UCLA with Alcindor. I would take the Bruins against, say, the 1972–73 Philadelphia 76ers, who finished 9–73, the worst record in the annals of the NBA. Or certainly Dallas of 1993.

One Dream Team member who regularly gets overlooked is Coach Chuck Daly. Daly didn't rule with an iron fist, but with a light sweep of the hand. He distinguished himself not so much by what he did as a coach, but by what he didn't do.

You do need a coach for any team—and Daly did a great job. The key was to figure out what's best for Jordan, Barkley, Malone and the rest of those guys. Daly did that. He didn't come in, start blowing his whistle and make decisions based on what was best for the coaches or the Suits. He always put the players first, which is easier said than done. When that happens, top players usually make a commitment to doing whatever the coach says. Look at the way the Dream Team responded to Daly's tactful leadership. A heavy-handed coach's methods will never work with elite players. Coaches who are only interested in promoting themselves, in increasing their own self-importance, can't survive at the professional level. They can only survive when the players are at a developing stage in their career and are too young and too inexperienced to know how much power they really have.

I've traveled the world teaching basketball. I've seen the quality of basketball players in other countries. The NBA is twenty years ahead of the rest of the world. In a perfect world, the 2016 Olympics could be up for grabs when it comes to the gold medal in men's basketball.

The world, though, is not a perfect place. We live in a world that, at times, seems to be headed in the wrong direction. The political turmoil, the social instability in so many parts of the world keeps teams and individual players from ever developing their full potential.

Look at the places where the good basketball players have been coming from: Lithuania, the Balkans, Latvia, Estonia? That area is a disaster. The former Yugoslavia? That place is worse than Africa. It certainly isn't where you would go to work on your game.

Who knows how long it will take until some sort of political stability is reached. In the grand scheme of things, basketball isn't that significant a concern. The simple fact remains that political unrest stunts the growth of the sport in those countries. Nor does it help those sports programs when so many of the international players come to the United States, learn the game at our colleges, and don't return to their original countries to pass along their skills and information to the younger players and coaches.

Having international players in the NCAA and the NBA is a good idea. These players improve with each game. Granted, there are a lot of poor players out there. But there are also some very good players who enhance the game with their talents, like Detlef Schrempf and Sarunas Marciulionis. These guys are tough, competitive players. Marciulionis, to his detriment, plays so hard he breaks down too much. I enjoy watching him play, I just wish he could stay healthy.

I'd like to see more international competition involving NBA players. Commissioner David Stern has made an effort. It was Stern who introduced the McDonald's Open, which is a tournament involving three foreign club teams and one NBA team. We need more events of that type.

A few years ago Stern was visiting China and he was approached by a guide, who somehow knew of his connection to the NBA. Through an interpreter, the man requested one thing from Stern.

"I am a great fan of the Oxen," said the guide. "Please bring them to China."

It wasn't until later that the interpreter told Stern that a mistake had been made in the translation.

"Not Oxen," said the interpreter. "Bulls."

There are about 250 million potential basketball fans in the United States and five billion in the rest of the world. You can watch NBA games in more than a hundred foreign countries these days, compared to a handful nine years ago. It isn't by accident that retail sales of NBA-licensed merchandise in the overseas markets has soared from $25 million in 1989 to $125 million in 1991.

My former boss, Red Auerbach, might have started the whole thing. Thirty-one years ago, Red took the Celtics on a world tour. He knew the game had to be shared, that it wasn't the private domain of the United States.

"It's not whether you win or lose . . . It's
whether *I* win or lose."
—*Anonymous*

When things were at their absolute worst in the early days with the Trail Blazers—when some of my teammates hated my guts, and I theirs and their selfish, money- and statistics-driven style of play, when the fans and team management were unaware or not concerned that I had a broken foot and were accusing me of being a malingerer when I was hurt—I would call up the team owner in the middle of the night and tell him I was quitting.

"I hate this," I would say. "I hate everything about this. This is terrible. I can't do it anymore. I quit."

Then I'd hang up the phone, toss and turn the rest of the night, unable to sleep. By daybreak, I'd call him back and rescind the previous evening's announcement.

I used to do this regularly: Get upset. Quit. Not quit.

One day it finally dawned on me that I wasn't the one with the problem. It was them. My teammates didn't share my love, passion and commitment for the game. They were the guys who didn't appreciate the game's beauty. They were the guys who were butchering the game with their indifferent, selfish play.

I told myself, "Don't let these guys drive you away from the sport you love. It's your game. It's your life."

I stopped making those nighttime retirement calls to the owner and concentated on changing the existing order of the Trail Blazers. I still despised the level of selfishness I saw on the Trail Blazers during my first two years there, but a few key trades eventually took care of that problem.

Basketball and I were meant for each other. I always felt that the game was made just for me. It always came so easily, to the point that I thought I could do whatever I wanted to on the court (except stay healthy, of course) and not feel any pressure to have any other facets to the rest of my life.

The championship rings that I was able to win are not found on my fingers. I had them fitted for my father, who also has an NFC championship ring my brother Bruce gave him. Bruce played for the Dallas Cowboys when they played in Super Bowl X in January 1976.

My dad was much more interested in music and literature than he is in sports. I'm convinced that there were years when he didn't fully understand what I even did for a living. Yet he never discouraged me from playing the game.

I tried to thank him as best I could. I can remember when I was a kid and I told him, "Dad, one day I'm going to make it to the NBA, win the MVP award and I'll give you the car."

"That's fine, Bill," he said.

Years later, I won the award. My dad still has the pickup truck I gave him.

Actually, I'm not much for keeping basketball mementos. There are no framed jerseys, or mounted basketballs, or plaques or trophies in my house. I wanted a home, not a museum. I didn't play the game for mementos or memories.

I played for the joy of it. I played so I could ride my bike through the streets of Portland in the Trail Blazers' championship parade in 1977. During the parade, I had to abandon my bike because of the crush of people. Someone recovered my bike from a thief; he agreed to return the bike on the condition that he got to meet me. Such a deal!

I played so I could experience the fun of having the city of Cambridge, where I lived during my all too brief stint with the Celtics, throw a special victory parade I'll never forget. "Bill Walton Day" they called it in Cambridge. Cops were cheering. Celtics fans were going crazy. There was a motorcade. Sirens were wailing. It was wonderful.

I played so I could learn from John Wooden.

I played so I could face the very best. I lived to play against Jabbar. During that championship season in Portland, we swept the Lakers, 4–0, in the Western Conference finals. Jabbar was incredible during that playoff, but there was one sequence when I scored something like 14 consecutive points against the Lakers. My dad later asked me about the game and I told him it was as if everybody else was playing in slow motion. I felt I was the only one playing at regular speed. I enjoyed that feeling, and wish it had happened more often.

I played because of the mental challenge. Basketball's like a really fast-paced game of chess, where every move had its benefits and repercussions. You would compete against another player not only on a physical level but also on a mental and psychological level.

Good players know exactly what they can and can't do. The best players know there's not a skill that can elude them. The minute they detect a weakness in their own game, they go out there and work on it until the weakness becomes a strength. The best players also spend a lot of their time worrying how they're going to make their teammates better.

The nicest thing that people ever said about me as a basketball player was that I made the players around me perform better. To me, there is no more meaningful compliment.

Of course, no one made me play better than Maurice Lucas. He was tough. He had a great desire for perfection and winning. He played with pride and understood the responsibilities of leadership. He was always ready to play.

Lucas wasn't the best player I ever played with. Larry Bird earns that distinction. But Lucas made me a better player than any other teammate. I'm not entirely sure how he did it.

Lucas had a very unconventional leadership style. He would walk into the locker room, usually late, sit down next to me and say, "Bill, who do we need on our team to play great tonight for us to win?" I'd give him several names, at which point Maurice would approach those players on an individual basis and, in his own endearing way, threaten to kill them if they didn't perform as he demanded.

I've been anxious, anxious that I might lose a game while playing on a great team. I've been anxious for the game to get started. I'm a wreck when not playing. When you're playing, you control the outcome of the game.

When I was playing, I could hardly wait for the tip-off. Forget the warm-up period. Forget the national anthem. Forget the halftime. Forget the timeouts. Let's just get going and *play*.

When you're playing well, you want the game to go on forever. Nothing else seems to matter. The fans are going crazy. There is a festival atmosphere in the stands, not quite like a Dead show, but close. Nothing matters outside the lines. You're in the zone. You can't hear a thing. All you see is the ball and the basket. You see your teammates and their every move. You see your opponents and their every mistake. It is an incredible feeling, one that you don't want to see come to an end.

As a kid I thought I was going to be successful at basketball. There was something about the game that clicked with me. I knew I *had* to be good at it, which is why I never thought twice about shooting thousands of shots by myself each day. I'd go out and play on my dirt basketball court, then run around the block, then practice dribbling the ball, then jump rope, and then want to do it all over again.

In the first game I ever played—I was a fourth-grader on the end of the bench for the sixth-grade team—Rocky Graciano inserted me into the lineup with only a few minutes remaining in a blowout game. I was in long enough to attempt one pass to a wide-open teammate standing under the basket. But I misjudged the distance and instead heaved the ball directly through the hoop, nothing but net.

Rocky came up to me after that game and said, "Bill, I thought you had talent for this game. I thought you would be good at it. But I never dreamed it would come quite that easy for you."

At night I used to lie on my back in bed and practice shooting the ball. I played a game: How close could I get the ball to the ceiling without actually touching it?

During the day, I'd position myself in front of the large mirror that hung over the fireplace mantel of our family home and practice my jump shot, my pivots and my rebounds. I used to compete with my brothers and sister to see who could touch our eight-foot ceiling. The older we got, the more competitive we got. At one point, we were trying to see who could touch the ceiling with his elbow, and eventually his head.

Basketball heaven was having the key to your high school gym—a little-known fact that we tried to keep from Gordon Nash, my high school coach.

Some of the players for the San Diego Rockets used to call me at home and ask me to open up the gym. I'd rush down there and find Calvin Murphy, Rudy Tomjanovich, Elvin Hayes, Don Kojis and Pat Riley anxiously waiting to play. I'd open it up and we'd run all night.

Those were good times. It doesn't get much better than high school. I got to play with my brother Bruce at Helix. Bruce was a pretty good basketball player, an even better football player. He played on the offensive line at UCLA and went on to play with the Cowboys for several seasons. Our body types couldn't have been more dissimilar: I was tall and skinny, the ectomorph, and he was only about 6' 5", but considerably more muscular.

One game we were playing El Cajon High School and I was having a terrible time. I was guarded by some thug whose only job, it seemed, was to constantly harass me with every cheap shot imaginable. I spent most of the first half ducking elbows and dodging chest bumps.

On one play, after the game had flowed upcourt, I heard the crowd moan, as if it had witnessed some sort of terrible traffic accident. I turned around and there was Bruce standing over the now prone El Cajon player who had been guarding me.

I didn't have any more problems that night.

Bruce was fond of teaching lessons on the court. He was the first enforcer I played with. He taught me how to develop moves going right—the hard way.

We had a small dirt court in the backyard. Near the edge of the left side of the court was a sort of cactus bush. On the right side, a three-foot drop into nothingness.

I preferred going to my left. Bruce kept telling me that I

was too predictable, that I needed to learn how to attack to my right. I was stubborn. I kept going left.

Bruce decided enough was enough. Whenever I made my move to the left, Bruce pushed me into the cactus bush. I still have the scars.

I learned to go right.

Today's young players seem somewhat different than when I grew up. They don't seem to have the same desire to go out and play the game on their own. They're always waiting for their parents to organize their activities, or sitting mesmerized by the mind-numbing wasteland of television.

Young players need to be going to the playground and learning the game themselves. The real skills learned in basketball come from years of free, non-coached play, the years of just hanging out on a court and shooting jumpers, having fun.

By doing that, they learn to shoot the shots, to dribble, to make the mistakes with absolutely no penalty. It's a dream come true. They can pretend they're Bird, or Magic, or Jordan, or Shaquille, or whoever they want to be. Maybe just themselves. Most importantly, they learn to win in order to keep the court.

John Wooden got me involved in the teaching aspect of the game. After I graduated from UCLA, I started to do clinics at his summer camps. It was an extreme challenge. To be the teacher up front you have to have it all together. There can be no bull. Young players can instantly tell the difference between someone who wants to help them become better players and someone who wants to listen to himself talk.

By doing clinics, I became a better player myself. I was forced to analyze and examine my own game. To teach, you have to understand and believe what you're saying. Before

I could do that, I had to take a look at my own approach to the game and determine where I was and where I was going.

Those were good times. Greg Lee and I traveled around California putting on clinics for kids, split the fees and used the sessions as a good way to work out. We taught by example, showing the kids exactly what we thought they should learn.

When I got hurt and later was forced into early retirement, I had to change teaching techniques. I couldn't demonstrate techniques and plays anymore because of my physical limitations. I had to simply talk the game.

I kept it simple. One of the most important things for young players to understand is that they need to shoot the ball every time they get it. To play like Danny Ainge. They need to go down to the gym, play in pickup games, get the ball and take it end to end, as if they were Magic Johnson, and shoot it each and every time.

One thing I tell young players is that when you're playing one on one, you should never turn your back to the basket and break down a little guy. You might score, but big deal—you're not learning how to play. It doesn't take any real skill to bump someone smaller than you out of the way.

I had the misfortune of watching some of that Jabbar vs. Dr. J one-on-one exhibition in 1992 on pay-per-view. When I saw Jabbar using that big butt of his to back down Dr. J, I said, "Goodness gracious sakes alive." I couldn't believe it. How embarrassing. What a disgrace. I turned it off.

The worst thing you can do is push kids into games they don't want to play. My four children all play basketball. That's their choice. I don't pressure them to play. Unfortunately, others do.

All I hope for, besides their health, is that my children find something in their lives that provides them with the same amount of happiness basketball has provided me. I try to give them opportunities that will give them as much joy as I had, whether it's basketball, music, literature, whatever. If I can do that, I've partially succeeded as a parent.

I've made every mistake possible, not only in dealing with my children but also in my own life. But that's part of life's experiences, of growing up, of maturing.

When I was a good player, I was at the top of the salary structure in the league. It was nice, but it wasn't the driving force in my life. When I graduated with honors in 3½ years from UCLA, I told my agent that only three things mattered to me: I wanted to play in the NBA, not the ABA; I didn't care how much money the ABA offered, I wanted to face the very best competition possible—I wanted to be in the big leagues. I wanted to play in Portland. I didn't want anybody to tell me that I had to get a haircut or had to shave.

"That's it," I said. "You take care of the money."

Money isn't everything. Usually the only people who say that are the ones who have a lot of it. But I really would have played for nothing.

If you let money be the motivating factor or the driving force in life, then you end up making decisions based solely on the bottom-line. That's a mistake. People fail to realize that if you play and live with passion and fire, the money will come. Achieve excellence in anything and you can't help but achieve financial security.

I've been so lucky my entire life. I've been around so many people who are motivated by greatness, by perfection, rather than by greed and money. John Wooden, Jack Ramsay, Larry Bird, Jamaal Wilkes, Greg Lee, Lenny Wilkins and Maurice Lucas, to name a few, weren't looking for a soft couch. They rarely cared about how much money they made. They were more concerned first and foremost about the quality of the job they performed, about reaching the highest level of excellence possible.

Players today don't want to discuss what kind of game

they've got, or what moves they're working on, or where their team ranks in the standings. Instead, they want to talk about how much money they make—or even more distressing, brag about how much money they lost gambling.

There has been an evolution of sorts, from players who loved to compete to players who spend far too much time thinking about their stock portfolios. If some of those same players would think about becoming great ballplayers, the money would take care of itself. They'd have twice as much money as they do now.

A lot of today's players want the game to hurry up and be over with so they can sit around and brag about how much money they made that night and how they didn't have to do very much to earn it.

Not everyone is like that of course, but enough to cause concern.

Thankfully there were players such as Michael Jordan, who was the perfect example of a guy who had pride in his game.

In a game in the 1993 season at Utah, Jordan and the Bulls were trailing by 20 points late in the third quarter. The Jazz crowd, thinking a Utah rout was on, started booing Jordan for things he had said about their fine city. The fans were going nuts.

I remember watching Jordan come alive with the booing and sensing the game was over if he didn't take charge.

He started taking the ball to the hoop and making just about every shot. Nobody could stop him. The Bulls got back into the game and eventually won. That shut the crowd up, which is one of the all-time great feelings in sport—to quiet the crowd on the road.

I was that way. I listened to the crowd, fed off it, but rarely acknowledged it. I wanted to use the energy of the fans to make me feel great. Jack Ramsay always stressed using the crowd to make your body feel golden. He also taught us not to let those fans, or the refs or anything else, get into your mind; that's going to distract you from focusing on the ultimate goal: relentless pressure and execution until finally the other team cracks and breaks.

I always felt that, when playing on the road, if the crowd wasn't booing me and I didn't have four fouls by the start of the fourth quarter, well, I wasn't really doing anything. You never wanted to go down the stretch of a big game without having used your fouls. Saving fouls? What a waste.

It is sad when I see people like Jordan become recluses because of their fame. Years ago I made the conscious decision to deal with the attention, rather than hide from it.

At UCLA it was virtually impossible for me to go anywhere or do anything because of the fans and the media. Everything we did or said was reported in the papers, on TV or on the radio. It's a difficult thing for young teenagers to go from being private citizens to public figures and have their every move monitored and on the lips of everyone around you. I rode a bike to class so I wouldn't be stopped so many times by other students. I enjoyed walking to class and I also enjoyed meeting other students and new friends, but I had work to do too. Just because I was inconvenienced didn't mean I sat at home, reluctant to venture into the outside world.

Some people talk about how they dislike being famous, how they can't stand the attention. I don't believe that's true at all. I think it's the greatest thing in the world to be acknowledged by people for your success and achievements. People love sports. I've got my own favorite entertainers and I introduce myself to them on the street. I'm a fan too.

It amuses me when someone says, "Man, you've changed since your UCLA days." Of course I've changed. I sure hope I have. I've learned a lot about life since then.

I've lived my life in a fishbowl since I was seventeen years old. It's difficult to make all life's mistakes on the front page of the newspaper.

In spite of all that, I probably wouldn't change much if I were to live my life over. I would like to come back as another player, though. I'd like to be a combination of Trail Blazers forward Jerome Kersey and former NBA guard Mike Evans, who played for four different teams before retiring after the 1988 season. Kersey and Evans could run and jump and play all day. They also had no qualms about taking wild shots and playing a wide-open game. I look at guys like that—guys who can play all day, every day—and I get so jealous. Some players don't realize how lucky they are.

I couldn't imagine not playing basketball. To me, basketball is what life is all about. It's the perfect game. You don't need anything but a ball, a pair of shoes and a hoop. Your ability to control that ball is what determines your success. If you can't control it, it's nobody's fault but your own.

That's the way life is too. Working to control your own destiny.

Bill Russell had an interesting way of assessing his control of a game. Immediately after the final buzzer, Russell would rate his performance relative to the skills he possessed. He would ask himself, "Did I play good offense? Good defense? Rebound? Make the passes? Make the shots I should have made? Do all the little things I should have done?"

Incredibly enough, the best score he ever gave himself was 70 on a scale of 100. Russell didn't grade on the curve.

In an interview Russell and I did during my first season in Boston while he was still active, Russell wanted to know if there was a game that stuck out in my mind as the best, a game worth a high personal rating.

I didn't know how to answer it. I never thought in those terms. There were times at UCLA and Portland and later at Boston when we would play really well. The ball would be moving. No plays, just constant motion. The game in its purest form.

There was no New York Knicks or Detroit Pistons thuggery and cheap shots; this game isn't about smashing people and butting heads. It's not about trash talking and statistics. It's about timing, running, jumping, competition, positioning and quickness. Those were the things I appreciated when I played.

I loved the game, not the statistics. I didn't have a favorite team or favorite game. It didn't matter, just as long as we won the championship. Fourth grade . . . seventh grade . . . high school . . . college . . . NBA—as long as we won the championship I didn't care. To me, winning is winning. You get the same feeling every time.

Some victories are more memorable than others, though.

Against the Philadelphia 76ers in the 1977 NBA finals, we (the Trail Blazers) weren't given much of a chance to beat supposedly one of the great teams of all time. They had Dr. J, George McGinnis, Darryl Dawkins, Caldwell Jones, Henry Bibby, Steve Mix, World B. Free and Doug Collins, among others.

They also had a knack of saying the wrong thing at the wrong time.

We were down two games to none and headed back to Portland when Dr. J said that the Sixers had this series under control because they knew all of our plays, knew exactly what we were going to do.

Heck, *we* didn't even know our plays, so how could they know them? Our understanding of Ramsay's complex offense didn't come until the following season.

That was also the series in which the invincibility of Darryl Dawkins was dispelled by Maurice Lucas. Up until that time, most people (including Darryl) thought the massive Dawkins, who was nineteen, but stood 6' 11" and weighed 265 pounds, could clench his fists and everybody in the world would collapse at his knee and beg forgiveness.

Then came a fight, highlighted by Dawkins accidentally punching teammate Collins in the mouth. Collins did not have a good game in the series after taking some stitches. Some have argued that he did not have a good game the rest of his injury-shortened career.

The fabulous play of our small forward, Bob Gross, was instrumental in our winning the championship. Normally good for 11, 12 points a game during the regular season, Gross scored 25 and 27 points in the final two games to clinch the championship. Equally important was Bob's work on Dr. J. Julius got his numbers, but Gross made the big plays, the deciding plays. By becoming an offensive threat himself, Gross made Dr. J work that much harder. Had it not been for Bobby Gross, we wouldn't have won the championship. As many times as Ramsay threw Gross out of practice for misbehaving, we felt lucky to have Bobby. We often felt that Gross's dismissals were because of Lucas's and my transgressions.

What a wonderful team that was. We played so well together and understood exactly what had to be done to win. We became what Ramsay dreamed the game of basketball should be: fast breaks, teamwork, ball movement and pressure defense.

No player is bigger than the game. That's one of the hardest things for the aging stars and the struggling, soon-to-be-fired coaches to understand. The game keeps going on and keeps getting better, with or without them. No one is indispensable.

Isn't that the excitement of it all? You have to go out and get it done every day. You can't think that your job today is secure because of yesterday. The minute you start taking things for granted, you lose the edge.

I love being on the edge. I love the view. Like we learned in *Spinal Tap:* "We want to take it to eleven."

"I need a miracle."
—Bob Weir

There are moments in every person's life when you finally have to concede that things will never be as they
once were. Shortly after the end of the 1984–85 season with
the Los Angeles Clippers, I had arrived at such a moment.

We won only 31 of 82 games that year and failed once
again to reach the playoffs. We saw Jim Lynam get fired
and Don Chaney take his place with only 21 games left to
play. We were a team that should have done better, but
didn't. Our roster included Marques Johnson, Michael Cage,
a healthy Derek Smith, Norm Nixon, Junior Bridgeman
and myself, but something was missing, maybe a lot. After
plenty of postseason soul searching, I finally figured out
part of the problem: it was me.

I was no longer capable of taking a team to a championship level. I realized finally that that had been the case
since my injuries in Portland in 1978. I wasn't even a front-
line player anymore. My numbers that season—67 games

played, a 10.1 point average and 9.0 rebounds per game—were embarrassing and paled in comparison with the stars of the league. I was thirty-two, but my body felt much, much older. The injuries had reduced my game to mediocrity. In fact, I had no game. My legs were pretty much shot by the time I got to the NBA in 1974. I peaked when I was twelve, just before I tore up my knee. Everything was gone by the end of the 1985 season.

Something had to be done. Something drastic.

There were two teams at the top of my trade list: the Los Angeles Lakers and the Boston Celtics. The Lakers were attractive for lots of reasons. The organization was first-rate, thanks to owner Dr. Jerry Buss, general manager Jerry West and Coach Pat Riley. They had magnificent players in Magic Johnson and Kareem Abdul-Jabbar. They were close to San Diego. They had a championship mentality and tradition. In fact, the Lakers had just beaten the Celtics in the NBA Finals, their third title in six years.

I didn't expect to be a starter. Instead, I saw my role as a substitute, someone able to give Jabbar an occasional rest.

I called West first and told him about my plan. He was polite as always, but the conversation was a short one.

"No, thanks," he said. "We're not interested. I've seen your feet."

Then I called Celtics president Red Auerbach. Red wasn't available because he was having a meeting with Larry Bird. I left a message: "Red, please call."

When Red got the message he showed it to Bird.

"Larry, what do you think?"

"Go get him," Bird said.

Larry thought I might be worth the gamble because I could offer some backup help to center Robert Parish. Parish played 2,850 minutes during the 1984–85 regular season (second highest on the team, behind Larry) and another 803 minutes during the playoffs (fourth highest on the team).

By the time the Celtics made their way past Cleveland, Detroit and Philadelphia to face the Lakers and Jabbar in the NBA Finals, Chief was starting to fade a bit. By the end of the series, Jabbar was clearly in control.

Jabbar played nearly 200 fewer minutes than Chief during the playoffs that year. That makes a big difference.

When I finally reached Red, I explained my position and then held my breath. After a few seconds of silence, Red said, "It sounds like a good idea to me. I think we can find a spot for you on this team. Just don't say anything to anybody. Let us do it."

Auerbach remembered the debacle in Portland, where I used every means necessary to leave the Trail Blazers. Auerbach wanted me to keep my mouth shut this time. That's not my style, but I did it.

No problem. I had learned a very valuable and painful lesson when I left Portland. Trades don't happen in the press. The press and player agents will generate rumors, but those people aren't the ones making the trades. It just doesn't do anybody any good to air your dirty laundry in the media. It hurt me immeasurably in Portland. I'm glad I was able to somewhat recover from it. No matter what, though, there will always be emotional scars from that experience.

Eventually the Celtics and the Clippers began working on a deal. But the Clippers were dragging their feet, causing the negotiations to almost break down. The Clippers wanted me to pay them a lot of money—a year's salary, to be exact— or else they wouldn't go along with the trade.

One of the things I did before signing with Boston was to visit Chief. I was back in Boston negotiating, checking things out, and I asked M. L. Carr if he would take me over to Chief's house. I wanted Chief to know that I wasn't there to try to steal his starting job. He was the center. I was the substitute.

I still had an ego; you have to have one to survive and excel in the NBA. But I always knew what my role was to be on that team. Whenever I forgot, Bird would always remind me: "Get to the weak side and rebound."

Auerbach and the Clippers finally agreed on compensation. The Celtics would get me. The Clippers would get forward Cedric Maxwell, who had played on two Celtics NBA championship teams, a No. 1 draft choice and lots of my money.

During those negotiations I came to fully appreciate Auerbach's skills as a basketball man and as a human being. With Auerbach, there is no double-talk, no mixed signals. If Auerbach said something, you could believe it. He created Celtics pride by the way he treated people. He made members of that organization feel proud about who they were and what they were doing. That's a rare gift, but Auerbach was able to produce that kind of loyalty.

"Look, first of all, we don't have incentive contracts," he said during our negotiations. "You're on the team. We negotiate a fee and we pay you that fee no matter what happens."

The whole thing took five minutes. With the Clippers, it would have taken five months. My old contract with the Clippers was so delicate, so complicated, that I was basically paid by how many breaths I took while I was on the court. With the Celtics, it was refreshingly different.

In retrospect, it was a blessing that Jerry West turned me down. The Lakers, as great a team as they were, probably weren't for me.

I was overjoyed with the trade to Boston for lots of reasons. With literally the stroke of a pen, I went from a last-place team to a championship team. I suddenly got to play with all these wonderful players and learn from K. C. Jones, whose contributions should never be underestimated.

Boston was basketball heaven. I grew up listening to

Chick Hearn doing Lakers' radio broadcasts, but the Celtics were always my team. I admired the franchise and everything about it: the players, the team spirit, the giant shadows cast by those championship banners and retired jersey numbers, the fans, the Boston Garden, the smoke from Auerbach's cigars.

When I was kid growing up in San Diego, which is about as far from Boston as you can be in the continental United States, we didn't have a television in our house until the mid-1960s. It just wasn't a priority with my parents. And when we finally did get a TV, it didn't have any sound. It's funny the things you can remember from thirty years ago, but I can vividly recall watching Celtics games on that little black-and-white picture tube and immediately knowing who the great Bill Russell was. His style, his presence and his talents literally jumped off the screen.

Years later, when Russell was interviewing me for a WTBS NBA TV show, I told him about picking him out on the screen.

"It was probably because I was left-handed," he said.

When Larry Bird first came to the Celtics, Dave Cowens took him aside and gave him some advice about playing in Boston. "Don't go about it 90 or 80 percent, because the fans know basketball here."

There is something very special about Celtics fans. I knew it the first time I ever played in the Garden. It's not that they just love the Celtics—which they usually do. They love basketball. They've seen all the great players. They live the game. They know the history of the organization and the league. They know the championship players, from Bob Cousy, to Russell, to Bill Sharman, to Frank Ramsey, to Tom Heinsohn, to K. C. and Sam Jones, to Satch Sanders, to Don Nelson, to Cowens, to Chaney, to Jo Jo White, to Bird, Kevin McHale and Parish and Dennis Johnson. The fans in Boston really care if the Celtics win, but just as important, they care that it's a great game. They're accustomed to excellence. They want to see great basketball, the way it's supposed to be played—with teamwork, fast breaks, man-to-man pressure defense.

If the Celtics play poorly, those fans are the first to jump all over them. But no fans in the country have more passion and understanding of the game than the Celtics followers.

When I finally moved to Boston in the fall of 1985, David Halberstam told me that Cambridge was the only place for me to live. He hit it right on the head as I became the first professional athlete to live in that great city while playing for the local Boston teams. Halberstam introduced me to his circle of friends in Cambridge, including a realtor. When I told them of my interests and tastes in housing, the first house they took me to fit my needs perfectly. It wasn't until after I had purchased the home that I learned I had bought it from Gunther and Karen Weil who, along with Dr. Tim Leary, had used the house as a classroom for their psychology courses in the early 1960s.

I loved riding my bike through the streets of Cambridge and Boston, to listen to the fans scream and cheer as I cruised by. They weren't cheering me, they were cheering the spirit of the Celtics. They loved their team and they loved the game. It was great to live in a place where what you did for a living was so important to the people in that city. To be a small part of that was indescribable.

When I played in Portland, the fans were devoted to the Trail Blazers, but they didn't eat and sleep the game to the extent the fans did in Boston. When I signed with Portland in 1974 there was less than 1,800 season ticket holders. By 1978, Portland management limited season ticket sales to 11,000. Otherwise, only season ticket holders would have been able to attend games. When I left Portland in 1978, there had been 53 consecutive sellouts. Currently the Trail Blazers' sellout streak is approaching 726, the longest in the NBA. But, in April 1977, you could walk up the day of the game and buy seats to a Trail Blazers game. That wasn't the case in Boston soon after Bird arrived.

The Boston Garden is a shrine. It's where God carved the Ten Commandments of Basketball and gave them to Red Auerbach.

There is no better place to play basketball than the Boston Garden. When you first walk onto the parquet floor, the moment is frozen in time. You're at *the* Garden, the place where championships were won. To be a part of that history was so wonderful that you tingled with excitement.

I don't keep mementos, pictures or trophies in my house in San Diego. I send them all to Craig Sherman, a friend, who keeps those things at his house in Montgomery, Alabama.

I like to look to the future. I don't look back. Plus, I don't want my children to be constantly bombarded with that stuff. But my favorite piece of basketball memorabilia is a framed double postcard given to me by Charles Reilly, my neighbor from across the street. One year he gave me a postcard of Muni Gym in San Diego's Balboa Park, where my career started. A few years later he gave me a postcard of Boston Garden, where my career ended. He later took them and had them framed. The postcards now hang on a kitchen wall near the sink, so when I'm doing the dishes I can take a quick glance over my right shoulder and have my daily religious experience.

During a television interview Russell and I did in 1986, we took a walk across the Garden floor. Near midcourt, Russell stopped and looked around the place.

"I couldn't imagine a better place to play a game than the Boston Garden," he said.

"The only thing I can't imagine," I said, "is what took me so long to get here."

Russell used to say that the Garden had a comfort zone

to it. There was something personal about it. It wasn't one of these sterile, plastic arenas. It had soul.

Russell didn't pay any attention to the banners. That's probably because he helped put so many of them up there. I always glanced upward. During the national anthem or pregame introductions, I'd look into the stands in search of former players. Knowing they were in the crowd really fired me up.

The Celtics were everything I thought basketball should be. I've always wanted to have fun playing basketball. I also wanted to expose my four kids to the positive side of professional sports. They had seen so much of the negative aspects of it, what with my injuries and many disagreements with management, the fans and the media. I wanted them to see their father happy and I was happiest playing basketball, and playing it for a championship team.

I always played for the joy of the game. I've been very lucky. I've had to make very few decisions in my life based on money. Playing for the Celtics was a lifelong dream of mine. It was very difficult for me to leave southern California, but I was at the point in my career that I was going to do whatever it took to get back to the championship level. Even if that meant the East Coast. If it meant making some financial concessions to the Clippers, then fine. I would have paid whatever was necessary to get to the Celtics. It was worth every single penny I spent. I was able to play for the two greatest basketball families in the history of the game: UCLA and the Boston Celtics.

I thought it was going to be great playing in Boston, but it turned out to be better than I ever imagined and more . . . much more. It was everything I had ever hoped for. I couldn't believe how lucky I was to wear a Celtics uniform. It was an honor and a privilege.

Reputations follow players everywhere. Mine, according

to the Celtics, was: "A strong, sometimes overbearing personality. When healthy, a player capable of helping a team. Demanding of his teammates and to a greater degree, himself. Hates losing. Not afraid to speak his mind."

I loved everything about the new situation—the team, the city, the basketball atmosphere. Auerbach deserved the credit for creating this aura surrounding the Celtics. He had the ability to promote and sell the game in its early days. He was such an incredible worker. Every free moment he had, he was out there with promotions, doing clinics, teaching the game of basketball.

Auerbach built something that no other franchise in the history of sports has been able to duplicate. No other team has the dedicated following of ex-players that the Celtics have. UCLA is a very, very special family too, but J. D. Morgan, the Bruins' athletic director, was not able to stay around long enough to continue holding that family together.

When the Celtics have a party, such as Larry's retirement in February 1993, the team flies all the former players back for the event. Jack Ramsay had his number retired in Portland and the Trail Blazers didn't do a thing. I called and said, "Hey, I've got the night off from broadcasting and I want to be there for Jack's night. Will you please send me a ticket. Bring in Dave Twardzik, Lionel Hollins, Johnny Davis . . . all the guys, and it will be a great time. We'd love to be there."

The Trail Blazers' response was: "It's not in our budget." This from a team that is one of the most successful franchises in the NBA from a monetary standpoint. Yet they said they didn't have the money to cover the costs of a few plane tickets. I ended up calling Ramsay myself and wishing him congratulations.

The Trail Blazers didn't understand or didn't seem to care

that we gave everything we had to that franchise. We wanted to be there to honor our coach, to continue our link with our team.

Portland wanted to save a few bucks. The management didn't realize that when you're old and you can't play anymore, there's nothing more satisfying than returning home and celebrating the success of one of your own—in this case, Ramsay.

Auerbach understood. Guys such as Russell, K.C., Cowens, Bird, among others, gave their lives to the Celtics and Auerbach treated them accordingly. He never forgot their contributions. The younger Celtics players see that loyalty and usually, if they have any pride, want to be part of the tradition. Then they give their all for the franchise. It is a cycle that Auerbach has kept alive for decades.

The New York Knicks and the Lakers are pretty good at fostering that same type of environment, but Auerbach is in a class by himself.

It was Auerbach who hired Johnny Most as the play-by-play radio announcer. Most, his vocal cords hardened by the countless cigarettes he smoked, had this raspy, enduring, unmistakable voice that pulled you into the game. Once while broadcasting a Celtics–Milwaukee Bucks game, his lit cigarette fell into his lap. Over the airwaves you could hear a panicked Most saying, "Oh, my! I was on fire!"

Most was an enjoyable homer. He hated whomever the Celtics played, especially the Lakers. If the Lakers did something that Most disliked, he would say, "This is a typical disgusting play," or "The yellow, gutless way they do things here."

He was sixty-nine when he died on January 3, 1993. A lot of the players theorized he lived so long because he had so many toxins and poisons in his body from the cigarettes and whatnot that no disease could possibly survive his daily routines.

Auerbach, with his feel for the game and the wants of the fans, and Most, with his voice and his style, created an incredible basketball environment. Celtics games eventually became a happening, an event much like a Dead show.

It helped to have the great players. But again, you have to give Auerbach a lot of the credit for finding these guys and blending them into teams that won sixteen NBA titles.

It started with the playing style created by Cousy and Russell. Russell had a fiery pride and demanded to be treated as an individual and with dignity. Two things he rarely accorded to anyone else.

A look at the history of the Celtics indicates how incredibly fortunate they were to get three key players: Russell, Cowens and Bird. Those are the three who sent the franchise over the top.

They were the fighters and the great competitors with the necessary skills to dominate and decide games. There have been a lot of gifted players who have worn Celtics uniforms, but very few of them could control the flow of the game by their specific actions. Russell, Cowens and Bird were the only Celtics who could determine the outcome of the game by what they did on the court. Havlicek and Cousy came close.

When I arrived in Boston, the Celtics were already a championship team. They had won the 1981 and 1984 NBA championships and finished second in 1985. But once you've won the championship you realize there's no difference between second place and last.

The starting five was written in stone: Bird and Kevin McHale forwards, Chief center, Dennis Johnson and Danny Ainge guards. But gone from the roster were M. L. Carr, who retired after the 1985 season, Cedric Maxwell, Quinn Buckner, Carlos Clark and Ray Williams. The rest of the team now included Jerry Sichting, Greg Kite, Sam Vincent,

David Thirdkill, Rick Carlisle, Scott Wedman, Sly Williams (who only played six games) and me.

Before a game McHale would sit in the locker room reading the paper, telling stories and jokes. He always wanted me to tell him about what "really happened" with Patty Hearst, or why I got arrested at UCLA, or what it was like to be involved in a sit-in.

Chief would usually read his fan mail—out loud. K. C. Jones would be giving a pregame speech and Chief would start reciting those letters to me.

"Hey, Chief," I said, "I'm listening to Coach."

Chief came back with "It's okay, Bill. We're going to win anyway."

Bird would get to the game at about 4:30. Then he'd get dressed and go out on the court. For the next two hours, he would shoot. The ritual was almost always the same: three balls, three ball boys, two hours of shooting, a hot shower, a massage and then the game.

D. J. was fairly quiet. He just went about his business as best you could in that locker room.

All Ainge ever wanted to do was talk about money and golf. I still don't know why. He tithes his money to the Mormon Church and he cheats at golf. Whenever Danny would start bragging about his golf game, McHale would pull out a Bible from the depths of his locker, bring it to Danny and ask him to place his hand on it. "Now," Kevin would demand, "tell us what you really shot."

With the Celtics the motto was "It's not how many shots you make, it's how many you take." Nobody adhered to that motto better than Ainge. He had no conscience when it came to shooting, but that was fine. It was one of the reasons I liked him.

Then there was K.C. He was as classy as they come and perfect for our team.

K.C. knew how to motivate this team. He never said much before or after a game. When he did, we listened.

There were some games that season when we absolutely stunk up the place. We were terrible, absolutely terrible. A disgrace to the sport. We came into the locker room afterward and K.C. told us, the disgust in his voice evident, "Go take a shower and wash that mess off yourself. You were ugly tonight. Go get cleaned up."

Then during his next pregame speech K.C. said, "I couldn't sleep last night after watching that hideous performance. Well into the night the phone rang and it was Bill Russell. He had seen the game on satellite and he was so disgusted with our effort that he wanted to know where he could mail back his eleven NBA championship rings. He didn't want them anymore. Then Havlicek called. He had also seen the game on satellite and he wanted to know how he could get his retired jersey removed from the banner hanging from the Garden rafters. Then Sam Jones called and he wanted to know how he could disassociate himself from the Boston Celtics. Eventually, I got calls from all the former Celtics asking how they could disassociate themselves from this team."

The first time I heard the speech I was in tears. We were so fired up that we went on a long winning streak. We ended up with a 67–15 regular season record, the best in the NBA that season (fourth best in league history), and lost only one home game, which is still an NBA record. We eventually won an NBA record of 48 consecutive home games during 1985, '86 and '87, breaking the 44 straight the Blazers won when I was in Portland in 1976-78.

Great basketball teams have their most memorable moments on the practice court. The 1986 Celtics were no different.

Our practices were intense. That's what happens when

you have a good team, everyone wants to prove his worth. When we scrimmaged, things became quite spirited.

Chris Ford and Jimmy Rodgers were the assistant coaches. During those scrimmages, they doubled as referees and had to make all the calls. We would say the nastiest, meanest, most vulgar, degrading things to them when they made bad calls, which was every time they blew the whistle. As soon as they put whistles in their mouths, they were fair game . . . Chris Ford and Jimmy Rodgers . . . Agghhhh!

I loved the practices. Relatively speaking, I was healthy. It was wonderful to be running the court, competing, being part of a team. It was great when McHale or Bird would call me in the morning and warn me about that day's scrimmage.

"We're going to kick your butt," McHale would say.

"Don't bring that 1965 jump shot around here," Bird would add.

Bird and McHale always razzed me about something, mostly my history of injuries. When I started picking on Carlisle one day at practice, Bird said, "Hey, Rick, you don't have to take that crap from him. You've already played more games than him and you've only been in the league a year."

They always gave me the hardest time before the games. We'd warm up and then go sit down. As I took my seat I'd always tell the ball boy, "Okay, coffee—black—three aspirin, two towels, two hydroculators and a *New York Times*."

Originally it started with just a cup of coffee. Then the bench started adding things and it got to be a routine. Ainge, who never missed a chance to needle a teammate, started telling people that I was a little on the demanding side. "You know what? Bill thinks everybody in this world is a ball boy and he can just ask anybody to do anything."

The whole season was a joyride and I cherished every

minute of it. Teammates develop special relationships with each other and Larry Bird was extra special when it came time to look out for his fellow Celtics.

Bird agreed to make a commercial for a local Boston restaurant, the Scotch & Sirloin. In lieu of a fee for the commercial, Bird asked the owner, Harry Johnson, to consider making the restaurant the unofficial Celtics hangout. Bird just wanted a place where everyone on the team could bring their friends and family after a game and feel comfortable.

In exchange for the commercial, Harry said we could come in anytime and eat for free. All he asked is that we didn't forget to tip the waiters and waitresses. It was a great deal for us because it gave us a nice place to relax and unwind. And Harry, no matter how much food we ate (and it was always a lot), never once made anybody feel that they were abusing their privileges. Even though it was costing him a small fortune to do this, he always made you feel welcome.

For Bird, though, this was simply his way of taking care of his teammates, of trying to create a sense of team unity. Bird was obviously a special player, but his uniqueness as a human being made him even greater then he was as a player.

We were a confident team. We were the Celtics. We had an attitude. "Hey, we're going to win every game we play and we don't care who you are and we're not interested in what you're going to do to try to stop us." That's how it was at UCLA and eventually in Portland too. We knew we were going to find a way to win the game. That was the common thread.

Somebody brought a newspaper to practice one day on the road and said, "Hey, look at this. We're the underdogs tonight."

We couldn't believe it. Us . . . not favored to win? We thought it was a misprint, a joke. We spent the whole day talking about it. Even when we were warming up for the game, we kept looking at the other team and saying, "Hey, they're favored."

We killed them. We won by 30. We had an attitude.

Near the end of the regular season, we traveled to Milwaukee for a game at the Mecca. The Bucks, who were coached by Don Nelson, would win 57 games that year and advance to the Eastern Conference finals before losing to the Celtics 4–0.

On this particular night, K.C. decided to try something different. He told us at the shoot-around that the first-string Stat Team was going to have the night off. They were going to sit on the bench and cheer. K.C. was going to order them beer and popcorn. The Green Team was going to play. K.C. said we had been riding their coattails all year long and it was time for us to earn our paychecks.

He called together the second-stringers—Sichting, Carlisle, Kite, Scott Wedman and me—and said, "Okay, Green Team, you've been talking trash all season, living off the skills of the Stat Team. Now we're going to let you prove how good you really are. We're going to give the Stat Team the night off. Don't tell anybody about this, but we're going to start you guys and the Stat Team will come in and play a little bit in reserve."

As basketball teams go, the Green Team was not the most physically gifted group ever assembled. We didn't have much quickness or speed, but we played well together. Our main offense wasn't fancy. Good solid pressure defense generating fast-break opportunities for quick shots. In the set offense, get the ball to me, then get moving to get open, with the primary weapons being Sichting's and Wedman's perimeter shooting.

Sichting was marvelous that season. I was fortunate to win the NBA's Sixth Man Award in 1986, but you could have made a serious argument for Sichting too. He played in all 100 games that year, played more minutes than I did and made 57 percent of his field goal attempts, which is fantastic for a guard. I bet you that of the 235 baskets he made during the regular season, not more than 15 of them were layups.

Years later, I discovered Coach Wooden had something to do with Sichting's success. They both went to Martinsville (Indiana) High and Purdue. When a scholarship was established in John Wooden's name at Martinsville, the first recipient was Jerry Sichting.

Anyway, the Green Team (the second unit) got all fired up for the Bucks. It might have been a meaningless game in the standings (we had first place wrapped up), but it meant something to us. It meant a chance to start for the Celtics.

Milwaukee, which hadn't beaten us all year, was charged up. And Nelson always wanted to win against his old team.

By the time the public address-announcer was ready to reveal the starting lineups, the place was going crazy. The Milwaukee fans were charged to root against the stars of the Celtics: Bird, McHale, Chief, D. J., Ainge.

Then they announced the members of the Green Team and it was like letting the air out of a balloon. Everyone—the fans, the Bucks, Nelson—expected to see the real Boston Celtics, and instead, they got us. You could see the disappointment in their faces.

From the outset we could do no wrong. Wedman and Sichting were hitting jumper after jumper. I was back-dooring guys for layups. Carlisle was getting his share. Kite was all over the boards. The ball was moving and we were just killing them in the first quarter.

Toward the end of the first quarter there was a scramble for a loose ball near the half-court line. Kite was in the middle of the pile and got called for a foul. That was typical.

Whenever there was a collision involving players like Kite or the Lakers' Kurt Rambis, the referee always whistled them for a foul.

Lee Jones was the official. As Jones made his way to the scorer's table to report the foul, Kite, who was still sitting on the court, cradling the ball, threw the ball and it hit Jones on the side of the head. Jones threw Kite out.

Jones did what he had to do. I felt sorry for Greg. Here he was, ejected from a game where he was the starting power forward for the Boston Celtics. He had a chance to go out there and beat the Milwaukee Bucks and he literally threw his opportunity away.

When I played for the Celtics, I just tried to keep the pace of the game up. We had so many weapons available, I just wanted to make things happen as fast as possible, to keep the pressure on the other team. I still had certain playing standards that I tried to reach, but the circumstances were different as a backup. When you're playing 35 or 40 minutes a game, you can take some time to warm up, to get used to the flow of the action, to let the game come to you. When you're coming off the bench you don't have that luxury. You've got to make the most out of your 15 or 20 minutes. You have to be ready to explode right at the start.

Kite forgot about that part of the equation. Lee Jones reminded him by taking away the one thing Kite didn't have much of: playing time.

We did hold on to win the game, though I doubt it made Kite feel any better.

There was a part of me that missed being a starter, but more than anything I had missed being a winner. After spending six consecutive losing seasons with the Clippers, I had almost forgotten how revitalizing and rejuvenating a victory could be.

In a way, the 1985–86 season was the ultimate fantasy.

It was a second chance, a rare opportunity to be part of a championship-level team.

I made it through 80 of the 82 regular-season games and 16 of the 18 playoff games. This stacks up brilliantly compared to the fact that I missed a total of more than nine full seasons of NBA action in my thirteen-year playing career.

Compared to the previous season, Chief received 300 minutes more rest during the course of the regular schedule and more than 200 minutes of rest during the playoffs.

Bird once told Bob Ryan of the *Boston Globe* that I made every player on the second team twice as good as they were. It was nice of him to say that, but I always figured my main job was to make sure Bird, McHale and Chief arrived at the games on time.

Aside from winning, my favorite moments on the court came when I was out there with Bird. It is safe to say that our playing styles were complementary to each other. We must have utilized basic give-and-go plays a thousand times that season. All it took was a moment's worth of eye contact, or a little nod of the head, and off Bird went, the pass from me not far behind. The other teams never seemed to figure it out, but the Boston reporters and columnists who covered us on a regular basis knew. According to Ryan, everyone on press row would immediately pull out a quarter—winner take all—and bet on how many possessions it would take before Larry and I ran a give-and-go. The wagering would begin the moment they saw K.C. motion for me to enter the game.

The players had a few traditions of their own. When a guy was getting ready to enter a game, we'd challenge him. "Will you please just go *do* something. Once in your life. Please. *Do* something."

I did what I could that season. After a nightmare debut

against New Jersey in the season opener, in which I disgraced the game of basketball, I settled down and started playing better. In fact, from December to March 14, the night I fractured my wrist in a game against Atlanta, things were going almost too well. You couldn't wipe the smile off my face, I was so happy.

We rolled through that season playing with great confidence. Someone, somewhere, in a foolish moment, said, "Hey, guys, let's not drink another beer until we win the championship."

We instantly agreed.

"Yeah, this will be great!" we yelled. "No more beers until we win it all!"

Then we sobered up.

At one point in our quest for the NBA title, McHale put it all into perspective.

"Hey," he said, "we're going to win it *this* year, aren't we, guys?"

By the time the playoffs arrived, we were a very tough team. We swept the Chicago Bulls in the first round, won four out of five against Atlanta, swept the Bucks and then faced the Houston Rockets in the NBA Finals.

I'm not comfortable talking about personal accomplishments, but there was one particular play in Game 4 against the Rockets that I'm proud of. With only a few minutes left to play, McHale had the ball initially and got his shot rejected yet again by Hakeem Olajuwon. D. J. ran down the loose ball and he finally got it at half-court. He quickly looked up—he knew time on the shot clock was almost out, but we were playing on the road and he couldn't find the shot clock. Already on the move, I gave D. J. some eye contact, communicating to him: "You've got to go to the hoop right now." D. J. drove the lane and Olajuwon and this time Ralph Sampson went for the ball again. I was able to convert the stick back. We ended up winning, 106–103, to take a 3–1 advantage in the series. We closed them out in six.

Rick Carlisle later said that the 1986 championship season was a "great reprieve" for me.

"No one," he said, "knows why Bill was able to go through that season without an injury. It was a magical thing."

Carlisle is right. It was a reprieve and it was magical. To play on that Celtics title team, especially after the injuries I had suffered during my career, made that season my greatest personal playing accomplishment.

The next season was also memorable, but for all the wrong reasons. We had the No. 2 pick in the draft and selected Maryland forward Len Bias, who died of a cocaine overdose two days after the draft. Then came the injuries. I only played in ten regular-season games that year because of a series of stress fractures in my right foot. Wedman also was hurt and appeared in only six games. That forced K.C. to reduce his playing rotation to seven, sometimes six players.

Somehow we advanced to the NBA finals, but nothing came easy. After sweeping Chicago, it took seven games to eliminate Milwaukee and another seven games (and one miraculous game-winning play by Bird and D. J.) to eliminate the Detroit Pistons. Still left to play were the Lakers.

Even with Chief struggling to play on a sprained ankle and McHale limping up and down the court on a broken foot of his own, we managed to stretch the series to six games before losing the title to the Lakers. I was no factor. About the only thing I did the entire series was throw my warm-ups in Jack Nicholson's face as I entered game 6. I did a lot of watching from the bench, and when I did play, I was rendered ineffective by my foot and ankle injuries. For the record, my last Celtics appearance and, as it turned out, my last NBA appearance came in the decisive Game 6. What a sad and disappointing way to end a season and a career.

Still, for one remarkable, rewarding and exhilarating 1986 season, I never had a better time playing basketball. I was part of a championship team, part of a family and part of a community that lived and loved basketball. That's something I'll always have and cherish. After we won the NBA title, I answered my phone for the longest time with "World championship headquarters—what are you going to do about it?" That got to be quite embarrassing when some of the phone calls were actually official business.

The memory of that 1986 championship doesn't make it easy to watch the Celtics these days. Right now, the big question involving the franchise revolves around Dave Gavitt, the man in charge. Can he inspire the same kind of loyalty that Auerbach was famous for? Can he evaluate players the way Auerbach did? Can he restore the Celtics to their familiar place at or near the top of the NBA? Can he do what Auerbach did?

If the 1993 Celtics were an indication of things to come, then I don't like Gavitt's chances. At best, the Celtics were mediocre in the 1992–93 season. They played with little pride, no leadership, no style. Worse yet, Jerry West, who lost six championships to the Celtics, finally got his ultimate revenge by saddling Boston with Sherman Douglas and his huge contract.

I would not say Dave Gavitt is off to an auspicious debut with his personnel decisions. It's one thing to treat people right, which he does, but if you don't get the right players in there, you're just coddling losers. I hate that. That's what Donald T. Sterling, the owner of the Clippers, has done with his franchise.

Auerbach didn't do that. He had the genius to know how to put a team together, how to assemble the parts so they all fit. Wooden was the same way. West hasn't done it as long, but he's almost in the same class as Auerbach and Wooden.

So far, Gavitt hasn't shown that same knack. Look who he brought in for the 1992–93 season: Douglas, Xavier McDaniel, Alaa Abdelnaby. C'mon, who are these guys? This is the Boston Celtics. The trio of Douglas, McDaniel and Abdelnaby isn't exactly the foundation for a dynasty. It isn't McHale, Bird and Parish. It isn't even Kite, Wedman and Walton.

I mean, the X-man is a good player, but he's got his problems. He's a small forward who plays a post-up game. Tough to play a post-up game when you're 6' 7".

Douglas? Forget it. Abdelnaby? I doubt it. Portland and Milwaukee, two teams who have a long and successful tradition in judging basketball talent, dumped him.

Right now, the Celtics don't have any great or good players. Those kinds of players aren't in Boston, they're in Phoenix (Barkley), Utah (Malone), Orlando (Shaquille), Charlotte (Mourning) and Houston (Olajuwon). Seattle might soon join the list if Shawn Kemp ever develops his game.

The realities of today's NBA make it unlikely that the things Auerbach and Russell accomplished with the Celtics in the 1950s and 1960s will happen again in the league. These days, a dynasty is a relative term.

But the Celtics fans deserve a better product than what Gavitt has delivered so far.

The Celtics do have one advantage: History is on their side. When things have appeared to be the bleakest, the Celtics have always managed to respond to the challenge. If ever there was a time they needed history to repeat itself, this is it.

Hey, Red! Do something!

"I went to see the Captain . . ."
—Jerry Garcia

I used to think Larry Bird was a good basketball player. Then I played with him.

Larry Bird, like all truly great players, is much better than I ever dreamed. I think that today Larry Bird is the greatest forward in the history of the game of basketball.

At the start of the 1986 season, my first with the Boston Celtics, we played the Indiana Pacers in an exhibition game at Indianapolis's Market Square Arena. The schedule was such that we didn't have another game for several days, so Bird, Quinn Buckner (who had just been traded from the Celtics to the Pacers) and I decided to go to French Lick, Indiana, Larry's hometown. Our driver was a state trooper. Our transportation was a state patrol car.

We didn't leave Indianapolis until nearly midnight, but that was all right. We had some beers on ice, a designated driver, a full tank of gas and a destination. About 1:30 A.M., we passed through Bloomington, the home of Indiana University. Quinn had played at IU and Bird had originally signed with the Hoosiers and Coach Bob Knight before he transferred to Indiana State. I had never been to any of these places, so when we came to Bloomington I suggested we pay Knight a visit and say hello. I mean, we were in the neighborhood.

"Quinn," I said, "let's drop by Bob Knight's house. Let's go over there right now and play him two on two. You and him against Bird and me."

Quinn, one of Knight's all-time favorite players, was mortified.

"We can't do that," he said. "It's one-thirty in the morning."

"Sure we can, Quinn," I said. "Just give the driver the directions to his house and we'll be there in no time."

"Forget it," Quinn said.

Bird and I wouldn't take no for an answer. We wanted to go see Knight. But Quinn wouldn't break.

"How about if we call him?" Bird said.

"Go ahead, but I'm not giving you the number," Quinn said.

That's when we tried grabbing Quinn's briefcase. Too late: Quinn wouldn't let go. We piled on top of Quinn, hoping to pry the briefcase from his hands and get his private phone book.

Quinn finally calmed us down and we made the rest of the trip south in relative peace. By the time we got to French Lick, the sun was just beginning to peek over the horizon. The streets were deserted as we entered the town, but then Bird noticed a pickup truck parked off to the side of the road near the center of town. We pulled over because Bird apparently knew the guys in the truck. Bird knew everybody in French Lick and everybody knew him.

Anyway, these guys had just finished hunting. There were a slew of dead deer and several empty whiskey bottles in the back and guns everywhere. I was thinking, "Oh, great."

Bird didn't seem to mind. This seemed perfectly normal to him.

We talked to his buddies for a few more minutes and then drove to his house. Bird lived there during the off-season, and it was a sprawling place, complete with a full-court basketball facility, glass backboards, the works.

We got some sleep and then Quinn and I walked down the hill to Bird's basketball court and started shooting around. A little while later, we heard Bird yell from the house, "What ya'll doin'?" Before we could answer, a golf ball whizzed past us. We turned around and there was Bird with a golf club in his hand. He was standing on the hill next to the house, teeing off and using the basketball court down in the ravine as his target. Quinn and I were obviously in the way.

Lucky for us he was just warming up.

Later that day I coerced Bird into taking me to the house where he grew up. It was a modest place. A rickety hoop still stood guard over the dirt court where Bird had first practiced and played. Very much like the court I had in my backyard in La Mesa.

Bird told me the history of the place and probably figured that was enough. But I hadn't come there for a drive-by quickie tour. I wanted something more permanent. I had something else in mind.

As Bird looked on obviously puzzled, I pulled out a glass jar that I had brought with me. Then I borrowed a small spade from the nearby woodshed and dug up a patch of dirt from Bird's childhood court. I scooped the dirt into the jar, put a lid on it and kept it with me that entire season.

When I returned to San Diego at the end of the season, I drove to the house where I grew up, the same house where my parents still live today. I went to the dirt court where I first played and unscrewed the lid from the jar. I carefully sprinkled the prized dirt from Bird's boyhood court onto my own.

I wanted my four sons to be able to play on the same ground Bird played on. Maybe some of his special qualities would rub off.

Bird thought I was nuts. Larry will understand things a lot clearer now that he's had to go through a lot of the physical problems that wrecked my career.

I knew Bird was a very, very good player, but it wasn't until I joined the Celtics and saw him on an everyday basis, especially during our practices, that I came to realize that he was one of the chosen few, one of the all-time NBA elite.

You have to understand the difference in talent levels. There are good players, such as Clyde Drexler, Shawn Kemp and Chris Mullin. Then there are the great players. Bird was one of those.

The wonderful thing about practice is that it lacks the structure of the game. Players are out there having fun, experimenting and expanding their games. One of the joys of playing on the same team with Bird was watching him at our workouts. The shots he would hit, the passes he would throw, the steals he would make, the rebounds he would grab . . . Bird did them all as if they were the easiest things in the world. Great players do that, they make the difficult appear simple. I've never seen anyone work harder at the game than Bird.

One day we were scrimmaging against the Stat Team and we were killing them. Just embarrassing them. It was Bird, McHale, Chief, Ainge and D. J. against Sichting, Wedman, Carlisle, Kite and me. Actually, the second-string team had a perfect mix of players. Wedman and Sichting were wonderful shooters, Carlisle was a good ball handler and defender and Kite was a rugged rebounder, which all went well with what I did. It was as if Coach K.C. Jones and Red Auerbach had built a team of substitutes to complement the skills of his starters. It was a beautiful concept and it worked.

With each basket we scored against the Stat Team, Bird became more and more upset. We were ahead, 6–1, in a game to seven, but you would have thought by Bird's expression that it was game seven of the NBA finals. He was raging. He couldn't or wouldn't accept that *his* team was going to lose.

Bird was one of the great trash talkers of all time. He started telling us that the Stat Team was going to win, that it was time for him to take control. The more he popped off, the hotter he got.

The game became his. He started stealing passes, getting every rebound and making the most difficult shots imaginable. It got to be a joke. After his first shot went in, he looked at us and said, "Watch out."

We put another guy on him, but it didn't matter. He made a second shot.

"Watch out, I'm coming back," he said.

We put three . . . four . . . five guys on him. Same thing.

He had McHale, Chief and the rest of the guys standing wide open under the basket, but he wouldn't pass it to them. He'd just shoot and make everything.

With the score tied, 6–6, Bird grabbed a rebound on the defensive end and started dribbling upcourt. We were trying to tackle him, but he dodged each attempt. As he neared the half-court line, he pulled up for a jumper—a jumper!— and swished it to win the game. Unbelievable. Bird did this sort of thing all the time.

One night we were behind by a couple at halftime and K.C. started drawing up this play for us to run when we got back on the court. There he was, meticulously detailing exactly where everyone would be positioned for this opening tempo-setting play, when suddenly Bird jumped up and said, "To heck with this. I'm going to shoot a three-pointer and we're never going to trail again."

K.C. took a look at his beautifully diagrammed play and said, "Okay."

Bird made the shot. We never trailed again.

Another time, Bird made a three-point shot in a game, but the officials didn't count it. So when Bird returned to the huddle for a timeout, he was still upset. K.C. started drawing up a play, but Bird interrupted him.

"To heck with the play," he said. "Give me the ball and tell all the rest of the guys to get out of the way."

K.C. wasn't in the mood to have his authority challenged.

"Shut up, Larry," he said. "I'm the coach here."

And then he started diagramming his play. "All right, now, Dennis, you take the ball out and get it to Kevin. Kevin, you throw it to Larry and then everybody get the hell out of the way."

The game was in Phoenix and Bird walked out of the huddle and went straight to the Suns' bench. He stood in front of the Phoenix bench, turned to their players and said, "I'm getting the ball right here and I'm gonna put it in the hoop. Watch my hand as I follow through."

D. J. threw the ball to Kevin. Kevin threw the ball to Bird and Bird made the shot. The ball went in, of course, and K.C. later said, "That's what you call arrogance."

Bird tested his teammates. In my very first regular-season home game, we were playing the Milwaukee Bucks and during a timeout, K.C. told me to inbound the ball to Danny Ainge.

Then I saw Bird, who was shaking his head no. As we broke from the huddle, Bird walked past me and said, "Don't give the ball to Ainge. Only give it to me or D. J."

I didn't think twice about it. When the ref handed me the ball, I promptly threw it to D. J. Later, after we had beaten the Bucks by nine, Ainge asked why I hadn't followed K.C.'s instructions.

"Uh, I didn't think you were open," I said.

What made Bird extra special were his qualities as a human being. Those qualities enabled him to become a superstar. He had a willingness to assume responsibility for his own fabulous play and a total dedication to lead by example.

Bird, more than any other player I've ever seen, knew exactly what was going on with every other player on the team. He had an uncanny sense of understanding the moods, the psychologies, the problems, the joys, the ups and downs of everybody on the roster. He would be able to avert potential problems by addressing them before they jeopardized the delicate balance of the team.

Like any great player, he spent a lot of time thinking about his own game, about his own jump shots going down. Shots don't go in by accident. There is a process involved in getting your game together that involves visualization. Bird, in his own personal way, would think everything through. But what separated Bird from nearly every other player I've known is that he would also sit and ponder the thoughts of the other players. He understood his teammates and, more importantly, he understood the limits of their skills.

Sometimes there would be situations where, say, Chief might be injured and I knew, just because of the way K.C. rotated players, that I'd probably see a significant increase in my minutes.

Mentally, I was always ready to play. Even more so when it meant more minutes. Bird knew this too. When he would get to the game on the particular occasions when I was scheduled to play more, he would come straight up to me in the locker room and tell me, "Look, let's get something straight. I get all the shots around here. Even though you may be getting more minutes tonight, it doesn't mean you get Chief's or Kevin's shots. Those shots are mine. You just rebound and stay over there on the weak side."

I was one of those players who used to watch NBA games all the time. I had made a deal with one of the Boston stereo outlet stores to provide Kevin, Bird, Chief and me with satellite dishes and a bunch of other stereo equipment. In exchange, I did some public relations work for them.

While watching these games, I'd figure out all kinds of new plays that we could use against the opposition. I'd have all these wonderful plans in my mind, jot them down and then give them to K.C. Not that it would matter—as soon as Bird got the ball, he'd shoot it anyway.

I'd stay up half the night watching the games from the West Coast.

One night while watching a game, I came up with a great idea for a play. I was so excited I couldn't wait until the next day's practice to tell Bird. So I picked up the phone and called him at home. It was well after midnight, but that didn't matter.

After a couple of rings, Bird answered and, without even saying hello, he said, "Bill, that play just won't work. I get all the shots around here. Now go to sleep, get some rest. That way you can play defense, get some rebounds and block some shots. Now quit bugging me."

Then he hung up.

Of all the positions on the court, it might be the most difficult to control the game from the forward position. That's because those darned guards always have the ball and when they do finally decide to give it up, it's usually to the center.

None of this bothered Bird. He wasn't bashful about wanting the ball, or taking it if you didn't get it to him. That was fine with me. I like players who are aggressive, who aren't afraid to take responsibility for the outcome of a game.

As much as Bird loved to shoot, he was rarely a selfish player. Instead, he was always the first guy to inbound the ball, the first guy to think pass.

During the 1986 season, the year we won the NBA championship, Bird led the team in field goal attempts *and* assists. In fact, only one player (John Havlicek) in Celtics career regular-season history has scored more points and only two players (Bob Cousy and Havlicek) have dished out more assists than Bird. In the playoffs, no Celtic has more points or assists than Bird.

When I look back on my own career, I was extremely fortunate to have played with three great post-feeders, guys who really knew how to get the ball inside: Greg Lee at UCLA, Bob Gross at Portland and Bird at Boston—that is, if Bird could ever get the ball away from Ainge.

There were times when Bird got caught up in the statistics. We were playing the Dallas Mavericks at Reunion Arena in 1986 and, as usual, we were killing them.

The Mavs had entered the league as an expansion franchise in 1980 and had never beaten the Celtics. When we had them down by 20 or so points in Dallas that night, our dominance seemed secure. Bird already had scored almost 40 points in three quarters and all was well.

But then Bird apparently decided he wanted to break his 60-point Celtics scoring record he had set a year earlier against Atlanta. So he started taking every shot. Meanwhile, it all fell apart and we blew the lead and lost the game.

The only thing broken that night was Dallas's losing streak against the Celtics. It was such a big deal in Dallas that the Mavericks made a video of the game and sold copies to their fans.

And Bird? He ended up with 50 points, but he was also the worst player on the court. I told him that in the locker room after the game, but he already knew it.

You could probably count on one hand the times Bird let his stats cloud his thinking. Bird lived the game of basketball. He was the antithesis of the player who is so prevalent in the NBA today. Most of the guys in the league these days think basketball is nothing more than walking out there, running up and down the court and shooting jump shots. Not Bird. He was the ultimate competitor.

No matter what it took, Bird would do it—or destroy himself trying. That's the reason he had to retire. Despite the wear and tear on his body, especially to his back, he never avoided his responsibility to the team or tired of his role as a Celtics leader and captain.

Bird relished his status. If we were on the road, Bird would do interviews with the local radio or TV reporters and promptly start talking trash about the other team. As the tape recorder or minicam whirred away, Bird would announce how he planned to light the other team up and that no one could do a thing about it. As if that weren't enough, Bird would then ask what the scoring records were in that particular arena because, well, he planned to break them.

Bird loved it, but McHale and Chief groaned every time they caught Bird's act. It was McHale or Chief who had to guard the other team's best front-court players, while Bird was always assigned to the opposition's weakest offensive player.

In a one-on-one situation, Bird was a poor individual defender. You didn't want to put Bird on Dr. J or Dominique Wilkins and say, "Okay, now go shut this guy down." That wasn't Bird's game.

But in a team defensive scheme, Bird fit perfectly. We had McHale, who, before his mobility was dramatically reduced by injuries, was a fabulous and versatile defensive player. McHale could guard anybody. In our scheme, he would usually guard the high-scoring front-court player. Then Chief, who was an underrated defender, would guard the big post-up center. That freed up Bird to do what he did best: make plays.

How many small forwards led their teams in rebounding? Bird did it regularly. He ranks fourth among Celtics career regular-season rebound leaders, behind three centers (Bill Russell, Dave Cowens and Parish).

Bird was a player who knew what was going to happen a split second before everyone else. Sure, there's an intuitive sense involved, but Bird's attention to detail and preparation is what really allowed him to excel.

As great a player as Bird was, he was a better human being. He is a moral, ethical and honest man whose loyalties run extremely deep.

Bird used to say that when the day came for him to retire, there would be no fanfare, no farewell tour, no ceremonies. He wanted to be like Russell and just walk away from the game. In his own autobiography, Bird wrote that his only wish was to be able to walk onto the parquet floor one last time and say thank you. He got his chance on February 4, 1993, when the Celtics and the city of Boston paid tribute to their hero.

The Celtics pulled out all the stops for Bird's farewell. They flew all of Bird's old teammates back to Boston (first class) for "Larry Bird Night." No one who had anything to do with that night will ever forget the excitement in the air that was as great as, if not better than, at any game. It was in marked contrast to the Trail Blazers, whose team often seems to be managed by accountants rather than entertainment people.

Before Bird got to Boston in 1979, the Celtics were in awful shape. The team stank and attendance was terrible.

Celtics front-office people actually used to go over to Fenway Park during Red Sox games and put season-ticket applications under each car's wiper blades. Things were in desperate shape for the franchise, which had gone 32–50 and 29–53 during the two seasons before Bird's arrival.

All that was forgotten on February 4, 1993. You couldn't get a seat in the place. Scalpers were getting up to $500 for tickets to "Larry Bird Night." Steven Riley, the Celtics vice president for ticket sales, said it was the toughest ticket to get since the seventh game of the 1984 NBA finals. The demand for press credentials was incredible. The Celtics issued a special pass just for this event. A local television station and local radio station broadcast the entire show live. Larry Bird.

Bill Russell was easily the most successful player in Celtics history, but Bird was the most popular. He became the people's choice. He played in a different era than Russell and, in his way, was more accessible to the average Celtics fan.

Just about everyone in Celtics basketball history was there that evening. The members of the 1981 NBA championship team, Bird's first, were seated near one corner of the floor. The 1984 Celtics title team was seated nearby, as was the 1986 championship squad. In another area of the floor were lots of Celtics dignitaries, such as Don Chaney, Satch Sanders, Jo Jo White, Havlicek, Bill Sharman, Ed Macauley and Frank Ramsey. It was like a Hall of Fame reunion, with all the great Boston players assembled in one place.

Even Bobby Orr, the former Boston Bruins hockey great, was there. That made sense. Before every Celtics home game began, Bird used to look up at Orr's retired jersey number, which hung from the rafters. Bird used to say it gave him inspiration.

NBC's Bob Costas was the emcee and he did an excellent

job of keeping Bird relaxed and talkative and the evening on the move. Video highlights of Bird's high school, college and pro career were shown, and after each segment Bird would reminisce. Bird said that night our 1986 Celtics team was "the best team I've ever seen in the league." That made me feel very proud—proud to be a part of something Bird thought was special.

It was fun to watch each championship team take its turn on the stage with Bird. What the crowd didn't know is that shortly before the players were summoned to the stage, a Celtics official took us to the locker room, where *our* warm-ups were waiting. It was such a terrific experience to walk into that locker room again and relive some of those memories. Some of us hadn't left the Celtics under the best of circumstances. On that 1986 team alone, K.C., our trainer, Ray Melchiorre, and I had enjoyed less than fond farewells. But Auerbach was forced to make what he considered to be the right decisions and I respect him for that. That's how it works. In college basketball, you have to leave when your eligibility is up. In pro basketball, you never want to leave. Auerbach though is the Celtic who has to tell you when it's time.

What an absolutely electric feeling it was to be introduced in the Garden once more. The spotlight was shining, the crowd was roaring and, best of all, you were getting ready to share a few more good times with Bird. All seemed right in the world. The whole Bird ceremony made me feel great, made me happy to be alive, proud to be a Celtic. It reminded me of my days right before I committed to UCLA, when just about every college coach in the country was offering me money or cars or whatever to sign with them—except John Wooden. All John Wooden offered was the chance to be a part of something special. That's how it was with the Celtics too.

I told a couple of these stories to the crowd and tried my

best to describe what kind of person and what kind of competitor Bird was. I didn't need to say much. Most of those same people had watched Bird play hundreds of times. They knew what kind of heart he had. They lived his greatness. He had lived for them.

The rest of the evening I spent as a fan. I listened as Cedric Maxwell recalled the first time he faced Bird in practice. Bird kept draining 20-foot jump shots in Maxwell's face. "I'll always remember thinking," Cedric told the crowd, " 'Boy, this white guy can play, can't he?' "

I watched as Magic Johnson paid tribute to Bird, saying that Bird was the only player in the league he ever feared. "Because," said Magic, "this man would find a way to win that damn game."

Auerbach did his part as well. Auerbach is the guy who picked Bird in the draft. The guy who signed him. "But the only regret I have," Red said, "is that I never coached him."

I think Bird enjoyed the ceremony. He's like every superstar, in that he loves his time in the spotlight, to have the focus, the pressure, the emotion and the excitement zeroed in on him. As always, Bird delivered that night. I was lucky to have a small seat up close.

There are few players who have the universal respect of their teammates and peers. Bird was one of those players. We loved him. We loved his talents, his arrogance, his sense of humor, his toughness, his kindness and his caring. Some people used to make a lot of fuss about the alleged friction and rivalry between Bird and McHale. There was no friction, but there was always a sense of competitiveness. You have to understand that Bird is only a happy and satisfied person when he's the defending champion. Larry Bird, in my opinion, has only been truly happy three times in his life: when he won those three NBA titles.

Every player wants to win, but there are a few players who, unless they actually win the championship each year, can't seem to shake the frustration. That was Bird. I imagine Bill Russell was like that too. Money . . . material goods, those come with success. But when you're one of the really, really top players, you want the ultimate success—the championship. Anything less is a letdown. To Bird, there was no difference between second place and last place.

I was a very frustrated player. Nobody missed more basketball in the history of the game than me. But I could identify with Bird's philosophy. I hold him in such high esteem because he approached the game from the mental aspect. To him, basketball was a game of position, timing, conditioning, teamwork, skills, angles and the accumulation of slight advantages over time that enable you to gain a decided, noticeable edge at the end of the contest. The players who understand that concept are usually the ones who win all the time.

Bird also had a supreme confidence that was contagious. We were getting ready to start practice one morning when K.C. said, "Okay, you guys are playing pretty well these days. If any one of you can make a half-court shot, we're out of here."

Bird didn't hesitate.

"No problem, guys," he said. "Head to the showers."

No one moved. Had you seen Bird that day, you would have known why. He was limping around like an old man. He was beat up and bloody. He played so hard, expended so much energy and was the object of so much physical abuse from the other teams that when he showed up for practice the day after a game, he usually looked terrible.

We should have known better than to doubt his word. Bird went over to the ball rack, picked out a ball, bounced it a few times, took a couple of deep knee bends, walked out to center court, took a jump shot and then admired his work as the ball snapped the net.

K.C. looked at the basket, then at Bird and then at us.

"Okay, we're out of here," he said. "Let's go."

K.C. tried the same thing later that season. This time—and this is how wild and perfect that 1986 season was for the Celtics—none of the players could make the shot. We all tried, including Bird, but nothing worked.

"Well," said K.C. reluctantly, "I guess we've got to practice."

Just as we started onto the court, somebody yelled, "Don't forget Ray. Ray hasn't shot one yet."

Ray Melchiorre, the team trainer, was not exactly in the prime of his youth, so you can understand why we weren't real confident about our chances to have a short day.

"Sure, I'll try it," Melchiorre said.

Ray had to get ready first. He had to take his gun out of his belt. He carried one all the time. He said it was for protection, in case he had to defend the honor of the Celtics. Then he stepped to the half-court line and unleashed the ugliest shot I have ever seen in my life—until it swished through the net. Then it was absolutely gorgeous.

Again, K.C. looked at us and said, "We're out of here."

K.C. was an excellent coach, but a coach can only do so much. In Bird, he had the perfect player to complement his direct style. Bird was like a coach because he had an influence over our team that was incredible. He is so perceptive about human nature and the game itself. Our opponents didn't have any choice but to listen to Bird too. He loved to talk trash—but in a fun and positive way. Plus, he always backed it up with fabulous play on the court.

I was with the Los Angeles Clippers in 1985, but I still remember watching the highlights when Bird set a Celtics record by scoring 60 points (32 during a 14-minute stretch) against the Atlanta Hawks in New Orleans. In a video called *The Secret NBA*, footage of that game is included. At one point, Bird hit a shot that had several players at the end of the Hawks bench laughing, high-fiving each other and waving towels. Mike Fratello, who was the Atlanta coach back then, later saw a replay of their reactions and fined them $100 each. Big deal, it was worth it to watch Bird play.

Bird was never afraid to say what was on his mind. Part of that security came with his status as one of the league's very best players.

He was always the first guy to stand up for someone who wasn't in a position of power. He was the first guy to defend someone if they were being unfairly criticized by the media or by management.

When McHale played in the 1987 NBA Finals with a broken foot, Bird was quick to question the tactics of the Celtics front office. He told reporters, "You're in the Finals, and they say, 'If you don't want to play, you don't have to.' That takes all the pressure off them, and it makes it look like Kevin's decision. I'd say, 'Go on home.' "

Not many players would stick their necks out like that for a teammate. Bird did it all the time.

He also didn't mind needling his own teammates.

I hit a shot one night and a few days later Bird was still all over me. He was quoted in the paper the next day. "You saw what happened the other night when he hit that hook in the fourth quarter?" Bird said of my shot. "We didn't score for five and a half minutes. He hit us with the stun gun."

When Bird hurt his elbow one time, a reporter asked him how it was. Bird told him, "I don't think I have the Bill Walton Syndrome yet."

Bird was my worst critic, but I never took it personally. It was his way of trying to make us better players.

In my very first regular-season game with the Celtics, a road game against the New Jersey Nets, I was horrible. I was an utter disgrace to the sport of basketball. I couldn't do anything right. Basically I couldn't hold on to the ball and kept fumbling it away. It was one of those games where you go back to the basics and reexamine your whole routine and approach. Considering this was the first game of the season, that didn't say much for me.

We blew a 19-point lead and lost the game, one of only 15 defeats we would suffer the entire season. As we walked to the locker room, I started to apologize for my performance, if you can call it that.

This time Bird took it easy on me. He said it was only one game and that everything would be fine. He was right. We won 17 of our next 18 games.

That night against New Jersey, I deserved the worst from Bird. He took pity on me. That didn't last long.

With Bird, there was rarely any malice in his comments. But there was lots of humor. Before the start of a 1986 playoff game against the Milwaukee Bucks at the Garden, there was a brief ceremony honoring me for winning the NBA's Sixth Man Award. We won the game, and afterward, someone happened to mention my award to Bird. Gracious as always, he said, "Sixth man? Hell, he was our eleventh-best player tonight and Milwaukee's best."

The great thing about playing with Bird, as well as with the rest of the Celtics team, was that you could have a horrible game and not be devastated by it. The pressure wasn't entirely on your shoulders. You had guys like Bird, D. J., Chief, Kevin and Ainge on your team. Hey, with that group you're probably going to win the game and go home happy no matter how crummy your own individual performance was.

Now that Bird is retired, I think he'll learn to enjoy life without basketball. He has a wonderful family, all the money he'll every need or want and a great basketball legacy. He realizes he can't physically play anymore, which helps make the transition a lot easier. It will take time for him to become comfortable with retirement. He'll need to get rid of the pain in his back, but as soon as that happens, he'll be happy.

During one off-season, Bird was supposed to play in Magic Johnson's all-star game in Los Angeles. Bird wanted to come out to Southern California and get ready for it. So he and his family stayed in my house at San Diego. I figured I'd show them the sights, relax and maybe work out once in a while.

Bird had other ideas. He came out here wanting to work out.

We lifted weights. We ran. We trained. Every day we played grueling, high-intensity games of one on one. We played the first few games on my garage court. But the court was so small that Bird couldn't get free of my defense, he couldn't back up far enough. So we said, "Enough of this, we're going down to Muni Gym and a full regulation-size court."

There were stakes involved, big ones. The loser had to go buy beer and sodas while the winner sat in the Jacuzzi and waited for the other guy to return from the store.

On the last day of our workouts, just before Bird was going to leave, it came down to the last game. I couldn't miss. I was hitting every shot I took. I was on fire.

During that very last game, I said, "Larry, I'm up ten to one. The game is to eleven and I've got the ball. I'll tell you what I'm going to do. I feel sorry for you. You brought your family out here. Here I am abusing you, beating you so bad. So I'm going to give you a chance. You can have the ball."

Bird wasn't stupid. Given the choice of me having the ball with a chance to close him out or his getting the ball back so he could make things respectable, Larry was going to take the ball.

So I gave him the ball and he hit a shot. It's 10–2. He

hit another shot. It's now 10–3. Then he hits another. And another. And another one after that.

That son of a gun ran off ten straight jumpers in my face, despite my using every illegal tactic I had ever learned.

I've been buying that guy beer ever since. What a mistake. Always put somebody away when you've got the chance. Finish him off. Especially Larry Bird.

"Sometimes the light's all shining on me. . . .
Other times I can barely see."
—*Bob Weir and Jerry Garcia*

Among the nicest and most satisfying rewards of my new career as a broadcaster is that I get to work every day *and* I don't get hurt physically. The only time I use ice now is when I want to drop a few cubes into a cocktail after the game.

It wasn't always that way. Ice and I used to be close personal friends. During the course of my injury-riddled career, I was, unfortunately, intimately related to heating pads, whirlpools, syringes, crutches, canes, casts, splints, wraps, scalpels, operating rooms, recovery rooms, intravenous tubes and, most devastatingly, pain.

No one in the history of basketball was injured as often as I was. I missed only three games of a possible 90 while at UCLA, but I missed 762 games during my fourteen-year NBA career. Those 762 games are the equivalent of nine lost seasons. That frustration was overwhelming.

The end of my career (though I didn't know it at the time)

came in 1988. I was with the Celtics and had spent the entire regular season recovering from major surgery on my right foot. The surgery, which was similar to the procedure done on my left foot seven years earlier, was designed to relieve the stress generated by running and jumping, hopefully ending the long string of stress fractures.

Near the end of the regular season, I joined the team for practice and began to test the foot. Everything seemed to be going okay, but I wouldn't know for sure until the first serious scrimmage session.

I wasn't the only anxious person. Members of the Celtics management and coaching staff wanted to activate me in time for the playoffs, but they wouldn't do a thing until I gave them the green light.

The scrimmage came . . . and I went. The foot couldn't take it. Every time I ran hard, the pain began that all too familiar surge and nearly exploded. I felt as if another stress fracture was imminent.

The trainers took me into the locker room and left me to soak my foot in a bucket of ice. I was all alone. Just me and a thousand thoughts, a rolling slot machine.

A few minutes later, Jan Volk, our general manager, walked in and said he needed to know whether to put me on the playoff roster. With tears in my eyes and sadness and defeat in my heart, I said, "Jan, I can't do it."

And that was that. I never played again.

When reminiscing about my career, I tend to remember two things: the losses and the injuries. I remember the four defeats at UCLA and the 762 missed opportunities in the NBA.

A memory that is particularly painful is from a season earlier, when the Celtics played the Lakers in the 1987 NBA finals. I spent most of my entire life, every moment of it as a basketball player, planning, training to beat Kareem Abdul-Jabbar. That's what I had prepared for. That's what

I wanted more than anything, to play Jabbar, to defeat him.

In 1987, the stage was set. Celtics vs. Lakers for the NBA championship. Walton vs. Jabbar for my personal satisfaction. To me, it was a lifetime of dreams come true.

Except that when it came time to play, I was useless. Oh, I made a few token appearances, but I couldn't run. My foot was broken. It's tough to play basketball when you have a stress fracture in your foot. It was all very embarrassing, as Jabbar, and anyone else I was assigned to cover, totally abused me on the court.

It was an awful experience for me because along with the pain, I could also feel the doubt. Some of my own teammates didn't believe I was hurt. Some of the Celtics officials didn't believe I was hurt. Some of the media didn't believe I was hurt. And some of the fans didn't believe it either.

I played in only ten games during the regular season that year. When that happens, you become an outcast of sorts. Out of sight, out of mind, is the way it goes for injured players in the NBA.

As I tried to get my foot and ankle in good enough shape to return for the playoffs, only two teammates seemed to understand what I was going through: Dennis Johnson and Robert Parish.

Both D. J. and Chief were already in the NBA when I was with the Trail Blazers. D. J. had played for the Seattle SuperSonics and Chief had been a reserve with the Golden State Warriors. Because of the division schedule, at the time we saw a lot of each other. In fact, those Portland–Golden State games were always ferocious affairs. Mostly because of Rick Barry, who played for the Warriors, but partly because I couldn't stand the thought of traveling to Oakland and then losing in front of all my friends from the Grateful Dead.

D. J. and Chief were in the league when the navicular bone in my foot split in half. When we later became teammates in Boston, they regularly told me, "Hey, Bill, just make sure you don't cripple yourself."

I've had many disappointments in life, but very few regrets. However, one of them involves my often deciding to play when hurt. I didn't let pain be my guide. I didn't say, "If it hurts a lot, don't play." Who knows what sort of irreparable damage I suffered during those games?

Maybe it was guilt that drove me to do it, or some sort of peer-pressure, macho thing associated with athletes. I'd like to think it was my love for basketball. Whatever it was, it had its limits—limits that I learned to apply. Learned the hard way.

Late in the 1987 season, I limped into the Boston Garden, put on my uniform and took my usual place near the end of the bench. The stress fracture in my right foot was on fire.

By then, the media was all over me, but what could I say? I could hardly walk, much less play basketball.

Near the end of a very close game, the fans in the always sold-out Garden started chanting, "Wal-ton, Wal-ton, Wal-ton." K.C. Jones looked at me, as if to say, "Can you give us anything?"

My eyes misted over. The crowd . . . K.C.'s hopeful face—it was too much to take. I knew I shouldn't play. I knew I couldn't play. I wanted so desperately to be on that court.

I didn't know what to do. Then D. J. came over. As the fans continued their cheers, he leaned in and said, "Don't do it, Bill. Don't do it."

I didn't. To this day, I don't know what hurt more: my foot or not being able to play. I had learned my lesson, but it had taken a long, long time.

Injuries are such a personal thing. You can't simply tell your body to heal. If that was all it took, all top players would still be playing. The body heals at its own pace and doesn't concern itself with the media, or doctors' prognoses, or the playoff schedule. I used to have a quote from Arnold Schwarzenegger taped to the refrigerator in my kitchen. Arnold said that anything is possible in your mind. But it is your body that is the machine, that executes those thoughts and turns possibilities into reality. He called it the "magnificence of the body."

If it were only up to the mind, I would have never missed a game. Larry Bird would still be playing basketball and so would I. But the body breaks down and it finally just won't work anymore. That was the big problem in my life— my body just broke down.

For reasons no one will ever know, my feet weren't meant for basketball. It certainly wasn't hereditary, since no one else in my family, including my older brother Bruce, had any similar problems. No, it was just me.

When you talk to as many doctors as I have, you become something of a specialist. I've got a stack of X rays as thick as the LA phone book. I've heard every diagnosis and prognosis. I've digested so much medical information that people now ask me what's wrong with them.

My particular foot condition is one of the reasons I ended up in Dr. Wagner's office. You didn't get to Dr. Wagner unless you weren't getting better. He was a last resort, the guy who only dealt with cases that nobody else wanted or that nobody could figure out.

"I'm sort of the end of the line," he would tell me. "People see me after they see five, eight, ten doctors and then I usually figure it out."

I wasn't the first patient Dr. Daly had referred to Dr. Wagner. But it was Dr. Wagner who had the reputation for making the kind of foot and ankle diagnoses that other orthopedists sometimes failed to come up with.

Dr. Wagner's waiting room was always packed with people. It resembled a religious shrine like Lourdes, with the crutches, canes, wheelchairs and other orthopedic devices.

Everyone was afflicted with some sort of unusual foot or ankle problems. These were people in really, really bad shape. I was one of those people.

Sometimes it was hard to enter that office. You were admitting that your situation was all but hopeless. Nor was it an uplifting experience to see the similar looks of despair on your fellow patients' faces. There we were, assembled in Dr. Wagner's chamber of dismay, despair and last chances.

There was a day, several years before my ankle-fusion surgery in 1990, when I sat waiting in one of Dr. Wagner's examination rooms feeling sorry for myself. As usual, Dr. Wagner's schedule was completely full, so I waited, the whole time growing more disheartened by my condition.

You can imagine the discussion I had with myself (these discussions were usually the best ones): "Why me? What is the doctor going to find this time? How long will it take to recover? How will it affect my playing career?" The usual.

I stared at the four walls, feeling completely alone and in the way, when I noticed a man on crutches making his way down the hall. He saw me and instantly made a beeline toward my room.

I wasn't in the mood for visitors, but that didn't stop him from coming right in and closing the door behind him. I wanted to tell this guy to go find his own waiting area. I felt terrible and the last thing I wanted to do was chat with a total stranger.

I considered calling security to shoo him away when he seized the moment.

"Bill," he said, "I need some advice."

Advice? Oh, great!

"Listen," I said, "this probably isn't the best time . . ."

He interrupted.

"Bill, I recently had both of my legs amputated right above the knee and I need to know how you stay so positive. How do you stay so up?"

Me? Up? I started to smile. As I looked at this big, strong, healthy, handsome guy I said to myself, "Bill, you big dummy, you are the lucky one."

We talked for a few minutes (and eventually became friends away from the office) before he returned to the general waiting room. Not long after that, Dr. Wagner walked in.

Actually, Dr. Wagner was never alone on rounds. There always seemed to be a medical entourage with him. Doctors from around the world would come to watch him work and learn his surgical techniques. He would never look at your medical chart or study your X rays—at least, not at first. Instead, he would grab your foot, look you right in the eyes and start twisting and yanking.

"Does that hurt?" he said after a tug of the foot.

"Yes!" I said.

You couldn't lie. In fact, it was impossible to fool Dr. Wagner. He wasn't examining your foot so much as he was examining the reaction on your face. He was looking right into the windows to your soul, and no matter how hard you tried, it was difficult to mask the pain.

Once he was done with the examination, Dr. Wagner acted very much like a construction foreman. There was no mincing of words. He was a blue-collar doctor and he used blue-collar explanations when detailing what needed to be done.

Dr. Wagner would often hold my foot and make his surgical recommendation in easy-to-understand language.

"Bill," he said, "I've got to cut this off and bring in the wrecking ball here."

———

My injuries were not the kind caused by colliding with somebody and breaking a bone. My injuries came from simply playing too much basketball. I always thought my body, from the ankles up, had been designed for no other reason than to put the ball through the hoop.

Basketball was the game I loved, so I played it every minute I could from the time I was eight to the time I was thirty-six. With each step, with each pivot, with each jump and corresponding landing, I weakened the twenty-six bones in my foot, taking a bit more away each and every time.

If you were jogging, when your foot hit the ground the stress from impact would be absorbed and dissipated through the muscles, tendons and ligaments in your foot, ankle and leg. If I were jogging, when my foot hit the ground the heel would fail to flex and all the stress would go directly into the bones. Imagine bending a paper clip back and forth . . . back and forth. Eventually the metal weakens and snaps.

That's exactly what happens with stress fractures. They eventually ended my career as well as that of several other good players, notably Andrew Toney and Doug Collins.

When I first developed my foot problems, stress fractures were not readily diagnosed in athletics. Stress fractures had been studied in the military, but that was about it. In the 1970s, X rays that didn't show any clear and clean breaks were assumed to indicate there was no injury—just malingering dregs. Doctors weren't even looking for stress fractures.

Some of the knowledge gained by the medical community regarding stress fractures was provided by my feet. It's a distinction I could do without. In some cases, the radical and experimental operations performed on me were almost completely new. I was a guinea pig.

Sometimes the procedures would work, sometimes not. What was particularly disappointing was that I would get better, return to action and then, when I least expected it, suffer another fracture at another part of the same bone.

That's when I got scared. It got to the point where I would ask, "When is it going to break again? Is this step going to be my last?"

I became a little paranoid. The mind is always the last place to heal.

One of the most difficult things about being an injured athlete is that there's really nothing you can do with your time or your life. When you're injured all the time, as I was, you have to learn to deal with the loneliness, the boredom, the therapy and being ostracized by your teammates, coaches and fans. For someone like me, who lived for competition and for the game, it was often just too much.

I'm a very frustrated person. I need the high that comes from being successful. That's why basketball was so much fun. You could go out and win a game in two hours and have instant gratification. The real world is obviously a bit different.

I don't believe I would ever have voluntarily retired from basketball. There are some guys who will just go on until they can't anymore. I was one of them. I destroyed my legs, my ankles and my feet because of that obsession. In fact, there was only one off-season during my fourteen years in the NBA when I didn't undergo surgery or, in some cases, multiple surgeries.

I'd do it all over again. Definitely. In a minute. There is nothing like being a basketball player.

I might think differently if the doctors hadn't been able to work their magic. I'm lucky that the pain I had in my feet and ankles is more or less gone now. Yes, I've learned to sit down. But had that blowtorch and those stabbing swords remained, I don't know if I would have been in such a hurry to repeat the cycle.

My NBA career did not exactly have a dynamic beginning. Just before my rookie season with the Trail Blazers

I had to have knee surgery. Then I had foot ailments that forced me to miss 47 regular-season games.

The next year I broke my ankle and missed 31 games. We also missed the playoffs for my second consecutive season (the Blazers had never made the playoffs) and Lenny Wilkens was fired. The fans were all over me. Steve Jones, who played on that 1975–76 Trail Blazers team, once said that the Portland community expected me to be the next Jabbar, to do what Jabbar had done in Milwaukee—instantly win a championship.

Said Jones, "That was really the emotional state of the town. The fans were saying, 'We got Dollar Bill, we're on our way to the Promised Land.' Except that all of a sudden Bill's a revolutionary and he's a revolutionary who gets hurt all the time."

A revolutionary? I always considered myself mainstream, a developing young man aching to express myself and, in a way, prove myself too. It was everyone else who was out in right field. During that season I broke my nose, then dislocated several fingers on both hands, then limped around with some broken toes. I asked Steve if he'd take a ride with me. I needed some advice.

"I don't know if I'm ever going to get to play," I said. "I mean, I can't stay healthy. Every time I turn around I'm getting hurt. I want to play. I need to play."

Steve didn't mince words.

"Bill, you're going to get over these injuries. You're going to get another contract. You're a seven-footer. You're white and you can play. You'll get another contract, believe me. So stop worrying about that stuff and start figuring out a way to play. And while you're at it, put away that ugly bank jump shot of yours and find something that will work for you. And get healthy."

I hurt my ankle again in 1977 but was forced out of only

17 games. Portland ended up winning the championship. I thought we'd just keep winning them too. We were supposed to win. This was our destiny.

It all fell apart in the next ten months.

In 1978, we were 50–10 and rolling when a number of our key players got hurt. I returned for the playoffs, but broke my foot in the series against Seattle. Steve Jones later said it was the basketball gods playing a cruel trick on me. We lost to the SuperSonics. Then I decided I wanted out of Portland.

I wasn't alone. I think the Portland fans and media also wanted me out.

That crippling foot injury caused me to miss the entire 1978–79 season. So dissatisfied was I with the quality of the diagnosis, treatment and care I received from the Trail Blazers' medical staff that I filed a malpractice suit against one of the team physicians, Dr. Robert Cook. He told me nothing was wrong with my foot. The Trail Blazers' management applied subtle, but constant pressure on me to play.

I played, or at least tried to, but I shouldn't have. I also took painkilling drugs and, against my better judgment, allowed Cook to administer painkilling injections of Xylocaine. I'm not proud of that. I initially resisted, but ultimately allowed my trust in the medical staff and my desire to play basketball to outweigh what should have been my first priority: my health. I jeopardized that and I have paid a steep price for that mistake ever since.

Three months before the 1978 season began, I asked to be traded. A year later, I was a San Diego Clipper.

And thus began six dreadful, frustrating seasons of foot injuries, surgeries, rehabilitation and more injuries. After one of the surgeries, I opened my eyes in the recovery room and my first postoperative sight was a naked 300-pound woman lying in the adjacent bed.

The nadir came when I had to miss almost the entire 1979–80 season and all of the 1980–81 season because of the stress fractures and subsequent surgeries. I was declared permanently disabled and the Clippers received a large insurance settlement. I had so much free time that I attended Stanford Law School during those two years.

When I returned to the NBA in 1982, the Clippers' doctors were very careful and protective of my playing schedule. Initially, I couldn't play at all. Then I tried once a week. Then it was two times a week. Then it was every other day. Unlike the Trail Blazers, the Clippers were very supportive. They handled my injury situation with sensitivity and professionalism. Dr. Daly, the team physician, deserves a lot of credit. He provided me with honest counsel, advice and care, and he also arranged for me to meet with the country's other leading orthopedic specialists. Dr. Daly wanted me to get better—not because it would help the Clippers, but because it would help me. It was a refreshing attitude.

Lots of other people also were interested in finding remedies for my stress fractures. Hardly a day went by that I didn't receive letters detailing the medicinal benefits of some homegrown concoction. Hardly a day went by that I didn't try them.

The longer you hurt, the more intense the pain, the more desperate you get. When things were really grim after the dark days in Portland, I got a letter from someone who explained exactly why the foot injuries continued to torment me. According to his reasoning, my feet were in such awful shape because a witch doctor in the Philippines had placed a curse on me. The ever-helpful fan even enclosed a detailed map of the Philippines, complete with clues and paths to take in search of the witch doctor. His advice was to track down the witch doctor and get the curse expunged.

Bad times have a way of making you appreciate life more.

Now, whenever things appear really bleak, my choice is: "It's either this or the Philippines."

One of the strangest suggestions I ever heard concerning my foot ailments came from a mechanical engineer in San Diego. The engineer, apparently respected among his peers, asked if he could meet with me about an exciting new idea he had concerning my physical problems. Not one to dismiss unusual concepts or miss a chance, I agreed to a meeting.

The engineer unveiled a set of blueprint plans which featured some sort of mechanical device. The device had pulleys, levers, hydraulics . . . the whole works.

"And what I am supposed to do with this?" I said.

"You wear it," he said. "It will make the foot non-important in the game of basketball."

I've had my share of disappointments, none greater than my inability to help professional basketball take hold in my hometown of San Diego. Once again, my injuries were to blame for the franchise's demise and eventual move to Los Angeles.

If I had been healthy and been able to play during my time with the San Diego Clippers (1979–85), there would still be an NBA team in the city. Instead, the Clippers are in Los Angeles. I am responsible for that sad situation.

I'd still like to be out there today, mixing it up with some of these young guys in the league. I would have loved to have played against David Robinson, Alonzo Mourning or Shaquille O'Neal. That would be fun.

One of the biggest mistakes I ever made was not playing against Wilt. Wilt retired the year before I played in the NBA. We used to play against each other in beach volleyball games, but we never played basketball.

Still, I had a chance to face him on the court and I blew it. Wilt regularly played in summer pickup games at Pauley Pavilion, but I never joined in. I really should have gone down to Pauley and played the great Wilt. What a waste.

The last time I played a game of basketball without a broken foot was in 1986, the last year the Celtics won the world championship. I played briefly in 1987, but that doesn't count. When you're injured, you're not really playing the game of basketball. Instead, you're doing a job. Just putting in time.

After the ankle-fusion surgery in 1990, I spent the next 2 ½ months in almost total seclusion. My home had become my recovery room. A nurse was hired to take care of me as I went through the morphine withdrawal and all points beyond. I had to wear a sixty-pound cast that stretched from hip to toe. I could barely move. The bones in my ankle and foot were basically loose. Now it was time for them to grow back together—a long, tedious process that took ten boring weeks.

Then one day—and I still remember the exact joy I felt—the pain went away. Poof. Gone. The bones had joined together just as the doctors had said they would.

I didn't know what to do. I didn't realize the pain would simply disappear. After dozens of surgeries, I had dismissed the idea of a life without the mind-numbing pain. Pain was a given, or so I had told myself. You fought through it. You coped with it. You endured.

No more of that. I celebrated.

Nowadays, I can ride my bike, but I can't play basketball, other than to stand stationary under the hoop or out on the perimeter and shoot layups or short set shots. The desire to play the game is still there, but my body can't.

From a physical standpoint, my life is a series of short walks from chair to chair. After all, I've got four bolts in my ankle, which produces just one walking speed: very slow. That was the trade-off. In exchange for the ability to live a relatively pain-free life, I had to forfeit my physical mobility. My right ankle no longer flexes. It is as if someone placed two two-by-fours perpendicular to each other, nailed them together and said, "Here's your new ankle and foot."

All things considered, it was worth the sacrifice. The truth is, I've been off to the races ever since. Things have never been better.

Sometimes I ask myself, "Why me?" But the truth is, I have very few complaints. There are many other people with far worse injuries. It's best to count your blessings and maximize the good things in life. You can't sit around and mope and moan and wonder what might have been.

I missed 762 professional games. For nine years I did everything I could, but it just wasn't enough. I wish I could have done more—all I ever wanted was more.

Maybe I should have gone to the Philippines.

"Just give me some truth."
—*John Lennon*

"Just remember, I made you . . .
I can break you."
—*Rudy Martzke*, USA Today *columnist, to me,
at the 1993 NBA finals in Chicago*

Once my basketball career was over, I had to look to the future, realizing that with my unique talents there was only one direction to go. I'm 6' 11". I've got red hair, a big nose, and I walk with a limp. I've got four steel bolts in my ankle. I have a severe speech impediment. . . .

Television. What else?

Becoming a broadcaster was probably the most remarkable (and unlikely) development in my life. I had a significant stuttering problem until my late twenties. Because of the stuttering, I was an intensely shy and private person. I never had much of a relationship with strangers or the media while I was playing. That isn't the smartest thing to do if you hope one day to enter the mass communications industry.

When a series of surgeries, including the ankle-fusion procedure, forced my premature retirement from basketball, a job in broadcasting was the last thing on my mind.

I was angry, frustrated and not the least bit sure what my next move would be. My playing career had ended in such disappointing fashion in Boston that it took three full years of operations and rehabilitation until I could even begin to think about a new life.

After overcoming the physical and mental withdrawal pains that come with leaving the game, I began to focus on my future.

During the 1990 NBA finals I was just three months past my ankle-fusion surgery. I was on crutches and still had a huge cast on my leg. But I had to go to Las Vegas for business involving the Grateful Dead, a book convention and a golf tournament.

I shared a hotel suite with Tim and Barbara Leary and was so exhausted from the travel, the meetings, the difficulties of getting around on crutches, the general weakness caused by the operation that I had to take a nap.

The phone rang. Tim answered.

"Hi, I'm looking for Bill Walton," said the caller.

"Bill's resting," Tim said. "Can I take a message?"

"Well, this is Pat O'Brien, CBS."

"Pat? This is Tim Leary."

Pat and Tim were old friends. So Tim woke me up.

"Bill, Pat O'Brien, CBS," he said. "Portland and Detroit are opening up the NBA finals. It's the first time Portland's been back to the finals since 1977, when you guys won it all. We thought it would be most appropriate if you came on the halftime show."

"I can't, Pat. I've got a cast on my leg. I'm on crutches. I only have some shorts and T-shirts with me. I can't get around."

"But, Bill," he said, "there's nobody else we want except you."

"No way, Pat. I don't have anything to wear."

"Don't worry about a thing. We'll take care of everything."

Back and forth we went. I finally said he was wasting his time. I wasn't going to do the show.

Fifteen minutes later he called back.

"Bill, we've got to have you on."

"No," I said, and repeated all my reasons for declining his invitation.

"Bill, please. I promise we'll take care of everything."

"Okay," I said, completely worn down. "I'll do it."

O'Brien kept his word. The limo picked me up at the hotel, took me to a nearby clothing store, where I bought a shirt, tie, jacket and slacks (which were slit up the side so I could wear them over my cast)—all courtesy of CBS.

The limo then took me to the airport, drove onto the tarmac and parked right next to the plane. I was wheeled up to the plane and soon thereafter was flying to Detroit.

I landed in Detroit and there was a limo waiting for me at the plane. I was whisked to my hotel.

A few minutes before halftime, I was wheeled onto the set and placed in a chair. The cameramen shot me from the waist up, so none of the viewers could tell I was wearing a cast.

Pat started talking about the 1977 Portland championship season and then turned to me and said, "Bill, what do you miss most about not playing."

"Well, I've had a lot of trouble, but the thing I miss most is waking up in the morning and knowing that in a couple of hours I would be going down to the gym to kick somebody's ass."

O'Brien's eyes glistened with joy.

"You can't say that," he said. "We're on TV."

Uh-oh. I didn't know it was live.

Not long after that CBS appearance, longtime NBC

broadcaster Charlie Jones, who lives in the San Diego area, called me up and asked if I would help him out on a video project. I was flattered and quickly said yes. Charlie is a true professional and one of the most underrated, hardest-working and versatile broadcasters in the business.

During a break in the sessions, Charlie asked me, "What are you going to do with your life?"

"I'm not sure," I said. "I'm looking for something."

"Well, I've been in broadcasting fifty years and I really think you ought to try it. I think you'll like it."

"Me? Broadcasting?"

Charlie made a couple of calls, introduced me to a few of his friends. I've been off to the races ever since.

I had a poor relationship with the media during most of my career. I was reluctant to give any information that might lessen my chance to win. The razor-thin difference between winning and losing is not something you give away. Anything I said could and would be used against me by the opposition. I didn't want to provide a reporter with any sort of information that might endanger my team's chances of winning. I was friendly enough with the media, just not a fountain of usable information.

I was protected by John Wooden during my days at UCLA. At my request, Coach Wooden restricted the media's access to me. Watergate totally changed the media (along with almost everything else), but I still remained very reluctant to agree to any sort of interview. I felt uncomfortable with the attention focused on me as an individual and self-conscious because of my stuttering.

It wasn't until I was twenty-eight that I really learned how to speak. For so many years I had used basketball as a sanctuary, a hiding place from the outside world. On the basketball court, I didn't really need to speak. I usually just yelled at the refs. Or to the coach—something about getting some rebounders in here. The game itself became my form of communication. Whenever I had a problem, I could always go play ball and suddenly everything would be clear, the day would be bright and sunny, even in Portland.

One night at a social function in Los Angeles (I was with the Clippers at the time), Hall of Fame New York broadcaster Marty Glickman, who used to do the Knicks games, pulled me aside. Glickman cut straight to the chase.

"Bill, that stuttering—it's just totally unacceptable. How are you going to go through life like that? You can't talk."

"I . . . I . . . I . . . I . . . I . . . I . . . know," I said.

Glickman gave me three pieces of advice that were perfect in their simplicity and John Wooden–like in their practicality and fundamentals.

First, he said, chew gum. "The gum will warm up your mouth and strengthen the muscles in your mouth and jaw. If the muscles are strong, then they'll respond to the instructions given to them by your mind."

Then, he said, slow down your thoughts. "Don't think ahead. Think about what you're saying right now. Your mind is racing too far ahead of where you're trying to talk."

Finally, I should practice reading out loud. "The sports pages. A book. The side panel on a box of cereal. Anything. Just read something out loud and do it all the time."

I immediately went to work. I'd start every day by popping a stick of gum in my mouth. It was like my stretching exercise. Then I'd stand in front of a mirror and practice reading out loud. I identified problems with particular sounds—with *w*'s, *th*'s and *d*'s—so I'd search out words with those sounds and repeat them until I mastered the words.

I did those drills every day. Still do. I never go on the air without first warming up. It's a routine—I never played basketball without putting my left shoe on first. I always dressed left to right.

People who have known me for a really long time can't believe that I've learned to talk. "How did you do it?" They can't believe that I make my living as a broadcaster. They knew me when I would barely say a word. Now you can't get me to shut up.

The first game I ever did as a broadcaster took place during the 1976 season, my second with the Trail Blazers. I was injured—as always—and it was driving Lenny Wilkens crazy. It wasn't that Lenny questioned the severity of my broken foot; it's just that he became extremely frustrated with the situation. I was the reminder of what could have been.

At one point, Lenny decided it was best that I left the bench. I think Lenny simply wanted me out of his sight. He was tired of seeing me and not being able to play me.

"Gawdangit, Bill," he said, "get off this bench and go see if Bill Schonely [the Trail Blazers' radio announcer] will let you sit next to him. You can go talk about the game."

I'm not sure who was more surprised at the order: me or Schonely. Schonely was very aware of the severity of my stuttering, but he stuck me on the air anyway. It was brutal.

A few months after deciding to pursue a broadcasting career, I found myself in New York on other business. I called Howard Cosell at his office at ABC. I didn't know Cosell at all, other than watching him on TV like everyone else. But I admired his work. He was my favorite broadcaster, regardless of the event. He was the only broadcaster I ever turned on the TV for just to hear what he had to say.

"Howard, this is Bill Walton and I'm in New York. I was wondering if I could come over and pick your brains. I'm embarking on a career in broadcasting and I'd like to get some tips from you, some pointers."

Howard sounded put upon, as though I was wasting his time. He said he was too busy, that he had no interest in helping me.

"Please," I said. "Just a half hour . . . fifteen minutes . . . anything. Please."

"Oh, very well."

I took a cab to the ABC studios, walked into his office, sat down and hoped for the best. Howard looked at me and said, "Young man, you're going to be a fine broadcaster because you're an intelligent person. Only a smart man would be wise enough to ask me for advice on how to become a successful broadcaster. You just made the best move of your life."

Howard Cosell and I then spent the rest of the day together. I tagged along as he ran his errands, lunched at the Friars Club, went to *his* podiatrist. He still seems angry, busy and put out when I call for advice.

The ability to learn how to talk is easily the greatest thing I've ever done. Winning two NCAA championships and two NBA titles was nice, but I knew that was going to happen. But learning how to speak has given me a whole new life. I have been set free.

Learning how to talk and learning how to be a broadcaster are two different things. In 1990, I was a rookie at both.

One of the most difficult things for a basketball player is accepting the fact that there are other criteria for whether you get a job, criteria other than your skills. When you're a good basketball player, they can't keep you out. Team management will tolerate your personality in order to reap the benefits of your performance. That idyllic situation is not available in other jobs.

I was always lucky as a player to have great coaches and teammates. I've been very fortunate in broadcasting as well. CBS hired me to become an analyst for its college basketball package. Then came opportunities with the CBA, the Dallas Mavericks, the Los Angeles Clippers, the Pac-10 Conference, Roy Firestone's *Up Close* show on ESPN and, most recently, NBC's *NBA Showtime*.

I started at the bottom, where I belonged. Too often ex-players think they're owed something, that they shouldn't have to pay their dues as they make the transition to their new careers. They're so accustomed to making big money and being pampered that they can't or won't make the necessary sacrifices when starting over in their post-NBA career.

I was willing to do just about anything. I had a lot of difficulty getting entry-level jobs because there was so much apprehension about my speech impediment.

Just prior to the 1991 NBA playoffs, the Portland CBS affiliate KOIN contacted me about working on their sports broadcasts. Even though there was little money involved, I jumped at the chance to learn the broadcasting business. I started with the postgame show. That role was quickly expanded to the broadcast news, and soon I was doing live remotes. Goodness gracious sakes alive, I was a broadcaster.

Most coaches lie awake at night thinking, "What are my players doing now?" My TV and radio producers were lying awake at night thinking, "What is Walton going to say tomorrow?"

I don't limit my critiques to any particular team or player, whatever the level. During my first year with CBS, I was assigned an NCAA tournament game featuring Indiana and Florida State. FSU was the decided underdog, but Coach Pat Kennedy's team, led by forward Douglas Edwards, played great and dominated the first half. Edwards played like Elgin Baylor during those first twenty minutes and had his team poised for an upset.

At halftime, the Florida State sports information director came over to me and said that Edwards had a stomachache and probably wouldn't play in the second half. I filed the information away.

Edwards came out for the second half, but he was a zero. As the game immediately turned and Florida State's double-digit lead was erased by a charged-up Indiana team, I remembered Edwards' stomachache.

"Well, at halftime the Florida State people told me that Douglas Edwards had a stomachache," I said. "But this is championship-level basketball. You have a chance to lead your team to victory. You can't let a stomachache stop you. What Douglas Edwards should do is go into the locker room and have somebody stick their finger down his throat so he can puke."

A few minutes later our game producer, Bob Stenner, received a call from Ted Shaker, Executive Producer for CBS Sports at the time. Shaker's message: "Bill, this is CBS. We don't talk about puking on prime-time television during the dinner hour in New York. Please make the proper amends."

On Roy's *Up Close* show last season, I mentioned that the Michigan Wolverines were overrated and underachievers.

Later, during an interview with Steve Wieberg of *USA Today,* I said, "They haven't accomplished anything," I said. "Making it to the Final Four, that's not a great accomplishment. Winning it is."

John Wooden is fond of saying, "A lot of coaches and a lot of teams have gotten very famous by winning one championship." Here are the so-called Fab Five of Michigan—Chris Webber, Jalen Rose, Ray Jackson, Jimmy King and Juwan Howard—and they haven't won a thing, not even a Big Ten Conference title. Yet people are giving them credit for accomplishing so much.

Michigan had the most talent, the most potential, but hadn't shown me that they were capable of winning the NCAA championship.

The Wolverines were a capable group that never seemed to come close to playing really well and dominating. I just don't think Michigan played a successful or fulfilling style of basketball. They didn't control the flow of the big games. They were in the game, but they didn't control it—and that's the difference between teams with championship rings and teams who finish second.

Webber and I saw each other less than forty-eight hours after Michigan's embarrassing loss to North Carolina. In a classy move, Webber and Wolverine coach Steve Fisher traveled from Ann Arbor to Los Angeles for the John R. Wooden Award ceremony. He made the effort, while all but one of the other candidates, including the winner, Calbert Cheaney from Bob Knight's Indiana Hoosiers, failed to show.

Midway through the media luncheon, I was called up to the podium by the awards emcee, Tommy Hawkins. Once there, I spoke briefly about my own disappointments and failures while at UCLA, including the heartbreaking loss to North Carolina State in the 1974 national semifinals. With Webber in mind, I said, "You should be congratulated on a tremendous season. Your courage in being here today should also be applauded."

Webber and I had a nice, cordial chat at a private luncheon later that day. I wish him the very best in his pro career. I wish he would have remained in school, though. Maybe he does too, now that the chance to play with Shaq has passed.

I learned to play and love basketball as a child, listening to Chick Hearn on the Lakers' radio network while in the kitchen doing the dishes. Four broadcasters announced the majority of my games: Fred Hessler at UCLA, Bill Schonely with the Blazers, Ralph Lawler with the Clippers and Johnny Most with the Celtics. I rarely heard any of their comments, which was probably just as well. I couldn't stand to listen to the broadcast of my team's game when I was injured.

When I was a kid, we had one radio speaker in the

kitchen. I listened to Chick as I did my homework or did the dishes. I would sit there just about every game as Chick's distinctive voice filled the room. The Lakers weren't my favorite team—the Celtics were—but that didn't matter. Chick made every game so exciting, so thrilling. So memorable were those moments that I asked my parents to save that speaker for me. It's now in my house.

Chick is the master at describing a scene or a play on the court. He does it with so much enthusiasm that you can't help but get caught up in the moment.

I owe so much to him. Chick doesn't just tell you about a play, he explains it. He explains why some players are good and why others aren't worth the trouble.

When I became a player myself, Chick taught me how to appreciate the game, how to be up every day. Few people have had a bigger impact on my career as a fan and as a player than Chick Hearn. My vision of basketball comes directly from Chick Hearn.

Chick Hearn's work ethic is inspirational. Chick has such passion for the game and his work that he'll arrive early to the arena and actually practice calling the action. There won't be anybody on the court, but that didn't stop Chick. He would call a make-believe game so vividly that you'd swear it was real. He's just like Bird, who came out early to shoot jumpers or practice free throws. When the actual game begins, Chick is ready to go.

Chick is the first guy to get all over his Lakers. Announcers who make excuses for the poor performances of the players or the coaches do the game and its business a disservice. Viewers and listeners deserve an honest broadcast.

I'd like to be his broadcast partner someday. But Chick has a tendency to dominate. Most of the time his partner, Stu Lantz, is reduced to saying, "Yes, Chick," or "You're absolutely right, Chick."

There are lots of things I should have done in my life. I

should have converted those easy shots against North Carolina State in the national semifinals. I should have stayed on the bench when I was injured. I should have sought Chick's advice when I first got into broadcasting.

I've never really spent very much time with Chick, which is my loss. In a way, though, I feel as if I know him. By listening to his broadcasts—he has done almost 2,700 games, dating back to November 20, 1965—I know his sharp sense of humor, his sense of pride, his sense of entertainment, his sense of perfection and performance. He's a showman. He's onstage. He's one of the main reasons to watch or listen to a Lakers game, more so now than ever before.

The only way you get better in anything is with practice. I love to work. I'd do a game every day if I could. It amazes me when players and coaches say they're upset because they have to play so much on Christmas. That's the best day of the year to work, besides the last two weeks of the season.

Three years ago I did a CBA game on Christmas Day on the radio from Bakersfield, California, and I didn't get paid. The team folded the next day. Two years ago I did the NBC studio show on Christmas.

Phil Jackson, the Chicago Bulls' coach, often complains that he hates being part of NBC's made-for-TV Christmas special. His reasoning is that "Christmas is always a family day. It's a giving day, a holy day for Christians and a meaningful day of peace and light. To mar it with a game in which you have to come out and fight with guys who are going to foul you on every possession [the Bulls were playing the New York Knicks] turns it into something else. We're not going to be able to enjoy the day."

How can you not enjoy a day when you're in the spotlight? The moment is yours. It's the ultimate Christmas present. It is one of the top honors in sports to play on the big holidays when everyone is home watching you.

The big events drive me. The crowds, the noise, the tension, the anticipation, the uncertainty of the outcome. It's like rock and roll: Just turn it up and speed it up. And get quickly to eleven.

As a player, I experienced those feelings every game. The same is true as a broadcaster. When the red light goes on, you have to be ready. You can't come back to Bob Costas and say, "Why don't you let me think about that for a while." Or "I'll get back to you later on that one, Bob."

Analyzing a game isn't difficult. I always look for people who come to win, who come to give you everything they've got. Larry Bird did it. Magic Johnson did. Michael Jordan did it. In the world of rock and roll, Jerry Garcia does it. They're going to give you a great effort and show every time they step onstage.

One of the terrific things about being a basketball player is the team. A group of guys traveling the world, winning games, taking names, celebrating your successes. I thought that was over when my playing career concluded.

I'm on a new team now. A team with lots of guys who still travel around the country, taking names and celebrating our victories.

It hasn't always been that way. At the lower levels of broadcasting—cable and local over the air—there's very little sense of team, much the way it is at Muni Gym, where you're on your own. Everyone for himself.

My new team is coached by Dick Ebersol and Terry O'Neil. They have given me my most recent opportunity to grow and expand. But like all my other Hall of Fame coaches, they've had to occasionally caution me about throwing the outlet pass down the center of the court.

My teammates today are Peter Vecsey and Bob Costas, extraordinarily talented journalists and broadcasters. Vecsey, the only man with enough credibility (or is it credulity?) to ravage Magic Johnson while singing the praises of guys like Benoit Benjamin and Sherman Douglas. Vecsey's quick wit and thirty years of experience of being lied to makes him the voice of reason on our team.

Bob Costas is a man whose talents I have come to rate along with the very best that I've ever come across: Jabbar. Bird. Wooden. Ramsay. Garcia.

Words and stories flow easily from Costas: the exact opposite of me. Costas' honest encouragement, direct instruction, frank guidance and teaching by example have taken me farther than I ever could have gotten by myself.

If he could just explain to me what it is he sees in baseball.

As for Rudy Martzke . . . I just hope he was kidding.

It's not how high you jump; it's where you are and when you jump. *RON RAY, HELIX HIGH SCHOOL*

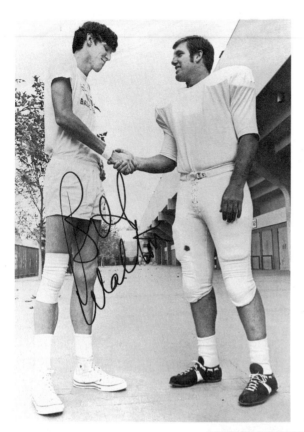

Getting some late
afternoon advice from
older brother Bruce
outside Pauley Pavilion
before we joined our
separate teams.

Off to a good start
under the coach's
watchful eye.

Comfortably and confidently meeting the press—still trying to
get the ball from main man Jack. *DAVE OLSEN*, THE COLUMBIAN

A great team gone astray.

Starting the fast break, my favorite part of the game.   (left) *PATRICK DOWNS, LOS ANGELES TIMES SYNDICATE* (below) UCLA

The '77 Blazer reunion at Lake Tahoe, Cal., 1991—bring on the stat team. *CRAIG SHERMAN*

A happy day with Lori: you could have been a flower.
KIRBY LEE

On the garage court that was too small for Larry Bird, the
Waltons—Adam, Nathan, Luke, and Chris—learn the
fundamentals of life: here, controlling the jump ball.
CRAIG SHERMAN

With my "teammates" after the 1993 Hall of Fame induction speech that lasted longer than my career. *MOKE*

Celebrating Red's 75th birthday in one of my many tuxedoes, drifting and dreaming, dizzy with possibilities.   *STEVE LIPOFSKY*

At the '86 Celtic championship parade with oldest son Adam—
Jan Volk didn't think this was the appropriate time and place
to have a beer—right!

Leaving the final game of the 1986 NBA Championship. "Just do something"—and "Kevin, about my number . . ."

Arguing with the band about the set list.

My hero, Peter Vecsey—"the voice of reason." *NBC*

Smiles all around—something you wouldn't see if I was still wearing my "old" uniform.

Wilt asked, "Okay, Coach Wooden, we're all here, now who gets to start?" Wooden's immediate response: "Well, is there anyone here who won three NCAA championships?" *GEORGE B. FRY III*

With my mom and dad at the Hall of Fame, 1993.
CRAIG SHERMAN

CHAPTER 9

"Got two good eyes,
but we still don't see . . ."
—*Jerry Garcia*

I was in New York last year, walking down the street, minding my own business, when some guy, a perfect stranger, saw me and yelled, "Why don't you play the game and stop crying, you big baby!"

The guy was repeating a line from a *Sports Illustrated* commercial, which features clips from a video called *The Secret NBA*. In one of the clips (which lasts about three seconds), my entire relationship with referees was captured on film forever—or at least as long as *Sports Illustrated* keeps running that commercial.

I was with the Boston Celtics at the time and we were playing the Houston Rockets in the Garden. Something happened—another missed call, another bad non-call—and I complained to the nearest referee, Jess Kersey. I liked to complain. Some called it whining. You must continually argue your case if you ever expect the judge to see your case through your eyes.

As we started to run upcourt after the play, Kersey turned to me and said, "Why don't you play the game and stop crying, you big baby."

That kept me quiet . . . at least until the next terrible call. Then I was back arguing my case.

I generally respect the refs, empathize with the demands of their job and feel they're seriously underpaid. I also don't hesitate to take a few verbal jabs at them.

Last season, when the basketball world was raving about incoming European star Toni Kukoc, I couldn't help but mention on NBC's *Insiders* segment that he was in for a big surprise.

"The only similarity between the NBA and European basketball," I said on the air, "is the inconsistent officiating."

I don't envy referees. They've got a very demanding, difficult and pressure-filled job. At the lower levels of play, they often decide the outcome of games.

The pay isn't what it should be, about $50,000 for an NBA rookie ref and about $9,000 for, say, a college ref assigned twenty regular-season games in the Pac-10 Conference. It's no surprise the quality of officiating is so shaky.

Their professional lives, especially the lives of NBA referees, are nothing to daydream about. They're on the road all the time, usually by themselves, and, like the players, they've got to take their share of abuse from the fans and the media—except that the players get paid a lot more to hear it.

Former NBA ref Earl Strom, a players' favorite because of his style, courage, integrity and personality, likes to tell the story about a game he did in Syracuse years ago. It seems that a woman in the crowd kept heckling him throughout the night. In fact, every game Strom did in Syracuse, this woman was there to rip him. No matter what call Strom made, it never failed to infuriate the woman.

Strom, like all refs, had rabbit ears. He never missed a thing.

"Hey, Earl," she said, "If you were my husband, I'd feed you rat poison."

"If you were my wife," retorted Strom, "I'd eat it."

Strom and I normally got along, which isn't always the case with players and refs. Some players go out there and don't care which refs they irritate. You can't do that if you want to win everything. You've got to learn the psychological makeup and the psyche of each and every referee. You've got to deal with them on a mental level.

The whole purpose is to convince a ref to see the game the way you're seeing it as a player. In a way, you've got to educate him, to teach him.

I was never afraid to tell a ref he missed a call, but the timing was critical. Some guys, such as Kersey, would get right back in your face, which didn't bother me. Other guys, such as Strom, would take a step back and say to themselves, "If Walton complained, gee, maybe I better take a better look at it."

Just as players sit around and talk about other players and refs, refs sit around and talk about other refs and players. For the most part, I think the refs respected me—at least, that's what Strom says. Sure, I did my share of second-guessing on calls, but for the most part, I got along with the refs.

There were exceptions, of course. Strom once told me that certain refs couldn't stand my attitude.

"Jeezus," they'd say, "that Bill Walton is a pain in the ass. I can't deal with him."

"No kidding?" Strom would ask. "I get along fine with him, but that damn Rick Barry—now there's a pain in the ass."

Strom's personality never mixed with Barry's. That's the

way it is sometimes. Players and refs have different flash points, which can produce all sorts of reactions.

Midway through my NBA career, a young referee named Terry Durham, who used to officiate a lot of our practices when I played for the Trail Blazers, finally made it to the top, the NBA. When my relationship with the Blazers went sour I became a very unpopular person in Portland because of my criticism of the Portland medical staff and my insistence on being traded.

Durham grew up in the Portland area and I swear he held a grudge against me. Every time he did one of our games, every call went against me. A guy could put an elbow through my face and Durham would swallow his whistle and pretend he hadn't seen a thing.

This went on for months. One day I saw Darell Garretson, a career NBA referee who is also the league's chief of officiating. I told him I was struggling with Durham and why I thought I was getting the short end of the stick.

Garretson talked to Durham and set up a meeting between us prior to a game both of us were working. When the time came, I told Durham exactly what was on my mind.

I related my frustrations, my dismay that every call always went the other way. I reminded him of his link with Portland and told him that I felt he still harbored resentment against me because of the situation surrounding my departure from the Trail Blazers. I told him I didn't feel he was acting like a professional.

Durham denied it all, of course.

The meeting certainly helped me relax as a player. I was able to let off some steam, make my feelings known and go about my business. I had done my part. Now it was up to Durham to do his.

I often criticize the quality of officiating in the NBA. I don't have anything against the refs (they're absolutely essential to the game). I just think they should be so much better. There are too few good referees and too many "I'm just happy to be in the league, happy to have a job" types.

Part of the problem is that a lot of refs don't handle the heat-of-the-big-game situations very well.

Just about anybody can call fouls and violations. All you need is a rule book and a memory for that. The trick is applying those rules once the game starts. It seems that in today's game, refs are taught how to memorize, rather than how to officiate and how to properly blend into a game and how to let the flow create a beautiful, entertaining event.

The sad thing is, progress in this area seems to come very slowly.

The salary scale is another reason for inconsistent refereeing. Mediocre pay usually means mediocre performance.

I have the greatest admiration for Stern and the job he has done. But the NBA simply doesn't pay enough to attract the best-qualified applicants. Just think how much better the officiating would be if more former players—people who really understood the inner workings of a game—were recruited and paid a decent enough salary to make it worth their while. Instead, some NBA refs, after working a whole season, must go scrounging around for their next meal. Some of them are freed to go to places like Puerto Rico to do summer-league games during the off-season so they can supplement their income.

As usual, politics plays a part in the quality of officiating.

The reviews are mixed on Garretson. Some people think he does a wonderful job. Others, such as Strom, aren't so sure.

Garretson is the director of officiating in the NBA. When NBA refs started grumbling last year about their wages and benefits, even going so far as to discuss the possibility of another strike, it was Garretson who stepped in and squelched the mini-uprising.

Garretson does have a powerful weapon on his side: the performance ratings (as if you can numerically evaluate something so subjective as a ref's performance). If a ref doesn't get a high enough rating, he is left out of the playoff rotation. If he doesn't make the playoffs, he misses out on that playoff paycheck. For a referee who works through the NBA finals, that can mean about an extra $40,000.

It's probably safe to say that Garretson has the majority of the refs under his wing. He knows it. He likes it. The NBA knows it. It likes it. The other refs know it. Tough.

A lot of the refs compete for Garretson's favor, instead of concentrating on results. When the ratings are calculated, the opinions of the NBA's operations staff, of which Garretson is a key member, counts for 60 percent of the total, compared with just 40 percent for the coaches and general managers and 0 percent for the players.

To some extent, the high quality of their work makes some refs relatively immune to petty politics. Guys such as Jake O'Donnell, Joe Crawford, Jack Nies, Hugh Evans, Ed T. Rush, Mike Mathis and Jack Madden usually do very well on the ratings.

Then there's Ed Middleton, who last year was rated as the tenth-best ref by the coaches and general managers. But by the time Garretson, operations chief Rod Thorn and the observer scouts were done with him, his rating had plummeted to seventeenth. Confounding.

Your success or failure as an official shouldn't be based on who you know or how often you have to wipe your nose. It should be based on performance. There are just too many instances of officials ratting on each other in an effort to move up the ratings ladder.

Another inadequacy is the lack of former players as refs.

There are a lot of referees who are intimidated by the NBA star players. They simply can't imagine a star player making a mistake out there, so they never call a thing on the guys with the big reputations.

From a physical standpoint, most of the refs are so short and so little that they have no idea of what a big man can do on the basketball court. Some of them can't understand how someone so tall could make such an athletic move or show incredible range. It is that lack of understanding and imagination that creates missed or incorrect calls.

It's difficult to ask someone so small to recognize the difference between goaltending and a perfectly timed blocked shot. They've never been up that high, how would they know?

Some changes need to be made, beginning with a system that would increase the salaries paid to entry-level refs, thus making it more attractive to ex-players, people who have an actual feel for the game at the major-college, CBA or even NBA level.

You don't necessarily have to be a former player to be a solid referee. But it would help. The world's best basketball players deserve the world's best referees. I don't think they have them right now. Generally, the refs are at the lowest level of proficiency in the NBA. You need stronger personalities. You need referees who aren't afraid to stand up to Michael Jordan, or Charles Barkley, or Karl Malone, or Clyde Drexler, or any of the stars in the league and say, "Hey, that's the way I see it." You also need refs who are willing to say they made a mistake and who are willing to work on their weaknesses.

Many times in my NBA career a ref would come into a game with an attitude. The best refs enter a game relaxed. They know the players are mean, fired up and ready to kill. As keepers of the peace, officials have to be ready to defuse those situations and prevent a violent explosion that could cause serious injuries.

Mediocre refs let their personal problems, their personal insecurities and their personal jealousies enter into their game-day thinking. They lack poise and confidence. Those are the worst. A disgrace.

Strom used to look for three things when assessing a referee: his judgment, his common sense and his courage.

Players want the same things out of a ref. They want someone who not only knows the rules of the game but knows how to use the rules to make the game better. Smart refs understand that the game has progressed beyond the original rules, that allowances and compromises have to be made. Flexibility is the key to stability.

Common sense is often in short supply among NBA refs. Surrounded by incredibly talented athletes and over- whelmed by the high stakes, refs sometimes panic. You get quick whistles . . . wasted fouls where a simple warning would suffice . . . an erratic flow of the game. In really im- portant games, ones where the very best referees are as- signed, rarely will you find a player in foul trouble or the game decided by fouls. Top referees try not to interfere with the game. They are there to enhance it, not dominate it or dictate its pace.

A ref has to have courage. He has to be willing to make tough calls in front of the home team's bench. He has to handle the heckling and be willing to admit his errors.

A lot of today's refs are too confrontational. A player or coach will approach a ref about an obviously bad call, but the ref becomes instantly defensive. They try to defend a bad call. Their actions are indefensible.

One of the toughest guys I ever played against was Artis Gilmore. Gilmore was 7' 2", at least 250, maybe 260 pounds, and he was strong. Gilmore thought the rules of the game, particularly three seconds, traveling and offensive fouls, didn't apply to him. He more or less considered them guide- lines, more than rules.

I was with the Trail Blazers at the time, and we were in Chicago for a game against Gilmore's Bulls. Strom was one of the referees.

In the waning seconds of a great game at the Stadium, the Blazers were up by three points, Chicago at the free-throw line to shoot two. The Bulls make the first one to cut our lead to two. No problem. Even if they made the next one we'd be up by a point and have the ball with only a second or so left.

Instead, they missed it. As the ball bounced off the rim, I had inside rebounding position. I set my body between the basket and Gilmore. I have him completely boxed out. The rebound is mine, the game ours.

And then . . . smash. Gilmore body-slammed me out of the way and I went flying into the basket stanchion. I heard a whistle as Gilmore grabbed the ball and dunked it.

"Good," I thought. "The game's over and I'm going to ice it at the line."

Strom saw a foul, all right. Only he called the foul on *me,* counted Gilmore's basket and sent the smiling Bulls center to the free-throw line with a chance to put Chicago ahead by one.

I went ballistic. My teammates had to restrain me from going after Strom, who should have called a technical on me. I was the one who had inside position, who had almost been knocked into the aurora borealis on Gilmore's muscle play. I was the one who should have been shooting free throws, not Gilmore.

On top of that, it was my sixth foul. I was out of the game. I was so mad I would have personally fed Strom rat poison.

Gilmore made the free throw. The Bulls were up one. The game was theirs. Strom had botched the call and cost us the game.

There was still a second left. We called time, which meant

we'd have a chance to advance the ball in order to inbound from half-court. We had two chances, slim and none.

Lionel Hollins, one of our guards, worked himself free and caught the inbounds pass near half-court. With his back to the basket and the buzzer ready to sound, Hollins turned and heaved a shot that kissed off the backboard and swished through the net.

I immediately charged Strom and pointed both of my forefingers right at Strom's stunned face.

"That's in your face! That's in your face! That's on you, Strom!"

What a disgrace.

Then I raced off the court. Hey, Strom had it coming. He deserved it. He blew the call. What a disgrace.

The college refs aren't any better. If anything, they're worse. They're terrible about calling offensive fouls, steps and three seconds.

Remember last season's NCAA championship game between Michigan and North Carolina? Never mind Chris Webber's timeout call at the end; what about Webber's blatant traveling violation, which was conveniently ignored by the officials?

Quit crying and play the game. But if something isn't done soon about the quality of officiating, there isn't going to be a game worth playing.

"Take me to the leader of the band."
—Jerry Garcia

I've been approached numerous times by college programs and pro franchises about becoming a basketball coach. UCLA once asked if I'd be interested in the job, as did a handful of other schools, but I always tell them thanks, but no, thanks.

There are many reasons for my decision, beginning with the fact that I can't kneel down or stand up for very long. My legs, ankles and feet won't allow it. And honestly, there isn't a coach in the business who isn't on his knees or feet the whole game, much less the practices.

I also enjoy broadcasting.

I also don't want to move. San Diego is my home, but there is no basketball here.

Getting fired isn't the problem—everyone gets fired, it's inevitable in coaching. The problem is that when a coach gets fired, he just can't pick up his things and go to the next corporation or business opportunity down the street. You've got to switch cities.

I am a single father of four fine sons, ages eighteen to twelve—Adam, Nathan, Luke and Christopher. I feel a tremendous responsibility for their development. It's important that they have a place they can call home, a place to seek shelter from the storm. It's important that *I* have a place I can call home. The ability to feel comfortable with the quality of your life is vital. Becoming a coach, requiring relocation, would jeopardize that quality.

Basketball players live in hotel rooms during most of their careers. So do coaches, as well as broadcasters. Already I live out of a suitcase even when I'm home. My broadcasting schedule is usually so crazy that I never bother to unpack. I love to travel, but the difference between broadcasting and coaching is that I know I'll always be returning home to San Diego when the road trip is complete. I've got a place where I feel safe.

On the other hand, coaches rarely have that luxury. They've got to be willing to take a job in Bloomington, Indiana, or Milwaukee, or Cleveland, or Starkville, Mississippi, or wherever. For someone wanting to become a coach, the location isn't as important as the opportunity. I'm not willing to do that—for myself or for my kids. I want them to grow up in San Diego.

I've had great teachers in my life. My father, John Wooden, Jack Ramsay, Red Auerbach, Lenny Wilkens, K. C. Jones and, in broadcasting, Charlie Jones. These people prepared me for life. Their lessons led me to believe that you can do anything you want. Anything. Absolutely.

I've got the best of both worlds. I'm a broadcaster, and every day my phone rings with new opportunities, people saying, "Let's do this, let's do that." I regularly work as a special instructor for basketball players. I've had the great good fortune to work with guys such as Shaquille O'Neal, Rik Smits and Luc Longley. I coach individuals.

Still, people continue to ask me, "Bill, when are you going to try coaching?" I coached every time I played a game. I coach every time I broadcast a game. I coach every time I'm watching a game from my living-room sofa. And you know what? I'm just like the real coach too: Nobody listens to me.

The coaching profession fascinates me. It inspires me. On occasion, it repulses and embarrasses me.

There are very few bad coaches and very few great coaches. Like their teams, most coaches are stuck right in the middle. Almost all coaches say the same things, draw up the same plays, wear the same kinds of clothes. What separates the great ones from everybody else is the ability to communicate, to relate, to lead, to sacrifice, to perfect personal skills, to become selfless. Leadership requires incredible sacrifice because you basically have to give up your own life for others. You end up living the lives of the players you're coaching. That way, you can help them attain higher levels of achievement than the students are able to reach on their own. It is the essence of teaching.

John Wooden obviously embodies those qualities more than any other coach I've known. But there are others who come close.

In 1973, UCLA advanced to the NCAA national semifinal (that's what it was called back then) and we played Indiana at the St. Louis Arena. Coach Wooden never said much about the opposing team. I wish he would have mentioned something about Bob Knight, the Hoosiers' thirty-two-year-old coach, and Indiana basketball. Maybe Wooden didn't know anything about him.

At the time, Knight had only been at Indiana for two seasons, but he was quickly making a name for himself.

That was the first year freshmen were eligible to play

varsity basketball. That gave Knight the opportunity to play and start Quinn Buckner. Neither Buckner nor any of his teammates did much as we took an 18-point lead at halftime and stretched it to 20 early in the second half. I carelessly got into foul trouble, got benched and watched as Knight's Hoosiers took full advantage of the opening. Indiana scored 17 consecutive points and Coach Wooden quickly got me back into the game.

A few minutes later, there was a foul called against Indiana center Steve Downing, who was whistled for his fourth foul as I drove to the basket. Downing picked up his fifth foul a minute later and we won, 70–59.

To this day, Knight says it was one of the worst calls he's ever seen. I, of course, thought the ref was in perfect position, had the clear angle and made the right call.

More than twenty years later, Knight is still at Indiana and still doing a fine job. I admire his results (three national championships, five Final Four appearances and countless Big Ten conference titles), I don't always admire his methods.

Knight has a rare gift of making people better basketball players and, even more important, better men. I have a great and growing respect for his coaching and leadership abilities.

I don't like the fact, though, that he's a bully and that he seems to enjoy needlessly abusing his massive power. Other people couldn't get away with some of the things he does. Most wouldn't even try.

The confusing thing about Bob Knight is that he can be one of the most charming people in the world, and a lot of times he is. I wish I knew Knight better. I saw a couple of his quotes from last season's NCAA Midwest Regional and it was interesting to see him reveal tiny bits of his personality. Someone asked him about his public image. He said, "It always amazes me. I'll see somewhere where a guy writes, 'Boy, I could never play for Knight.' That's usually something that's written, meaning I'm such a bad guy. Well, for most of you, it would be good for you to have a friend like me. Guys that say, 'I couldn't play for him,' better think, 'I bet there's no way Knight would have me on his team.' But that usually isn't done."

Could I have played for him? Probably not. He wouldn't have had me on his team. I was too good a player. Also, I'm a big-city guy. Bloomington doesn't exactly fit the bill.

Normally, people take on the personality of their environment. Here's Bloomington, a very reserved, very small town, and Knight is basically a national bully, someone whose personality you would think would fit into a town like New York, Chicago or Los Angeles. Instead, he lives in Bloomington. He probably couldn't be Bob Knight in New York, Chicago or Los Angeles.

I respect and admire the discipline that Knight brings to the game, the organization, the commitment to team play and the emphasis on physical and mental conditioning. But there seems to be so little joy to the play of his teams. His players regard their stay with him as an honor, but also as a sentence.

One real test of a coach or leader is how the players think of their coach years down the road. Knight, like Wooden, grows on his ex-players as they mature. It is sad to hear players, well after their playing careers are over, complaining about their former coaches. Rarely is that the case with Bob Knight.

I do not know Bob Knight as a person. He doesn't appear to always enjoy his life. Maybe in his personal life away from basketball he is an entirely different person from what we see on the court. He is a very intelligent person, which is one of the traits all the top coaches share. Still, you have to have the ability to think through things before they ever happen. Coach Wooden did that. Pat Riley does that. Before he ever utters a word or makes a decision, Riley considers every aspect of the situation, every repercussion. I'm not sure Bob Knight does the same thing. He sometimes seems to act first, think later. Kind of like me at times.

UCLA and Indiana were invited to play in the 1991–92 Hall of Fame Tip-off Classic in Springfield, Massachusetts. I was doing the national radio broadcast of the game. As part of the festivities, there was a luncheon honoring the two teams on the day of the game. It was a wonderful affair . . . until Knight was asked to say a few words.

Red Auerbach had spoken earlier and Knight immediately praised Red for his many accomplishments.

Then, for reasons unknown, Knight started complaining about what a drag it was to be in Springfield and how he and his team were wasting their time there.

Moments later, Knight noticed Dick Vitale sitting at a table near the front of the stage. Vitale, who is a huge fan of Knight's, was part of the television broadcasting team there to do the game.

Knight first mentioned something about Vitale's latest book, *Time Out, Baby!,* and then told the audience not to buy it. He said to buy Auerbach's book, but not Vitale's. "How can you believe anything a man says who sees the game of basketball with one eye?" Then he covered one eye and swung his head back and forth.

I felt like crawling into a hole, not only because of the boorish tactics of Knight but partly because of my own failure to stand up and say something. It is one thing to get on a guy because of his abilities or lack thereof. I strongly believe in open discussion and criticism, where criticism is due. I have no problem with ripping somebody for a legitimate professional shortcoming—those are just the facts, please. But I don't think you ever, ever criticize a man for a physical limitation . . . a handicap. Goodness gracious sakes alive, there were 1,500 people at the banquet. This was not a frat party. Absolutely nobody—and I'm not one of Vitale's biggest fans either—deserves that sort of treatment.

Some of the worst moments of our lives are the times when we fail to do something. I should have done something. I should have walked out. Knight's comments about Vitale were embarrassing, cruel and not even remotely amusing. Instead, I sat there frozen in my chair. I was unable or unwilling to act and I've never quite forgiven myself for that.

Knight is an enigma, a paradox. How else can you explain his kind of behavior? How can someone so smart, someone who has done so many wonderful things for so many people, be capable of such behavior? If he were a dummy, that would be one thing. But he isn't; he's a bright, compassionate person who has his players' and his program's best interests at heart 99.9 percent of the time. His record speaks for itself: His players get their degrees and they usually leave as better basketball players and better people than when they arrived. He teaches them to respect the purest aspects of the game and to act as model citizens.

I have no dispute with the way Knight coaches. At least he doesn't substitute incessantly to coddle bench players. He did a fantastic job with the Hoosiers during the 1993 season, especially after center Alan Henderson hurt his knee late in the season. My disagreements with him have to do with the way he treats people. As for myself, he's always been respectfully civil. There are members of the media who swear by him, others who would rather swear at him.

One guy who can't stand him is Charles Barkley.

Silly Charles. After all, how could Barkley possibly be upset with Knight's decision to cut him from the 1984 Olympic team in favor of Jeff Turner? Knight's U.S.A. team won the gold medal, but Barkley should have been on that team.

Maybe that's why Barkley went on Roy Firestone's *Up Close* show one time and basically said that his dream in life was to be locked naked in a room with Knight.

I don't think he meant it in a good way.

Knight has done a marvelous job at Indiana with basically inferior talent. There have been exceptions (Isiah Thomas, Buckner, Calbert Cheaney), but most of the Hoosiers' success is Knight's doing. He is a teacher, like Wooden. But unlike Wooden, Knight is a bully and his tactics needlessly hurt a lot of people along the way.

Just ask Vitale.

———

Of all the coaches I ever played for, Boston's K. C. Jones was the closest to John Wooden in terms of style and substance. Of all the coaches I see in the college game, Duke's Mike Krzyzewski is the most Wooden-like. He does the most with his team and the talent he has to work with, he's low-key and he lets his players play their game. The way it should be.

The beauty in Krzyzewski's program is that he's built it up to the point now where he doesn't really need to recruit. Instead, the players come to him, just as they did when Wooden was at UCLA. And the parents are the ones who are pushing the children there.

Krzyzewski has accomplished this at a relatively young coaching age (he's forty-six). Wooden wasn't able to do it until he was well into his fifties.

It all could have fallen apart for Krzyzewski after Duke got hammered, 103–73, by Jerry Tarkanian's powerful UNLV team in the 1990 NCAA championship game. That Las Vegas team was very much like the Michigan team of today, in that it had no respect for the opposition. Wooden and Krzyzewski would never let a team make that kind of mental mistake. They would make you believe that the opposition was very capable, even if it wasn't. You could be playing the worst team in the history of the game and still these two coaches could make you respect those players, make you compete against the ideal opponent . . . never the real one.

We opened our varsity careers at UCLA against The Citadel. Reporters asked Greg Lee about the opponent after the game and Lee said they were sort of like a good junior college team. The story appeared the next day, which prompted John Wooden to deliver a stern lecture on media relations to Lee and the rest of us.

We beat The Citadel by 56 points, but the margin of victory wasn't as important as the style and performance itself. Even if we killed a terrible team, John Wooden wasn't happy unless we played well.

Krzyzewski is the same way. He and Wooden understand the importance of playing against an ideal. They also know how small the difference between winning and losing is.

Krzyzewski had a chance to leave Duke a few years ago and become the coach of the Celtics. Dave Gavitt, Boston's senior executive vice president, wanted to hire him, but Krzyzewski ultimately decided that he belonged at Duke. Coaching in the NBA is so much different from coaching in college, but Krzyzewski would have figured it out. He's the kind of guy who is successful at whatever he tries. He's a humble man, not overly impressed with himself. He is extremely confident, and should be. But the difference between him and some of those slick-talking, pseudocoaches is that Krzyzewski isn't out there trying to sell himself. He's out there doing his job.

Krzyzewski played for Knight and later spent one season at Indiana as a graduate assistant on Knight's staff. You can see the many similarities in the way they approach the game. But Krzyzewski has his own distinct style. He is Knight without the venom and moodiness. He is Wooden without the squareness. Krzyzewski doesn't get overly excited about what he's doing. He's a basketball coach—nothing more, nothing less. His players seem to overachieve for him and they seem to have fun doing it. And they rave about him years later.

Can you imagine what it must be like for Christian Laettner, who played for Krzyzewski at Duke, played for the Dream Team and was chosen by an NBA expansion franchise, the Minnesota Timberwolves? One minute he's playing for the best college coach in the business, winning national titles and gold medals; the next minute he's playing on a Minnesota team that has guys who can't make plays, who won't or can't pass the ball and who don't care about winning. He's one of the few guys on that team who ever won anything. Thurl Bailey's North Carolina State team won the 1983 NCAA championship (thanks to a horrible shot by Dereck Whittenburg that was retrieved and dunked by Lorenzo Charles at the buzzer), but Thurl's about had it.

One of the biggest disappointments I had in my career—and I'm sure it's the same thing Laettner is going through—is that you think everything is going to be a step up when you get to the pros. You think the coaching is going to be as good, that the players are going to be as committed and life will be wonderful. Then you get there and the coaches can't coach and the players can't play. You ask yourself, "Wait a minute, what's going on here?"

Krzyzewski, in the same way John Wooden did with me, teaches his players the importance of teamwork, pride and sacrifice. It is amazing how few players truly understand those concepts and are able to live them.

I don't see any end in sight for Krzyzewski's dominance of college ball. He's the first coach since John Wooden to claim consecutive national championships and his team has been to six of the last eight Final Fours.

Another college coach doing a first-rate job is Kansas's Roy Williams. It was not happenstance that the Lakers' Jerry West wanted to hire Williams several seasons ago to replace Mike Dunleavy. Williams is a top coach who makes the most out of good, but not great, talent.

During the 1991 NCAA tournament, Billy Packer convinced the CBS Sports team to let me do a game, my first on network television. My assignment included a second-round NCAA tournament game between Pittsburgh and Kansas at the Southeast subregional at Louisville's Freedom Hall.

In addition to my usual pregame homework, one of the things I like to do is watch a team go through its warm-up drills. You get a chance to see the players move and shoot and jump. It obviously isn't the same thing as game competition, but everything helps you notice the nuances of a team and its personality.

As I watched Kansas, I couldn't believe what I was seeing. I couldn't believe the NCAA selection committee had actually extended them a tournament invitation. The Jayhawks looked very unimpressive, to the point where I had to make sure their 23–7 record at the time wasn't a misprint.

They did their little drills and I kept saying to myself, "Who are *these* guys? What are they doing here?"

When it came time to open the broadcast with a brief scouting report, I was ready.

"Well," I said, "it doesn't look like Kansas has any sort of chance at all today against Pittsburgh."

And then I rattled off some reasons why they would lose, returned to my broadcast position and then watched as Williams's Jayhawks dismantled Pitt. Amazing. The more I watched, the more I realized what a talented coach Williams was.

Kansas beat Pitt by 11 points. Then it blew out Indiana,

83–65, in the regional semifinal. Then it beat Arkansas by 12 to reach the Final Four. Then it defeated North Carolina in the national semifinal, before finally losing by seven to Duke.

Knight, Krzyzewski and Williams are three guys who have an incredible sense of the history of basketball and the requisite skills of basketball. The differences lie in their enjoyment of the game.

Two somewhat misunderstood college coaches are Dale Brown of LSU and John Thompson of Georgetown. Brown is one of my favorites. He has the two crucial ingredients for success in coaching: the ability to inspire and teach greatness, and the ability to rise above the roar . . . to see things in the proper perspective.

Some basketball people say he's not an X's and O's man. Big deal. So what? Drawing X's and O's is the most over-rated part of coaching. Coaching is people skills; X's and O's you can get from a book. In coaching, you've got to live a life of basketball. You've got to dream it, understand it and be totally committed to it. Brown does that. The thing I find most admirable about him is that he cares so much about his players and is so willing to learn, from whatever source. He has a positive influence on the way they live their lives, particularly after they've left LSU.

Thompson makes the same kind of effort. He teaches them the necessary skills not only to become successful basketball players but also to become successful citizens and move on in life.

My problem with Thompson is the way he coaches offensive basketball. I believe in the fast break. That's the best way to play basketball, forcing the action to wear down the opponent by generating easy scoring opportunities. Thompson's style is the exact opposite.

There is no questioning his skill as a teacher of defensive

skills. His key players through the years—Patrick Ewing, Dikembe Mutombo, Alonzo Mourning and now Othella Harrington—have all been enhanced by spending time with Thompson. Away from the court, Thompson has shown a willingness to become involved in the community and take stands on issues. I don't agree with all of his opinions, but, hey, I much prefer someone who has opinions to someone who always keeps quiet or who just blows with the wind.

But someone needs to tell Thompson to lighten up on the reins. I don't like it when a coach constantly closes practices to the public or to the media. The idea is to be proud of what you're doing, to show off your accomplishments. John Wooden used to have open practices all the time. We regularly had thousands of people watching and cheering us during workouts at Pauley Pavilion. John Wooden would always tell them they could stay if they behaved themselves and caused no distractions, which seemed fair enough. It was certainly not a rock concert atmosphere in the stands during practice. That much fun was saved for the game. I know having the fans there made me practice harder.

Some coaches, however, won't let the fans and the media observe practice because they don't want anybody to know that they're clueless about what it is they're doing. They're insecure, scared that an outsider might recognize their shortcomings as a coach.

John Wooden didn't care. He knew his methods worked. Thompson has had a successful enough career to feel the same way. Given his personality, which is confident and self-assured, you'd think he'd be more than happy to open his practices to the public. Basketball is a simple game. It's based on skills, conditioning and the ability to teach your players to function as a team. Thompson gets good players with decent basketball skills. They're disciplined and well-conditioned. And they always play hard and play together.

But Thompson's reluctance to show them off, to let them run, to teach an effective offensive scheme limits Georgetown's ability to achieve at its expected level.

Thompson, it seems, is always involved with the delicate issue of race relations.

It is disturbing that some black high school stars choose their college and basketball program based on the color of the coach. Frequently, high school basketball stars will announce their intention to play only for a black coach.

That's ridiculous. If you're a player, you want to play in the situation that's best for you. That situation could involve a black coach, a white coach, a coach of Oriental or Hispanic descent. It doesn't matter. But under no circumstances do you want to limit your choices based on any categorical division or exclusion. If you do, you're cheating yourself and you're cheating the rest of the world. You're also doing a disservice to the development of the society we live in. The whole point is to work toward a truly color-blind society. By saying "Black Only" or "White Only," you reverse the movement and progress made.

We certainly don't live in perfect harmony. Far from it. But the beauty of sports—and especially basketball—is that you play and work with people from every imaginable background. You make friends and enemies because of the unique, color-blind nature of basketball. Basketball opens up so many doors of opportunities and possibilities for its players. But it's what you do when you get through those doors that determines your character, abilities and contributions. Why limit those possibilities by saying something like "I'm only going to play for a black coach."

One coach who never gets his proper due is Jerry Tarkanian. Tarkanian was one of the greatest college coaches of all time and few taught individual defensive basketball better than he. His UNLV teams had a beautiful style of play and were responsible for some of the best individual games ever played.

My personal favorite was Tarkanian's 1977 Vegas team, the first during his run at UNLV to advance to the Final Four. The Runnin' Rebels faced top-ranked San Francisco in the first round of the West Regional and blew them out, 121–95. It was a great game and epitomized all the best things in basketball: man-to-man pressing defense, fast breaks and teamwork.

Tarkanian's failings had nothing to do with the game itself. Where he erred was off the court. Even after he had established himself as a legitimate coach with a top program, Tarkanian kept recruiting the wrong kind of players, the kind of players who would often get into trouble on and off the court. Players who would always be there with hat in hand. Not every player he signed was like that, but there were enough of them to hasten his departure. Those players contributed to his troubles with the UNLV administration and the NCAA. In the end, Tarkanian paid the price—he was kicked out.

The sad part is that Tarkanian was an accomplished recruiter who developed one of the most interesting and financially successful college basketball programs in history. Yet he left himself open to disaster because he failed to recognize (or chose to ignore) the warning signs.

Tarkanian's on-court philosophy didn't match his off-court methods. Few coaches adapted and transformed their style to changing players and times better than Krzyzewski. But when it came to recruiting, he didn't seem to be able to insist that people who played for him be good, responsible citizens.

Some coaches, especially during the early years of their careers, will cut some corners while recruiting. They do it to get over the hump, to put their program on the map. Most coaches, once they get over that hump, try to recruit a higher quality of player and person. Tarkanian did not always make that transition.

When he got to the NBA as the San Antonio Spurs coach, Tarkanian continued with that same style. Plus, he committed the cardinal sin of talking to Peter Vecsey every day. If you want to keep your job in professional basketball, stay out of Vecsey's column or out of his NBC *Insiders* report as much as possible. I think Peter Vecsey is the best pro basketball writer in the business. He is a fan's dream come true. But if you're Jerry Tarkanian, and you're feuding with the owner of the Spurs over team policy, you don't want to have your name in Vecsey's column every day. Peter is not the kind of writer who protects and shields people. He writes the news, and the news was that Tarkanian was peeved at the owner of the Spurs at the time, Red McCombs. The more Tarkanian talked to Peter, the better his chances of getting fired.

Tarkanian didn't realize how hard pro coaches work. When you're a pro coach, you don't sit on the bench and say, "Let's go." There are only three NBA coaches in the Hall of Fame. What a disgrace.

Pro coaches work extremely hard. The majority of them are really talented men. One of the great misconceptions about the NBA is that no coaching goes on.

More coaching goes on in a single pro game than goes on in an entire college-season schedule. Tarkanian apparently figured, "Hey, I'll sit there and watch the guys play."

Unfortunately, very few NBA players ever had the luxury in college of playing for a coach as good as Tarkanian. They didn't know how to handle the freedom they were given as players. And Tarkanian didn't know how to handle the special demands of being in charge of an NBA team. He never fully grasped the pro management mind-set, which values playing talent above all else. Every decision is based on skill. You can be a criminal, a druggie, a jerk of a person, have zero social skills, very little intellect, but, man, if you can play, there's always a spot for you.

Tarkanian also failed to realize those same management principles didn't apply to the fringe positions: the coaches, the administrators, the trainers, the support positions. If you're a player, they can't keep you out. Only in professional sports is that true. Tarkanian didn't completely understand the difference. He thought he was secure and protected.

His pro coaching career lasted twenty games. The coach with the winningest percentage in the history of college basketball finished below .500.

The realities of the NBA hit hard the day I signed my rookie contract with the Portland Trail Blazers in 1974. At the time, it was the highest-paying contract in the history of professional sports.

After I signed the contract, one of the owners of the team grabbed my elbow and said, "Bill, before we go talk to the reporters, I'd like you to step over here and meet the coach."

"Sure. Great. Let's go," I said, not having a clue who the coach was.

Just before the owner introduced me to the coach, he whispered in my ear, "Be real nice to him because we're going to fire him tomorrow."

Welcome to the NBA. After spending four wonderful, idyllic years with John Wooden at UCLA, things were definitely going to be different with the Trail Blazers.

The coach turned out to be Jack McCloskey, a solid basketball guy. He was replaced by Lenny Wilkens. Portland management wouldn't give Wilkens any control over player personnel, which is the kiss of death. Wilkens was in the same boat as the previous Blazer coaches. "Look at the guys you're giving me," he told management. "They can't play."

Well, some of them could play, but the others were cancerous to the team. Wilkens wanted to trade Sidney Wicks and Geoff Petrie and give more playing time to younger guys like Lionel Hollins and Bob Gross. Wilkens never got his chance.

Instead, they fired him, primarily due to my inability to play because of assorted injuries. In those two years, I played in only 86 games. That wasn't Wilkens' fault, but he took the fall. Then they hired Jack Ramsay and gave him the power to make wholesale changes (which he did immediately). I stayed relatively healthy and Portland won the championship in his first year there.

What a strange, confusing time those first two years were for me. I had passed up an even bigger financial package from the ABA and the opportunity to stay in Los Angeles so I could join the NBA. I wanted to play against the best.

Unfortunately for me—and for Lenny Wilkens too—I had to have knee surgery just before the beginning of my rookie season. Not a good way to start a career.

I joined the NBA with great expectations about how much fun it was going to be. I was shocked at how selfish and greedy so many of my teammates were. They were more concerned about how much money they were going to make or who got all the publicity than they were with winning games. It was a very negative situation for me right from the start, but Wilkens did as good a job as humanly possible with it. You have to be careful about giving too much credit to Ramsay and not enough credit to Wilkens when assessing Portland's early success as a franchise.

My first two years with the Trail Blazers were like playing in the Twilight Zone. I got so frustrated with the selfish attitudes of the other players and with my own crippling injuries that I constantly asked to be traded and seriously considered quitting the game altogether. I was a developing and maturing young man of twenty-one. I was experiencing life. I would give everything I had on the court, but off the court I wanted control of my own life. That's why I insisted that my contract with the Trail Blazers include a clause that allowed me to grow my hair as long as I wanted.

I felt bad for Lenny Wilkens because he was and still is a great guy and a top coach. He taught me a lot about basketball. He wouldn't have been fired had I been able to avoid injury. A simple twist of fate.

Lenny Wilkens soon will be the winningest coach in NBA history. Only Auerbach (938 regular-season victories) is ahead of him. All other active coaches, with the exception of Golden State's Don Nelson, are many fifty-win seasons away.

Soon Lenny Wilkens will become only the second person in the Hall of Fame to earn entry as a player and as a coach. John Wooden was the first. Lenny's future induction will begin to right the mistakes of the Hall of Fame.

Unbelievably enough, Auerbach, Ramsay and Red Holtzman are the three sole NBA coaching representatives in the Hall of Fame. More will follow. Nelson is a lock. So is Pat Riley. Chuck Daly is also a worthy candidate. I hope Phil Jackson stays around long enough to get enough wins to earn Hall of Fame status. He deserves it, but when things come apart in Chicago—as they inevitably will—Phil might not be willing to tolerate coaching in the NBA. Phil is an intelligent, interesting and diverse person. He might just walk away from it all. Maybe he should. It will be tough to coach players who don't measure up to Jordan. I hope he stays. It's important that Phil, with his skills and intellect, not succumb to the temptation to quit now that the river Jordan has run dry.

Basketball is a game of people. It isn't a nameless, faceless, mindless institution. It won't continue to thrive if people like Phil Jackson leave.

The crucial ingredient in coaching is the ability to inspire people, to take people to levels of achievement that they couldn't possibly reach on their own. Knight, Krzyzewski, Ramsay, Nelson, Wooden, Riley, Wilkens, K. C. Jones and Phil Jackson have all had or currently have talented players on their rosters. The key is to teach someone to play better than when he showed up.

It's one thing to be a good recruiter and have talented players. It's more important to be able to motivate those players and convince them that anything is possible, to push them even closer to their limits. "Hey, sure you're a good player, but are you as good as you can be?"

Coaches whose main purpose in the game is self-promotion are nothing more than glorified hucksters, charlatans and frauds. You probably know who they are. I know they do.

These kinds of coaches are always trying to use basketball as a way to become richer and more famous. They don't care about the game as much as they do about their bank accounts.

These are the same coaches who get fired all the time because the players eventually lie down on them. The guys just quit. It's easy to see why. The coach will come into the locker room and start talking about how they have to fight through the pain, how they need to win, how they need to sacrifice. All the while the players know this is the same guy who sold his soul for an extra dollar to the nearest advertiser. The players tune out the coach. They don't listen because they don't care. They don't listen because the coach hasn't been willing to make the same sacrifices that he is asking them to make.

Wooden, Ramsay, Jackson, Riley, Knight and Krzyzewski, to list just a few, have credibility. They make the commitment and their players know it. You can't buy credibility. Once you lose it, it's virtually impossible to get it back.

Riley is an interesting coach because of his total devotion

to and obsession with the game. Even though he's a great coach, Riley sometimes gets so preoccupied with controlling the game from the sidelines that he forgets that it's a players' game. This coaching trap causes the plays to lose their freedom and their creativity.

When teams go bad (discounting injuries), it's usually the result of a stagnant offense. This generally happens when the coach gets too involved in the game by calling too many set plays.

John Wooden was the exact opposite. Before a game he'd have his rolled-up program in his hand, point it at us and say, "Men, I've done my job. We've practiced all week. We're ready. The rest is up to you." Then he'd go sit down on the bench and ride the officials and the other team's top players.

K.C. was that way with the Celtics. Wilkens and Krzyzewski do the same thing.

Every coach at some point is guilty of overcoaching. Pat Riley doesn't have much of a choice these days. His lineup doesn't include a really great offensive player. Patrick Ewing is talented, but he's not among the top players in the NBA. He doesn't dictate the flow of a game and he doesn't attack like Hakeem Olajuwon. Riley must compensate. Sometimes Riley's coaching is done excessively. The Knicks' style of play is the exact opposite of the style that Riley's Laker teams played during the championship years with Magic Johnson and Kareem Abdul-Jabbar. Back then it was finesse, intelligence, maneuverability, speed and quickness that won games for Riley. Now it is defense, intimidation and brute strength.

Ramsay motivated players by staring into their souls. He would do this by walking right up to you, stepping on your feet so you couldn't move away and then looking into your soul through your eyes. After a long, dramatic pause, he would say, "Can you go . . . can you give me all you've got tonight? We need you."

No one taught me the skill of preparation better than Ramsay. He was a huge believer in watching games, film, charting tendencies, studying opponents ... anything to give him the tiniest edge. He loved to unleash that shrill whistle of his. Fifteen thousand cheering fans would be rocking the joint and we could still hear Ramsay's whistle. We'd look over at the sidelines and there he was, ordering some kind of slight adjustment in our defense or offense. He was the best at sensing when it was time to make a change.

Ramsay was sheer joy to work with, a real dreamer. He would push you and push you and then push you some more. You were able to reach your highest levels of performance and achievement because of his constant emphasis on excellence.

I played for some coaches who never understood the concept. They were too busy drawing up little plays. It would be a close game, very little time left on the clock, the players spent and exhausted, and the coach would have his chalkboard out trying to diagram plays that we had never seen before. That isn't a plan for success; it's a prescription for confusion and failure.

John Wooden would have none of that. With him, everything was accomplished through repetition at practice. When situations arose, you knew what to do because he had taught you over and over again in practice. There was no frantic drawing of plays in the waning moments of the game.

K.C. Jones was so cool under pressure. He was smart enough to let his players win or lose the games. He might say, "Get the ball to D.J. here and, D.J., you make the play." At which point, Larry Bird would interrupt and say, "Get it to me and I'll make it. I'm hot as can be."

Bird did that all the time. He made me proud to be his teammate. There's nothing wrong with players taking over a huddle. The importance of leadership by the coach is displayed in many ways. Often by what he lets others do. The coach has to have the final say. Every good player understands that. Every good coach understands that he needs the players' input. Charles Barkley put it best: Coaches make substitutions and players make plays.

I'm frequently accused of being too critical of coaches and players. Coaches are paid to get the most out of their players, and players are paid to fulfill their potential. Underachievers drive me crazy.

Near the end of my first season in broadcasting in 1990, I did some work for the CBS affiliate in Portland during the playoffs. At the same time, the *Oregonian* called and asked if I'd write a guest column during the conference finals between the Blazers and the Lakers.

After the Lakers beat the Blazers at Portland in Game 1, I pointed out in my column that the strategies and substitution patterns of the Blazers' coach, Rick Adelman, cost them the game. That was the only game in the series won by the road team.

The Trail Blazers have been accused of being a dumb team. They fail to play to their talent level. Everyone in that organization has to take the blame: the front office, which drafted and acquired the players; the coaching staff, which failed to correct the problem; the players, who seem perfectly satisfied with finishing second.

What kills the Trail Blazers is that they don't have a top player who's a natural leader. Clyde Drexler, Jerome Kersey, Terry Porter, Cliff Robinson . . . they're among the most physically talented players in basketball. But they don't have the one top player who can lead them and dictate the flow of the game. They always fall just short of their potential. A leader is someone who can walk into the locker room before a game and say, "Okay, this is what we need to do to win tonight. Now let's get going!"

Players in that position back up their statements with their performance on the court. When it's the coach in the role of the leader, he must have the hearts and minds of his players in his pocket. Adelman, apparently having neither, is unwilling or unable to succeed in that role.

Adelman is stuck. He needs a player who is capable of taking charge. A coach can't play the game for them. As smart as a coach might be, he has to get his players to think the same way he thinks, to see the game the same way he does. Riley did it with Magic and Jabbar (or was it the other way around?). Ramsay did it with Maurice Lucas, Lionel Hollins and me. Auerbach did it with Russell. Holtzman did it with Walt Frazier. K.C. did it with Bird. They think the same thoughts, they see the same game.

Adelman doesn't have an alter ego on the court and it shows.

Coaches can be some of the most frustrating and disappointing people to work with. The self-promoters are more interested in making a buck or getting their faces on the covers of magazines than they are in winning games. Those kinds of coaches seem to flourish in the college game. They give in to the whims and blackmailing tactics of high-profile high school recruits.

The vast majority of the cheating rampant in college athletics is at the instigation of the players. The players are aware that there are people out there who will give them whatever they want. The players seek those people out.

The real sham(e) comes when a coach or an athletic director, who originally had good intentions and wanted to follow the NCAA rules, succumbs to the degrading requests of these young punks. In pro basketball there's no shame in asking for the big stack, only pride in getting it.

The solution, obviously, is to just say no to these punks. But one of the unique things about basketball is that it's dominated by one player. During each game, each season, each era, everything is written in terms of the exploits and conquests of a single player. In today's game that player is Michael Jordan. Because of the difference one player can make, coaches are all too willing to take great risks to get that one impact player.

Coaches who confuse discipline with bullying are a disgrace. Lou Campanelli, who was fired by California midway through the 1992–93 season, can't seem to relate to the ever-changing athletes. Rather than adapt, they tighten the screws. They try to motivate through fear and denigration.

At Cal the players came close to a revolt. At the very least, the Cal players were beaten down by Campanelli's bullying. They tuned him out.

Finally Campanelli was shown the door, and boom, they reach the NCAA Midwest Regional semifinals (which, when I played college ball, was the first round).

Coaches are teachers. Unless you learn, you can't teach. Campanelli never learned to adapt to changing times and changing players. I've got no problem with what Cal did to him.

Coaches who have to be the center of attention during a game are annoying. They're everywhere; always prancing up and down the sidelines, yelling at their players, jumping up and down. They have these confused, pained, out-of-control looks on their faces.

Bad teams are usually coached by guys who fit this description. Their players spend the whole game looking at the sideline, waiting for their next order, instead of taking the ball and going to the hoop. They stand around and wait for the coach to tell them what to do. Television is a major culprit. The director is always cutting away to some sideline shot of the coach. Smart coaches—Krzyzewski, Williams, Dean Smith, for example—couldn't care less about the TV exposure. They want to win games. But the theatrical coaches, the ones who think more camera time means they have a better chance of attracting big-name recruits, miss the point. Winning attracts the top players, not televised sideline theatrics.

A good player doesn't want a coach who's running all over like a madman, who looks like he's out on a limb. He's supposed to be the picture of stability, the calm in the storm. He's supposed to exude poise and confidence.

Another annoying habit, especially of college coaches, is their addiction to substituting players. Some coaches feel they must substitute so much because they "need to keep the guys happy or else they'll leave."

Let them leave.

If a coach tries to play too many guys, it will end up hurting, not helping a team's chances to win. If you're constantly switching players, what does that say about the job the coach has done teaching and preparing these players to play? Stick with your five best players and have a back-court substitute and a front-court substitute available. As the season goes on, try to develop a backup to each of those substitutes. But basically, you're talking about winning or losing with those seven, maybe eight players. The games are too short. The more you substitute, the more you lose control of the game.

What Dean Smith did during last season's Final Four should have cost North Carolina the title. If the opponent had been a good team, it would have.

Smith used ten players in the semifinal win against Kansas and eleven players against Michigan in the final. Just because something works doesn't mean it's the right thing to do. Smith took a calculated gamble. It paid off, luckily.

If I'm the coach, playing for a national championship, and there are only 45 seconds remaining, and I'm leading, 72–69, as North Carolina was at the time, I don't think I want my lineup to be two starters (Derrick Phelps, George Lynch) and three reserves (Henrik Rodl, Pat Sullivan,

Kevin Salvadori). I want Eric Montross in there. I want the hottest player in the tournament, Donald Williams, in there. I want my other starting forward, Brian Reese, in there as well.

I was confused and distressed by the substitution pattern in the last five minutes of the game. I've never been a fan of that whole style of basketball. This wasn't the annual Blue-White game at Chapel Hill. This was for the national championship.

I'm happy, though, for North Carolina. The Tar Heel players seem to be genuinely good guys. And they also seem to be proud of their school, much the same way players from Duke and Kansas are proud of the basketball traditions at their universities. UCLA players used to be like that.

Barring the unexpected, Smith will finish his career as the all-time winningest coach in college basketball history. Only Adolph Rupp of Kentucky has more victories (875), but Smith, who began the 1994 season with 774 wins, is quickly closing the gap.

The coaching profession has some good young talent. But there are a lot of former players who should be in the profession. They're successful, they have high self-esteem, they'd make wonderful teachers of the game, but they don't want to be treated like crap. They don't want to go through the degrading process of having to recruit. They don't want to be abused by spoiled, rotten NBA punks who think coaches are there to be humiliated and embarrassed. They also don't want to start at the bottom of the coaching chain.

The better coaches today seem to be the ones who were marginal players during their careers. Knight, Smith and Krzyzewski certainly fit that mold. With the exception of Jerry Sloan, Lenny Wilkens, Wes Unseld, Dan Issel and, to a lesser extent, John Lucas, Don Nelson and Paul Westphal, there are no NBA coaches who enjoyed remarkable playing careers. And Sloan, who coaches the Utah Jazz, and Issel, who coaches the Denver Nuggets, made their marks because of their hustle, great pride, determination and outthinking their opponents. The game of basketball did not come easily to them.

Coaches who were marginal players have an appreciation for the game, they understand it better. They know what it's like to struggle, to have to survive on trickery, deception, conditioning and limited physical skills. And they know what it's like to be treated badly.

Then there is Bill Russell. Or Jerry West. Or Elgin Baylor. Or even Wilt, though you can't really say much good about his brief coaching experience with the San Diego Conquistadors.

Those guys are easily some of the greatest players in the history of the game and were arguably among the worst coaches too. They couldn't comprehend why every player wasn't great, or why every player didn't share their love of the game.

Russell, West, Baylor and Wilt made playing the game look easy. It wasn't work to them. The game flowed to them.

Coaching is different. Nothing comes easy in coaching.

"When you get confused . . . listen to the
music play."
—*Jerry Garcia*

One hot, muggy day on Cape Cod in the summer of 1989, a rainstorm had prematurely ended Kevin McHale's golf tournament. This forced my friend Moke, Kevin, me, a Boston Celtics entourage and the rest of the golf entrants into the clubhouse, where we spent the day telling lies about the history of basketball and the Celtics.

An early plane ride from Boston the next day forced Moke and me on yet another dawn adventure. Our return flight to southern California took us through Chicago, where we scrambled across O'Hare airport trying to make a tight connection. It was at O'Hare that we were approached by a group of colorfully attired travelers.

"Hey, Bill, are you going to the shows?"

Obviously these strangers were happily talking about attending Grateful Dead concerts, but we were clueless. Further discussions led Moke and me to believe that there might indeed be Grateful Dead concerts somewhere in the vicinity. Never one to jump to early conclusions given the myriad of rumors that constantly swirl around the Dead, Moke and I raced to the pay phone to call Frances Shurtliff in northern California. She answered the phone on the first ring.

Yes, there was a concert. Yes, the concert was that night. Yes, the concert was near Chicago—in fact, only an hour and a half by car from O'Hare.

After the airline officials ignored our desperate pleas to have our luggage removed from the plane, Moke and I headed to the rental-car counter with only our briefcases, our wallets, the name of the concert venue, the name of the band's hotel and a few phone numbers.

I first went to a Grateful Dead concert in 1969.

Twenty-five years ago.

I attended lots of rock concerts when I was in high school and college, but after my first Dead show I realized that I had found a home.

In the early 1970s I traveled up and down the state of California by both car and plane, showing up at whatever concert I could fit into my student-athlete schedule. On a number of occasions while at the show, I was approached by people inviting me to come backstage to meet the band. Being the shy, reserved and scared person that I was at the time, I simply ignored all those requests.

In 1974 I left UCLA and southern California and moved on to Oregon. That fall, shortly after I had arrived to start my NBA career, the Dead showed up in Portland.

Ecstatic with my good fortune, I was at the concert enjoying myself immensely when someone approached me and asked if I would please come backstage immediately. Since it was right in the middle of the show, I was in no hurry to leave my perfect vantage spot—you have a great view at concerts when you're 6'11".

This person was adamant. He wanted me to go backstage right away.

Apparently, some of the crew members of the Grateful Dead had noticed me in the audience. One of them had said, "Send the security into the crowd and tell that guy to get off his chair. He's blocking everybody's view."

Following up, another crew member glanced at the crowd and said, "That's not some guy, that's Bill Walton."

"I don't care who it is," said the first crew member, "get the guy off the chair so everyone else can see."

"But that guy's not standing on a chair. He's that tall."

"Get him out of there anyway."

I was having such a good time that I was not about to move. I told the security guard thanks, but I was happy right where I was.

"I'll go backstage when the show's over," I said.

Sensing he couldn't change my mind, he left disappointed. Afterward, I did go backstage, and enjoyed an experience that has ever since changed my life.

———

After reaching the rental-car counter and negotiating our way into a Cadillac at the economy-car rate, Moke and I were on the road to Alpine Valley, Wisconsin. Even though every hotel in town was sold out, at least we had a place to sit down in the band's hospitality suite. Moke and I and our Grateful Dead friends set about planning for our survival during what was to be three nights of dancing in the streets.

An extra hotel room was eventually found. Clothes and daily supplies were donated. Transportation was arranged. Moke and I were set: We were with the band.

The band has been everywhere. I've tried to be there with them. They can't always wait, and I'm often busy.

Egypt was one of the more interesting tour stops. All the stops are interesting, because it doesn't really matter where the show is, as long as it is. Some of the very best shows that I've ever seen have been in the absolute middle of nowhere.

Dead shows are always memorable occasions. The Grateful Dead went to Egypt in the fall of 1978. The site at Giza enhanced the experience, as did a total lunar eclipse that began just after showtime.

Our accommodations in Egypt were spectacular. We stayed at the Mina House Hotel, a walled estate that was originally an ancient hunting lodge. The hotel is situated adjacent to the great pyramids up on some low hills overlooking the Nile Valley.

Temperatures of 118 degrees forced even the most enthusiastic of us into submission during the day. The teeming streets of Cairo, an immense city, were our entertainment when the pool scene at the hotel got boring.

With the shows starting so late at night, your natural body clock had to be reset to Grateful Dead Standard Time. The shows didn't end until four-thirty or five the next morning. The band would stop, the festival over, and we would all make the half-mile trip back to the hotel just as the sun, a huge, burning ball of fire, was rising over the Nile Valley.

At Alpine Valley, Moke and I helicoptered to the concert with Bill Kreutzmann and Phil Lesh. Once there, we enjoyed a fabulous dinner, our first real meal since we left Kevin's golf tournament.

The show went on as scheduled and, as so often happens at outdoor Dead shows, it rained. Did it ever rain.

Moke and I stood in the rain for three nights dancing with 20,000 strangers. With borrowed clothes, some food and family spirit, Moke and I survived yet another Dead tour.

The Grateful Dead have done a lot for me, as well as for countless other people. The example that they set in leading their lives and running their business affairs make all Deadheads like me proud to jump in the air, flailing our fists, proclaiming, "I'm one of them . . . I'm with those guys."

The Dead used to play a significant part in my game-day routine. The moment I got out of bed, I'd turn on the stereo. All I had to go was crank up the volume, sit back and start to get psyched up for the game.

I was fierce on game days. By the time I got to the arena, I was not someone you'd want women and children to meet. The Dead helped me focus on the game. I would just let their music wash over me as I played the game over and over in my mind.

The more Dead I could hear, the better I felt. When I was with the Trail Blazers, I became friends with Bill Schonely's son, Rick, who was in charge of the sound system at Memorial Coliseum before the games. After a while, I started bringing my Dead cassettes to the game and he would play them during warm-ups.

When I was with the Celtics, Rick Carlisle and Jerry Sichting nudged me during a game at the Boston Garden and said, "Hey, Bill, listen to that. The organist is playing the Dead."

Turns out that the organist had learned how to play three or four Dead songs after my arrival in Boston. Once in a while, during the pregame drills or maybe during a timeout, the organist would work one of the songs into his routine. What a great combination: playing basketball at the Garden and listening to the sounds of the Dead bouncing off the rafters, the championship banners and Russell's retired #6.

Over the years I've tried to turn my basketball friends, as well as others, on to the Grateful Dead. Some have been interested. Some even have become Deadheads. Some were confused. Those people just didn't go to enough concerts.

The 1986 Celtics team was loaded with players who had only peripheral ties to the rock-and-roll scene that began in the 1960s. Larry Bird, Dennis Johnson, Robert Parish, K. C. Jones, Scott Wedman, Jerry Sichting, McHale . . . basically the entire squad constantly quizzed, chided and teased me about my relationship with the Grateful Dead. Always the team player, I tried to explain and help my teammates understand me and the Dead.

The Boston area is one of the Grateful Dead's most popular tour stops. On a number of occasions the Grateful Dead came to play a concert series at the same time that the Celtics happened to be in town. I was able to arrange for some of my teammates to attend. After the initial concerts, word quickly spread throughout the team that this "Grateful Dead thing" was cool . . . check it out.

At the height of the team's championship success in 1986, the Grateful Dead rolled back into town. By this point, the entire team was hot on Jerry Garcia's trail.

After an early-morning trip by me to that night's concert site and some begging and pleading to stage manager Robbie Taylor, I arranged a music fan's fantasy.

The Dead that night created a special seating area on the stage within a few feet of the musicians, yet totally private and out of sight from the rest of the fans in the auditorium. About twenty chairs were placed in this special seating area.

Knowing that the Grateful Dead always start on time, I

instructed my teammates to be sure to get there early. While we milled around before the start of the show, the intensity and the anticipation of the show began to surge throughout the building.

When Cameron Sears, the Grateful Dead's road manager, informed us that the show was moments away from starting, we made our way through the shadows to our specially reserved seats. Basically the entire 1986 championship Celtics team was there, with the exception of Danny Ainge, whose wife wouldn't let him go.

As we took our seats, members of the crew delivered four to five coolers full of our favorite cold drinks. As soon as we settled down, the band took the stage to the usual roar of the crowd, the same crowd that has made the Grateful Dead one of the most successful musical groups in history, selling out huge stadiums and arenas around the world about eighty nights a year for almost thirty years.

Few moments in one's life are as exciting and keep you on edge as when the final minutes leading up to a Grateful Dead show click down. The warm-up chords to the first song that was just chosen have concluded. Everything is in order.

As the band was about to begin, Jerry Garcia, primed for yet another virtuoso performance, stepped forward, glanced over his shoulder to the Celtics entourage at stage right, picked out Larry Bird and gave him a deep nod, as if to say, "This is what *we* do."

———————

The success of the Grateful Dead has been based for those thirty years on the same principles that make basketball teams and players champions. They have a love for their work, an insatiable desire for perfection and greatness, individual talent blended to encourage and support creativity, a craving for speed, a need to be up and going faster, a need to create, to build, to celebrate.

The Grateful Dead are as close to and as far from being a basketball team as you can get. The lifestyles are exceedingly similar, except that the Grateful Dead have no opponent (discounting the police, of course).

Life on the road: arenas, airports, hotels and a bunch of guys sitting around waiting for the game/show to happen, waiting to see who will be the hottest and the best that night.

The big difference between the Grateful Dead and basketball is who is in charge. The Grateful Dead are their own bosses. Basketball players work for the NBA.

Non-Deadheads find it startling that I've attended over five hundred Dead shows. But how many games has a Celtic season ticket holder seen Larry Bird play? How many times in John Wooden's twenty-seven years did Bruins fans observe him signal an A-okay to his wife, Nell, prior to the game?

The Grateful Dead are a creative group. Every measure is like a new trip downcourt. The players are the same, but the game/show is always different. It's never repetitive, it's never boring. The speed, creativity, timing, positioning and fluidity of both basketball and the Grateful Dead make them interchangeable components of my life.

For twenty-five years the Grateful Dead have given me a life of goodwill, family and fond memories. The Grateful Dead have been such an instrumental part of my life that it is appropriate that through them I have met the person who has made my life complete.

My fiancée, Lori Matsuoka, and I met at a party organized by the Dead. Her spirit has enabled me to continue my life's quest for perfection. Lori's and my appreciation of the Grateful Dead extends beyond the music, beyond the party, beyond the tour. We have been fortunate to have become personal friends with interesting, exciting and fascinating people whom we are also fans of. It is difficult to imagine a world, a life that does not include our friendship with the Grateful Dead.

Fortunately, they love playing music as much as I loved playing ball. It is wonderful to be a fan of entertainers who enjoy performing as much and as often as we like watching. Even though there are no more games for me, there will always be another show.

Lori and I are lucky. Just when we think that we're at the end of another road, the next Grateful Dead show is just around the corner.

"When Push Comes to Shove"
—The Grateful Dead

**"Dreams become something else altogether
when you try to make them come true."**

If you really want to talk Dream Teams, then don't bother
with the one that played in Barcelona at the 1992 Olympic Games. That was a nice collection of players, but an All-
Time Dream Team lineup would require quite a few roster
changes.

For instance, Christian Laettner . . . gone. John Stockton . . . goodbye. Clyde Drexler . . . glide right back to Portland. Patrick Ewing . . . thanks for stopping by the booth.
Scottie Pippen, Chris Mullin and David Robinson . . . a reluctant farewell. Charles Barkley . . . a very reluctant
farewell.

Selection to the Walton All-Time Dream Team does not
come easily.

For starters:

—Michael Jordan. Guard. Chicago Bulls.

When Jordan first joined the NBA in 1984, I was not a
big fan. His game has always been built on unique indi-

vidual skills, but he didn't seem to understand that there were four other teammates on the floor with him. The importance of teamwork can't be overstated. When people spoke of Jordan, it was in terms of personal accomplishments. "Jordan was going to score this many points," they said. "Jordan was going to dunk that many times."

Big deal. Anybody can score points and dunking is overrated. The people who are most impressed with dunking are generally the people who can't do it.

Give me players who understand how a team works, how a team wins games and championships. Jordan wasn't that kind of player at the beginning of his NBA career. I was convinced that Jordan was hype. Jordan was hot air.

Jordan changed his game, and I changed my opinion of him. Jordan is the real thing.

Since his arrival from North Carolina to the NBA, Jordan has completely convinced me that he is, for the most part, the consummate team player. He had occasional selfish lapses, such as when he referred to the rest of the Bulls as his "supporting cast." Give me a break. Playing basketball is about being part of a team. It isn't about a class system where the best player embarrasses his teammates by referring to them as mere extras.

There is nobody who can do what he did on a court. I played in the game the night of April 20, 1986, when Jordan scored 63 points against the Celtics in the second game of the Eastern Conference playoffs. No player in the history of the NBA has ever scored more points in a playoff game. I fouled out. Big help!

Jordan is the accumulation, the aggregation of the skills of every player in the history of the game. Those skills also happen to be packaged in the NBA's best-trained and most magnificent body.

What separated Jordan from the NBA's best players was his incredible discipline and his ability to embrace hard work. At the beginning of his pro career, Jordan reminded me of a younger, more modern version of Julius Erving. When in doubt, Jordan would shoot, just as Dr. J did in his glory days. Dr. J was a wonderful offensive star and a class gentleman, but he was much more fun to play against than to play with. There is nothing more frustrating than being on a team where the star player shoots every time, no matter if there are three defenders climbing all over him, no matter if two teammates are standing wide open under the basket waiting . . . praying for the pass that will lead to an easy layup.

Jordan used to play like that. Not anymore. He became the team leader, the perfect example of a team player. He fit his amazing individual talents into the team concept, a key requirement for basketball greatness. It is also the main reason why I've become Jordan's biggest fan.

Michael Jordan is the most underrated and, before his unexpected retirement, by far the most underpaid player in the history of the NBA. He was the only real choice for league MVP every season. But he should have also won every other award as well, including Most Improved, Best Defensive Player and Coach of the Year.

I teach the game of basketball at clinics around the world. I use Jordan as the example of what everyone should aspire to be, regardless of position. Not because of Jordan's jumping or dunking ability—lots of players can do that. Today Michael Jordan represents everything that is right in basketball. He has the ultimate gift: the ability to beat someone who is bigger, stronger, faster, taller and able to jump higher. He beats them because of his fundamental skills. He is the most fundamentally talented player in all of basketball. He's the kind of player who could survive a major injury, return to the game with less physical ability and still be able to perform at a high level, because his fundamentals are so good.

Dean Smith obviously taught him the right stuff at North Carolina. What Jordan didn't learn at Chapel Hill, he taught himself. He also benefited greatly when Phil Jackson replaced Doug Collins as coach of the Bulls.

Jordan was also the best-conditioned player in all of basketball, as well as the most disciplined. He had the ability to take control of a game in the fourth quarter when everyone else was fatigued. He rarely forced a shot or ignored a teammate who might have had an easier scoring opportunity. Watch the way he played defense, the way he anticipated, the way he thought on the court. Forget the dunks. Keep your eyes on Jordan as he moves up and down the floor. Try to observe the nuances of his game, rather than concentrating only on the jams.

I was disappointed and sad when Jordan announced his retirement. It wasn't like when Larry Bird and Magic Johnson retired. Those two guys left everything they had on the basketball court and fans who wanted more from them were being greedy. But with Jordan leaving at the peak of his success, the fans will always want more, much the way they wanted more from Wilt Chamberlain and Kareem Abdul-Jabbar.

Jordan apparently doesn't need to achieve competitively anymore. Maybe we've created a situation where the players no longer have to play the games at all. Kevin McHale suggested this during his final season in 1993: "Why even play the games anymore? Why not just have merchandise, card shows and autograph sessions? Everything is about money now."

I'm happy for Michael Jordan because he seems satisfied and comfortable with what he's doing. But he's wrong if he thinks that all of a sudden he's going to have a normal life. He'll never have that and I doubt he really wants that. After all, it was his own self-marketing that created what he is now.

I doubt he'll ever return to the NBA. Unless you're driven by that inner need to be the best, you're not going to be able to compete at the top of any professional level. Jordan might come back if he gets totally bored with retirement, but even then, it will be extremely difficult for him to regain the necessary level of conditioning.

For someone like Michael Jordan, basketball is his greatest freedom, his purest sense of escape, his last place of refuge and sanctuary. When he walks onto the court, nobody else is allowed to follow him. Now he doesn't have that anymore. He doesn't have that place where he can just be himself.

Jordan's retirement will also make my job as a broadcaster that much more difficult. Now I'm going to have to figure out who's going to win the championship every year.

Like Jordan, I valued my privacy. Although the reporters assigned to cover the teams I played on during those years might disagree, I liked the attention. I didn't mind venturing out into crowds. I liked going to concerts. I couldn't imagine missing a Dead concert because I was afraid of being recognized. Are you kidding? I liked having a life and the only way you're going to have one is by getting out and experiencing it. You can't see the world from your living-room couch.

For the most part, people are friendly enough. As long as you let them know that you're not always there to sign autographs, but to have fun, people seem to understand. Most of the time people simply want to say hello, nothing else. It doesn't take much to say hello back.

—Magic Johnson. Guard. Los Angeles Lakers.

Magic Johnson's career transcends the history of the game. He was probably the most versatile player ever to walk onto the court. Jordan might have passed him by now, but nobody could play all five positions as well as Magic. He personified what being a team player means.

Of all the players in the history of the game, no one played the game more like Bill Russell than Magic Johnson. Magic did whatever it took to win the game, scoring only when no one else could get the job done. He did his best when his best was needed and he did the things that few other players were willing or able to do.

Magic saw the game of basketball the way Bill Russell did. He saw a collective unit with a plan, a plan to win. A plan that was indomitable.

More than anything, though, Magic brought the issue of AIDS to the national forefront and forced us to deal with the disease far faster than we ever dreamed.

I don't think people who are HIV-positive should play competitively in contact or collision sports, most notably basketball, football, baseball, hockey and boxing. The HIV and AIDS are communicable diseases that are transferred by the mixing of blood. Every football game, basketball game, hockey game and boxing match produces blood, and plenty of it. Blood ranks a close second in the category of Fluids Lost During a Game.

Every doctor I've spoken with says the same thing: The chance of contracting the HIV virus or AIDS through contact with blood during a sporting contest is infinitesimal. I remain unconvinced.

I grew up in the age of Nixon. I grew up in an age when government officials said nuclear power was a safe energy alternative. I grew up in an age when our military leaders said the Vietnam War was a just and winnable war. So when our nation's doctors, who have only scratched the surface in AIDS research, tell me that the chances of contracting the deadly virus on the basketball court, on the football field, in the hockey rink, in the boxing ring is negligible, I don't buy it.

Of course, a person who has a communicable disease should be allowed to play basketball—as long as it is strictly on a recreational level and as long as that person tells the other players about his condition prior to the game. I'm all for Magic, and anyone else with the HIV virus, going out and playing the game for pleasure and enjoyment as long as everybody understands and is freely willing to accept the risks and dangers. But to play competitive basketball while infected with the HIV virus, where the stakes are incredibly high and the means to which players will go to win these games are even greater, is a mistake. We are talking about people's lives.

Few people understand the intensity required to play professional basketball. You have to have the mind-set of someone who, if they tried the same things on the real streets, would be arrested by a SWAT squad. So fierce is the action, so heightened are the emotions during a game, that you're ready to punch anyone out at a moment's notice. The top players, the ones who have deep pride in their game, work themselves into a frenzy before a game. It gets to the point where you are committed "to punch this guy in the face and I'm not going to quit punching him until he goes down. I don't care if he's eight inches taller than me or fifty pounds heavier. I will not be stopped. I will not be denied. I will not be intimidated. If someone tries coming to the hoop, I'm going to lead with my knee and my elbow and he will never come down the lane again."

You're ready to kill out there to win a game. At least, I was. When I see Isiah Thomas and Magic Johnson kiss before the game starts I wonder what's going on here. I think the players are far too friendly to each other in the game today. If they're on the other team, they're the enemy. That's the way I learned to play the game. That's the way I teach the game. You do everything you can to beat them, to embarrass them, have them cry in their beer and go home. After the game, if you want to congratulate an opposing player for a hard-fought effort, go for it.

It is that killer mentality, combined with the physical nature of the game and the possibility, however slight, of commingling blood, that convinces me HIV-positive players have no place in competitive basketball. Had any other player been diagnosed with the HIV virus and then made those findings public, that player wouldn't have had the chance to return to the NBA. Because it was Magic, an exception was made.

I was shocked when Magic said he intended to return to the Lakers and continue his career. I was shocked because I didn't think he was serious. When he did come back and performed so well in the NBA All-Star Game and later in the Olympics, obviously he believed differently than I do. People have different opinions. When everybody thinks alike, nobody thinks.

When he quit again, I was disappointed, frustrated and a bit angry. Quitting is not the answer to anything. Magic performed a disservice by doing so, mostly because he put the issue on the back burner. I think that the HIV and AIDS epidemic is one of the most pressing issues in sports and yet there is very little talk about it. Because it is considered, at least by the general public, to be a disease that strikes homosexuals and drug users, there is no sense of urgency regarding its dangers. That situation will soon change, simply because the virus is non-discriminatory. It only makes sense that those players who have the HIV virus shouldn't be allowed to participate in events where the spillage of blood is common. When a prefight blood test last April revealed that featherweight Ruben Palacio had tested positive for HIV, the World Boxing Organization stripped him of his title and barred him from entering the ring. The WBO did so because it didn't want to risk the life of another fighter.

I'm not an expert on HIV and AIDS. I've tried to learn as much as possible. I have a responsibility as a father, a broadcaster and a human being to stay informed on all issues. There is the potential for a problem on the playing field. It would be easy to go the other way, to say Magic and anyone else should be allowed to play. That's probably the safe and popular choice, one easily made by people who aren't playing anymore, like me.

Would I feel any different if I were still playing? It's easy to say what you wouldn't or would have done. It's a lot harder to actually do it.

—Larry Bird. Forward. Boston Celtics.

The best forward in the history of the game.

—Kevin McHale. Forward. Boston Celtics.

(Maurice Lucas and Elvin Hayes would be tied for second.)

Warming up before practice, Kevin and I would always play one on one, to get warm, to work on our games. We'd do the same thing after practice as well.

On one particular day late in the 1986 season, we were going at it pretty hard before practice started at Hellenic College. Of course, practice could never start until McHale actually got there. He was notoriously late to practice.

K.C. blew his whistle for us to come down and start practice at the other end. We ignored him. We just kept going.

He finally blew the whistle very loud and said, "Let's go!" As we walked down the court to join K.C. and the rest of the team, we were really talking a lot. We were shoving and pushing each other. We were into it. I was telling him that he had no game, that he wouldn't even be in the NBA if he didn't have Larry Bird passing him the ball all the time for layups, and if he didn't have Robert Parish playing center to guard his man all the time, to force the other team's best defensive player to guard Chief, so Kevin would have a stiff to play against.

He wasn't too impressed with my game either.

K.C. had seen and heard enough.

"I'm sick and tired of this," K.C. said. "I've been listening to this all season long. We're going to settle this right here once and for all. You guys are going to play one on one for keeps in front of the whole team."

K.C. lined everybody up. Red was there too, smoking his cigar. Havlicek and Cowens were in the building. They had armloads of basketballs that they wanted to get auto-graphed and probably sell on the memorabilia market.

I told K.C. that I needed a minute. I went over to the sideline to get myself ready. I made sure my finger tape and wristbands were properly adjusted. I made sure my knee pads were set, that my shoes were properly tied. I told my-self, "Bill, this is your chance. Here you are at the end of your career, broken down, can't play at all, and here you are going up against Kevin McHale. You've got to make the most of this one right here."

At the time, Kevin was the MVP of the league. He wouldn't actually win the award that year because he got hurt toward the end of the season. Bird won it, but McHale was having a phenomenal season.

We walked back to start playing and K.C. said, "Okay, you need a ref."

I looked up and down the whole line of guys. I stopped at D.J. On April 21, 1978, D. J. had played in the game in which I had taken a shot of Xylocaine from the doctor at Portland. It was the game when my foot split in half.

Before that, in the two-month period when my foot first went bad and I was trying to get better to play for Portland, they didn't know what was wrong with me. It eventually turned out that I had a stress fracture. They couldn't or wouldn't find it.

They took me to a hypnotist after everything they tried failed. The hypnotist had me lie down on a table and he swung the watch in front of my eyes. He said, "Your foot is feeling fine. Your foot is feeling fine. Now get your ass out there and start running."

That didn't work.

Then they took me down to the banks of the Willamette River at dawn one day and had me stand in ankle-deep water as the sun rose over the Cascade Mountains to the east. I was supposed to have a religious experience so my foot would get better.

That didn't work.

Then they took me to the training room and said, "We've got some Xylocaine for you." I eventually took the shot of Xylocaine, and man, did that feel great. That was before the game against D. J. and Seattle.

I went out there and played and the bone in my foot split in half. I spent the next twelve years trying to regain my form, which I never did.

But for one brief moment at Hellenic College in 1986, with D. J. as the ref, I went out and I kicked Kevin McHale's ass all over the court.

After I made the game winner, I tossed the ball to K.C. and said, "We're out of here."

"All right," he said, "let's go."

The first day I got to Boston I should have played Kevin McHale for his jersey No. 32. I wore that number at UCLA, Portland and the Clippers, but McHale had it when I got to the Celtics. When he was in high school, he wore No. 32 because I was his idol.

—Bill Russell. Center. Boston Celtics.

Russell is the best player in the history of basketball. In fifteen seasons of national-caliber competition, Russell led his University of San Francisco team to two NCAA championships and the Celtics to eleven NBA titles. He might have had a twelfth NBA championship ring had he not suffered a severely injured ankle against the St. Louis

Hawks in Game 3 of the 1957 finals. Even then, the Celtics took the series to six games, with Russell playing twenty minutes in the last game with a cumbersome ankle brace. The Hawks barely won, 110–109, thanks to Bob Pettit's 50-point game and Russell's injured ankle.

The only other team that won a championship during Russell's tenure was the Philadelphia 76ers in 1967. The Sixers beat the Celtics in the division finals and went on to defeat the San Francisco Warriors in the championship series. All of a sudden people were calling the Sixers the greatest team in the history of the sport. What about the eleven championship teams Russell played on? Philly wins one and it's the greatest? C'mon. What a disgrace. The Sixers wouldn't win another title until 1983. The Celtics, with Russell as center/coach, won the next two.

Russell was not only the best player ever to wear an NBA uniform; he was also my favorite player. To him, basketball was a mental game. He studied everything. He knew the best way to start the fast break, the best way to get a rebound, block a shot, set a screen, make an outlet pass. In his mind, the game was started on the defensive end and it was there that he set the tone, determining the way the game would be played.

Russell was the ultimate clutch player. All too often, though, his offensive contributions were carelessly ignored. He made a lot of key shots during his career. What made him so special was his knack of taking over a game at the precise moment his team needed him to do so. Very few players—Wilt Chamberlain, Kareem Abdul-Jabbar, Larry Bird, Magic Johnson, Michael Jordan—had or have that rare skill. Very few can control the game, every game, by virtue of their basketball talents, by their physical presence.

Russell was so cerebral in his approach to the game. He told me that he could watch an opposing player and, on the basis of that mini-scouting session, decide which of his many

skills he was going to use against him that night. I tried
to prepare for a game the same way.

One of the times while Russell and I spoke together in
his role as a television commentator, we discussed how we
would have played against each other.

"Well," I said, "I'd have to use my superior height and
strength, back you down and then dunk in your face."

He laughed. I think he thought I was kidding.

"It would be a good game between us," I said.

"That's true," he said, no longer laughing. "It would be
very interesting."

Russell told me the games he enjoyed playing the most
were against the smart players, whose numbers, he added,
were far too few. In his opinion, the smartest player he
matched wits with was Oscar Robertson, who combined intelligence with magnificent physical skills. And the second-
smartest player he faced? His nemesis, Wilt Chamberlain,
whom he said was smarter than 95 percent of the players
and coaches in the league.

Russell didn't win those championships by himself. Hanging from the rafters of Boston Garden are the retired jersey
numbers of some excellent players, including K. C. Jones,
Bob Cousy, Bill Sharman, Tom Heinsohn, Sam Jones, Satch
Sanders and Frank Ramsey. Only Sanders isn't in the Naismith Memorial Hall of Fame.

Russell also had Hall of Famer Red Auerbach, who
coached the Celtics to nine of the eleven NBA titles.

Not everything you learn about the game of basketball
comes from the playing court. I learned a lot from the books
I've read on the history of basketball. The best were Wilt
Chamberlain's *Wilt—Just Like Any Other 7-foot Black Millionaire Who Lives Next Door*, Bill Russell's *Second Wind*,
and Jabbar's *Kareem*.

But no book had a greater effect on the way that I approached the game of basketball than Russell's *Go Up for Glory*. I still have my first paperback copy of that book. The book had a profound effect on the way I approached the game and my life. I patterned my game after Russell's. I wanted to be just like Russell. He believed you measured a player's success by the number of championships you won. He considered defense the most important facet of the game. He played with emotion, joy and a fierce competitiveness. Along with Muhammad Ali, Jimmy Connors, Rick Barry, Oscar Robertson and Jabbar, Russell was one of my childhood sporting heroes.

The Walton All-Time Dream Team does not stand alone. It must face the Walton All-Time Opponents. After all, this is all about competition.

The starting lineup:

—Dennis Johnson. Guard. Seattle SuperSonics, Phoenix Suns, Boston Celtics.

You've got to have somebody to slow down Michael Jordan.

D. J. was an incredible clutch player. He would make the most remarkable plays in the world when it mattered most. He was oblivious to pressure. He was one of those players who could change the flow of the game with sheer determination. D. J. had no regard for his well-being when it came time for championship-level basketball.

D. J. has never received the proper respect for what he accomplished during his thirteen-year career. He played on three world championship teams (one in Seattle, two in Boston), was named NBA finals MVP in 1979, never once played on a team that didn't advance to the playoffs and ranks in the top three in postseason assists and in the top ten in postseason points and games played. If you broke down the statistics to include only guards, D. J. would rank near the top in almost every category. It's appropriate that

on the third banner hanging from the rafters of the Boston
Garden, only two retired numbers grace the sheet: Larry
Bird's No. 33 and Dennis Johnson's No. 3.

—Isiah Thomas. Guard. Detroit Pistons.

He is the best little man I've ever seen play the game. In
fact, it's embarrassing to talk about the great little men of
the game because basketball players are good regardless of
size. Mugsy Bogues is a good player. Tiny Archibald and
Calvin Murphy were good players. They don't need quali-
fiers attached to their careers.

Thomas had dazzling offensive skills. The scoring runs
he's capable of going on over short periods are amazing.
He's the kind of player who can get most of a 40-point game
in a single quarter.

Isiah isn't simply a scorer. Top players have to do more
than simply score points. Thomas has a great sense of
timing, of understanding the importance of positioning
and angles. He is a great rebounder, a creative passer
and a tenacious defender. His court sense rivals that of
the greatest players in the history of the game. He's got
it all.

Thomas doesn't have a lot of friends in the NBA. I'm sure
there are reasons, but I don't care what kind of people players are off the court. I'm here to play ball. I'm here to win
games. What other guys do when they're away from the
team, I have absolutely no interest in. I'm not picking these
guys to be my friends. I've got friends. I'm picking these
guys because of how they play ball. I'd rather play on a
team of jerks who win championships than finish second
with a great bunch of guys.

—Rick Barry. Forward. Golden State Warriors.

Until Larry Bird came along, Barry was the best forward
I ever saw play basketball. Rick and Larry were very similar
players. They could do everything, particularly on the offensive end of the floor. Only three other players—Wilt

(1962: 50.4 points per game), Elgin Baylor (1962: 38.3) and Michael Jordan (1987: 37.1)—have ever finished a season with a higher scoring average than Barry's 35.6-point average of 1967.

Barry, like Bird, was a poor individual defensive player, but exceptional on team defense. Barry wasn't as tall as Larry (6'7" vs. 6'9") and he didn't have the rugged body of a Larry Bird. But he could play the game.

—Wilt Chamberlain. Center. Philadelphia 76ers, Los Angeles Lakers.

Wilt could do and did do anything he wanted. He was one of the truly great athletes in the world. Forget basketball. Wilt could play whatever sport he wanted. He was criticized a lot during his career because his teams didn't win more championships. He dominates every page of the record books. He is also the kindest, nicest, sweetest, gentlest person you'd ever want to meet. There are not enough superlatives to describe Wilt's contributions.

—Kareem Abdul-Jabbar. Center. Milwaukee Bucks, Los Angeles Lakers.

A lot of basketball experts regard Jabbar as the best player who ever played the game. Nobody is even close to Jabbar in career statistics. He played seven more seasons than Wilt. He helped UCLA to three NCAA championships and won six NBA titles (one with the Milwaukee Bucks, five with Magic Johnson and the Los Angeles Lakers). Jabbar is one of the very few players—Wilt and maybe Russell being the others—who were dominant at every level of basketball, from high school to college and the pros.

Jabbar was the very best player I ever played against. I never played against Wilt or Russell, but I did face Jordan, Bird and Magic, and it was no contest.

Jabbar had the body, the basketball fundamentals, the strength, the conditioning, the heart, the pride and, of course, the skyhook. He had a tremendous style and part of that style was his ability to stay focused and disciplined. He was extremely organized, very predictable and still so very successful. If he had a weakness in his game, I never found it. I looked as close as I could.

My battles with Jabbar, next to winning championships, were the most exciting moments of my professional career. Jabbar's skills and body were fabulous, but it was his tremendous desire to win that set him apart from the others. He did not want to let his team down. Like all good players, he would complain to the referees about the fouls that were not called. Of all the guys I played against, Jabbar pushed and fouled the most.

Everything I did as a basketball player I did to beat him. I would be riding my bike up a hill, pumping iron, running, lungs burning with fire, the pain excruciating, all the while saying to myself, "Jabbar . . . Jabbar . . . Jabbar—I'm going to get him." He was my ideal opponent, my competition, my archrival, my motivation, my least favorite person. I admired and respected him and hated him at the same time. The night before a game against the Lakers, I would get to eleven very early in the evening and dream about killing him.

I have nothing personal against Jabbar. He was a fantastic player, but he was also my nemesis. Even now, my relationship with Jabbar remains cool, almost adversarial. We're opponents. I have the utmost respect for him, but he's on the other team. He's on ESPN and I'm on NBC.

To compare centers: Wilt led the NBA in scoring seven times and in rebounding eleven times in thirteen years. Jabbar won the scoring title twice and the rebounding title once in twenty years. Jabbar scored more career points than Wilt, but Wilt had a higher career scoring average.

Russell wasn't a prolific scorer like Jabbar or Chamberlain. He didn't have to be. He controlled the game with his defense and his mind, which is much harder to do. Russell had 4,000 more career rebounds than Jabbar in seven fewer seasons.

Dr. J didn't make either one of my teams. Dr. J was easily the most spectacular player I've ever seen. People talk about Jordan, and well they should. But Dr. J had a flamboyance that I've never seen matched.

Dr. J's hands were so big and his ability to hold the ball and maneuver it around while he was in the air was unparalleled. You could have perfect defensive position, yet he would still embarrass you with his creativity and maneuverability. Jordan could do many of those same things, but Dr. J was so much more dramatic, more theatrical. Plus, his Afro and beard made him scarier-looking coming at you. Jordan was a better basketball player than Dr. J. He had a much more accurate outside shot than Dr. J ever did. He was a better dribbler, passer and defender too. Jordan was everything that Dr. J could have been.

There are very few truly great players. Jordan was a driven athlete, the epitome of someone who came to play every game. The loss of Magic and Bird and Jordan from the game is worrisome because the values they brought to the game might be forgotten by the next generation of players.

There are other players in the game today who are good, but certainly not All-Time Team members. They have yet to show the ability to reach the very top level of play.

Guys such as Tim Hardaway and Chris Mullin of the Golden State Warriors are two of the most entertaining players to watch. They work hard at the game and they also play with boundless joy and enthusiasm. Hardaway is the best point guard in the game now that Magic has retired and Isiah has been slowed by age and injuries. Kevin Johnson of the Phoenix Suns is right behind.

Mullin is a classic team guy, a truly fine finisher. His game has blossomed under Coach Don Nelson.

Charles Barkley from Phoenix is another player I enjoy watching. Barkley's career suffered because he started out on top. He joined a Philadelphia 76ers team that was only one season removed from winning the 1983 NBA finals. That team included Dr. J, Moses Malone, Andrew Toney, Maurice Cheeks and Barkley. Bobby Jones came off the bench. Despite that talent, the Sixers were unable to make another run at the title. That hurt Charles emotionally. Now that he's on a winning team again, you can tell the difference in his personality and in his game.

Barkley has a bad habit of blaming someone or something else if he has a poor performance or his team loses a game. Barkley always uses the referees as an excuse. Charles never makes the mistake; it's always the referees who screwed up. The referees don't care who wins the game. They just do the best job they can and go on home.

Every time something goes wrong for Barkley, he claims it's racially motivated.

Barkley is a fabulous bsaketball player, one of the league's elite, but he suffers from a severe lack of personal responsibility. No matter how hard you try, you're not going to win every game and you're not always going to be successful at everything you do. A lack of success doesn't necessarily mean it's someone else's fault. He also takes steps regularly. His footwork is very sloppy.

Jordan obviously came closest to maximizing his abilities. Second on the list would be Hakeem Olajuwon, then Barkley.

Barkley is ready to take the next step up because of the lessons of humility taught to him in the 1993 season during the playoffs. I hope he will come back a better player because of the whipping he took at the hands of the Chicago Bulls. He set himself up as the world's greatest player, but was rudely brought back to earth by Jordan, Pippen and Horace Grant.

Barkley is young enough, smart enough and hungry enough to take that next step.

Karl Malone of the Utah Jazz does a nice job with his game. Malone has come an incredibly long way since his career began in 1985.

Too much emphasis in the game of basketball is on size and strength: the good players are the ones who can jump the highest and run the fastest. Success is determined by how hard you're willing to work to develop your skills, to outthink and outhustle the other guy. Basketball games are won and lost at the highest level because of a player's ability to use his mind. It makes little difference what your body looks like. Through weight training and physical conditioning you can make your body do just about whatever you want it to do. And through constant practice you can develop whatever skills you want. Bird and Magic couldn't run or jump a lick and they weren't close to being the biggest or strongest guys on the court. Their success was the result of hard work and mental preparation.

Three of the biggest upsets in college basketball history involved favorites with dominating big men. North Carolina beat the Wilt Chamberlain-led Kansas Jayhawks in triple overtime, 54–53, in the 1957 NCAA championship game; Houston defeated the Lew Alcindor (Jabbar)–led UCLA Bruins, 71–69, at the Astrodome; Villanova beat the Patrick Ewing-led Georgetown Hoyas, 66–64, in the 1985 NCAA championship game.

The beauty of basketball is that small guys always have a chance. The biggest and strongest players don't rule the game. Most often players such as Jordan, Isiah Thomas, Russell and Magic are the guys who determine the outcome. Wilt, Jabbar and Ewing weren't the reasons their respective teams lost those games. Size and strength don't guarantee success or anything else. Wilt and Jabbar were fabulous players, and Ewing, at the time, was a very good college center. But height is not everything in basketball. If it were, then Manute Bol, Mark Eaton and Chuck Nevitt would be the greatest players in the history of the game. Instead, they're terrible. These types of players have no concept that basketball is a game of position, timing and angles. When you're playing against any of those really tall guys, you only need to remember that they have one-track minds. They think all they have to do is stand under the basket and wait for the game to come to them. What they're actually waiting for is to get dunked on.

In the 1980s there was a trend to try to find the tallest and biggest players in the world and make them into basketball players. That didn't work. Don Nelson took a different approach. His philosophy has finally gained the proper attention. Nelson believes, like John Wooden, that talented basketball players win games. It doesn't matter what size you are, it matters how good you are.

Isiah Thomas and Tim Hardaway are relative midgets. Yet, at crucial times in most games, they're the players who are making the big plays, often right underneath the basket.

John Wooden and I regularly talk on the telephone about life, the world and developments in the game of basketball. On one of those calls in the fall of 1990 I was startled when someone else picked up the phone at his apartment, where he lives alone. It was a voice I didn't recognize.

"Uh . . . this is Bill Walton," I said, hesitantly, thinking I might have misdialed. "Is Coach Wooden there?"

"Yes, he is," said the voice. "And by the way, I know you're heartbroken that you didn't get to play for that fabulous coach at LSU, Dale Brown."

Dale Brown regularly visits Coach Wooden and I just happened to call when they were both there. Brown had recently read that I had been back in Indiana working with Rik Smits, the 7'4" center for the Pacers. A few days later, Brown called me at home in San Diego from Coach Wooden's house.

"Bill, I've got a player down at LSU that I'd like you to come work with," he said.

"Okay," I said.

"He's a center. Shaquille O'Neal's his name."

Dale Brown is an incredibly smart man. He recognized the uniqueness of Shaquille O'Neal. The season before, he had sat Shaquille down for four games and told him, "Right now, you can block shots, run the court and dunk the ball. But there's got to be more. You've got to learn a jump shot, a hook shot and how to pass. You've got to get a feeling of the game."

John Wooden was a visionary in his approach to basketball theory, player development and improving individual technique. John Wooden, when Alcindor and I were at UCLA, had hired former professional basketball players to provide physical contests in practice because of our physical dominance over our collegiate peers. Their job was to manhandle us on every play. They would push, shove, hack, foul, taunt and, in effect, do everything to take us out of our game. These daily muggings prepared us for what would happen during the actual games.

Before I went down to actually work with Shaq, Dale Brown sent me some videotapes of Shaq in action. Shaquille O'Neal's incredible potential was immediately obvious. The more tapes I watched, the more I could see that his athletic ability had kept pace with his size, which isn't always the case with big men. His physical skills were extremely impressive.

Shaq's first season at LSU was dominated on the court

by Chris Jackson and Stanley Roberts. Shaq was basically told to go to the weak side and rebound. But when Jackson left early for the NBA and Roberts flunked out of school, Shaq was thrust into the limelight prematurely and without sufficient help. This young, naive, but wonderful, caring and gentle person was in an incredibly difficult situation—difficult in the sense that everybody wanted a piece of him. I knew from my own experiences exactly what was going through his mind. I constantly stressed to him the importance of being true to himself all the time.

When I arrived for my five-day coaching stint at LSU, Brown's limo was waiting for me at the airport to take me to the Pete Maravich Assembly Center. I was taken immediately to the locker room, where I met Dale in the hallway. Dale wasted no time.

"C'mon," he said, "I want you to meet the team."

Brown took me straight into the locker room, asked for attention and simply said, "Men, this is Bill Walton.

"Bill is going to be here this week to work with Shaq and everyone else here," he said. "I want Bill to feel free to say anything and everything about what any of you are doing and anything I'm doing, as well as the assistant coaches. He is here to impart everything he knows about the game of basketball. There are no limits on what he can tell you guys, even if it's totally contrary to what I've been teaching you."

Few coaches would feel comfortable having someone spend an entire five days on the court with them. Even fewer coaches would want a guy like me to come in to teach their players possibly different techniques and philosophies than the ones taught by the staff. Most coaches aren't that secure in their abilities to do that. Dale Brown is.

I appear regularly on Roy Firestone's *Up Close* show for discussions of the issues surrounding basketball. Prior to the 1993 NCAA tournament, I was part of a roundtable discussion on college basketball with Jim Gray of CBS and Jim Rome, a San Diego sports talk show host. When the discussion swung to LSU's chances, Rome referred to Dale Brown as "a little bit of a wacko."

I felt once again like Billy Martin, constantly having to defend the honor of the New York Yankees. I jumped on Rome about having to defend Dale Brown again.

Dale Brown is many things. Too often people mistake passion and intensity and a zest for life as something other than normal. It's easy to call somebody in Baton Rouge a wacko while sitting in a television studio in Hollywood.

I've come to know Dale Brown very well during the past few years. His teaching ability, his leadership qualities, his strength of character and his willingness to stand up and fight for his beliefs set him apart in college basketball. I wasn't the only former player who worked with Shaq and the rest of the LSU team. Brown brought in Julius Erving to talk to the Tigers about dealing with the media and how to handle fame in a graceful manner. Jabbar spent a day trying to teach Shaq his unstoppable, rhythmic skyhook.

Shortly after I went to LSU, the NCAA passed a rule, generally referred to as "the Bill Walton Rule," that no longer allowed outside consultants to be hired as quasi-coaches. Apparently other Division I schools thought their programs were put at a disadvantage if this sort of thing were allowed to take place. In reality, the only person the NCAA is putting at a disadvantage is someone like O'Neal, who might benefit from an outside point of view. How can knowledge be a negative? Do universities limit guest speakers on an educational level?

Dale Brown has an insatiable appetite to learn. That's really the ultimate test of leadership—your willingness to learn and to listen so that your positions are constantly being refined. Things change. Smart people change and adjust their thinking based on what they know. Dale Brown is always in search of that extra information. When he takes a position on the issues of the day, he backs it up with knowledge and a solid foundation.

Mike Dunleavy of the Milwaukee Bucks is much the same way. Mike constantly looks for new ways and angles to be better at what he does. That way he can do a better job for the guys on his team.

While I was at LSU we did it all. Shaq and I watched films of his games, of other players' games. We watched films of the legends of the NBA. We spent time on the practice court. We went to dinner every night. We would hang out at his dorm room, talking about anything that popped into our minds. Except for the time he spent at classes and when he slept, we were always together.

No subject was too minor to discuss. Agents ... life on the road ... the media ... money ... school ... relationships with teammates ... temptations ... the business of basketball ... coaches. I wanted him to understand what was required to be great. To that end, I gave him a long list of books to read, including Bill Russell's *Go Up for Glory,* as well as Russell's second book, *Second Wind.* Also on the list was Wilt's first book, *Wilt—Just Like Any Other 7-foot Black Millionaire Who Lives Next Door,* Jabbar's books, *Giant Steps* and *Kareem,* and Muhammad Ali's *The Greatest.* I don't know if he ever read any of them.

I told Shaq the same thing I tell everyone I work with: become a complete player. Become Michael Jordan, Magic Johnson and Larry Bird.

It's easy to work with players like Shaquille because he's such a hard worker. He's extremely coachable and has tremendous desire.

I tutor a lot of basketball players, many of whom you wouldn't know because sometimes they don't amount to much. I get calls all the time from coaches who, not knowing how insensitive they sound, say, "Bill, I've got this seven-foot stiff. Will you come work with him and make him into a basketball player."

Shaquille is no stiff. He doesn't play basketball because he's big, he plays because he likes the game, the competition, the spotlight. Most of the big guys in basketball play because one day they were walking down the school hall and a coach said, "Hey, big fella, c'mon, you've got to play on my team." That introduction doesn't exactly generate a real love of the game.

The advantage Shaquille has over so many players his size is his great athletic skills. Some guys you literally have to teach how to run, how to start, how to stop. Players like Shaquille are the most rewarding to work with because they're bumping up against the edge of perfection. The less developed players require a more rudimentary approach. You have to show them the proper way to hold on to the ball, how to position themselves for a rebound. How to tie their shoes. All the stuff John Wooden showed us that first day of practice at UCLA.

Regardless of talent level, everyone—including Shaq—has to learn how to play the game like a guard, like Magic Johnson. You learn the game by going down to the gym and shooting the ball every time you touch it. Forget about passing. Forget about rebounds and defense in pickup games. Nobody else is working on those things, why should you? Be aggressive. Shoot every time, then shoot some more.

I tried to impress upon Shaq the importance of knowing your opposition. Jack Ramsay taught me that when I played for the Trail Blazers.

By the time tip-off arrived, I wanted to know everything about the guy I would face that night. I wanted to be able to read his mind, to anticipate his strategy. I'd watch games on my satellite dish and take notes. I'd read everything I could about him. I'd listen to every TV interview that featured him. I'd study the box score. I'd know his tendencies.

I'd know his travel schedule and his playing schedule. I'd know how his coach was going to use him. I'd know at what points during a game he usually needed to rest. I'd watch him practice. I'd watch him warm up. The more you knew about a player, the better you could attack his weaknesses.

Jabbar . . . Jabbar . . . Jabbar. Almost without fail, Jabbar would get the ball the first five plays of the first half and the first five plays of the second half. The Lakers did that to dictate the tempo and the style of the game, as well as to keep Jabbar interested in the game.

The Lakers pounded the ball inside to Jabbar whenever they needed a big basket. Everyone knew what he was going to do, but who could stop him? Jabbar had scouted the opposition as well.

When Shaquille was at LSU, he listed Michael Jordan as his favorite player in the school's media guide. Good. I hope Shaq follows the path of Jordan and dedicates himself to the game like Jordan did. Jordan came into the league with so much hype, but because of his values as a person and because of his goals and desire to be the greatest, he went beyond the hype of a guy who could dunk. Michael Jordan would be a great basketball player regardless of his size. With him, it's not a factor. It wouldn't matter as long as he could jump.

Michael Jordan would be a star whatever his physical skills were because he has incredible command of the fundamentals of the game of basketball. The way he breaks defenders down when he has the ball, the way he beats people would make a great teaching video on how to execute the basics of basketball. When Jordan gets the ball and has you one on one, he'll beat you. Period. That's how you play basketball. That's what players such as Andrew Toney, the exciting former Philadelphia 76ers guard, and Jabbar did. That's what Shaquille needs to get: an incredible command of the fundamentals of basketball so that he can break down a defender each and every time. Shaquille also needs to shoot the ball. Basketball is about making shots. A shot is anything that isn't a layup or a dunk. It can be a two-foot shot. It can be something as refined and polished as Jabbar's skyhook. But you need something. The guys you play against in the NBA aren't stupid—at least not most of them. They're going to make you shoot the ball and prove to them that you can do something other than dunk. Unless you can shoot, your game will never have a chance to be great.

Shaquille always thinks dunk first, dunk second and finally shot. It isn't a basketball mind-set I'd recommend, although it's imperative that your style of play include the concept of getting to the hoop. It's a big mistake to glorify the dunk.

Television has a lot to do with the dunk's popularity. Almost every basketball sports highlight includes a clip of a dunk. People get so excited about dunking probably because most people can't do it. As a basketball skill, the dunk is overrated. At the highest levels of basketball, there is very little dunking. In championship-caliber play, a player has to make shots.

Making shots requires intense mental preparation. Shot making isn't something you turn on and off like a spigot. You have to come ready, prepared. You don't come out for the center jump and say, "Okay, now it's time to play basketball." Smart players have already mapped out their strategy and played the game a million times over in their heads. Bad and undisciplined ballplayers arrive at the arena and haven't given the game a second thought.

Balance and versatility, two subjects that were both stressed repeatedly at UCLA, are important concepts. John Wooden taught you every skill and every move. He taught you how to get open, how to shoot and how to make and develop shots. He got you to believe the importance of balance and versatility, the ability to flow to the next option when an obstacle was placed in front of you. To adapt instantly so that there's nothing any defender can do to stop you. They can't keep you from winning, from dominating. All they can do is stick another defender on you, maybe two. That's when leadership comes into play. You try to give your teammates the ultimate gift, which is the gift of confidence. You inspire them to believe that "I can kill these guys just like he is."

If you're good, they've got to put two guys on you. Then it's four players vs. three and I don't care who's out there for the other team, you'll win that matchup almost every time. A great player who's not a team player doesn't breathe life into the rest of the squad. If the other players sense that the star doesn't have confidence in them, they'll become hesitant and unproductive. That was the beauty of Magic, Bird and Russell. They made all their teammates feel as if they were the greatest players in the world, that they, not Magic or Bird or Russell, were the reason the team won.

Shaq needs to learn that skill. To be great, he has to inspire.

Shaq can become a playmaker from the center position. Some people love to talk about the point guard being the playmaker. Whoever has the ball is the playmaker. It just so happens that the guards have the ball to begin the play. That doesn't mean they keep it. That doesn't qualify them as playmakers.

Bird was a small forward. He used to be the guy who would make all the plays and most of the great passes for the Celtics. Barkely makes all the plays from the forward position for the Suns. Jordan made all the plays from the shooting guard position. Jabbar, even after Magic came along, made a ton of plays for the Lakers. Wilt did it too, when he set up his finishers, Jerry West and Gail Goodrich.

There is no one in today's NBA game who can match Shaq's sheer athletic ability—his size, his strength, his power, his agility. One of the things he needs to master is the footwork of a Jabbar or Magic or Bird or Jordan.

Shaq couldn't get a break on all the calls he probably deserved in his rookie season. It is a rite of passage in the NBA. Referees were learning his game and Shaq was learning theirs. Shaquille is so big and so strong—much as Artis Gilmore, Darryl Dawkins, Elmore Smith and Wilt were—there will come a time when he'll be able to abuse the three-second rule, to say nothing of offensive fouls. There won't be a thing they'll be able to do about it either.

Vital to Shaq is his work ethic, something his father, a former career Army man, must have taught him. I really enjoy watching guys who work hard—when they play ball, the sweat just runs off their bodies like a river.

The biggest potential problem in Shaq's career has nothing to do with his physical skills; it concerns his attitude. He has to realize that his true success won't be measured by how much money he makes, how many commercials he films or how many products he endorses. His career will be judged on how many games and championships he helps his team win. Will he be able to reach the level attained by Jordan, Magic, Bird, Wilt, Russell and Jabbar? Can he learn to control the game from a winning standpoint? Can he walk onto the court and dictate the game from start to finish? Very few players are able to do that. Shaquille has the potential. Shaquille's destiny and future are in his own hands.

Shaquille and Alonzo Mourning, the wonderfully talented center from the Charlotte Hornets, are the future of this league. The media, the fans and even other players fuel the mentality that thinks there is a need to continually make spectacular plays. Shaq and Alonzo have to understand that it takes perfect, relentless execution of a series of smaller plays to win a basketball game.

Players like Shaq and Alonzo should hire retired players

like Kevin McHale to teach them the footwork, balance, skills and theories required to become a great low-post player.

Shawn Kemp is another player who is capable of joining this elite group. Kemp didn't play college basketball. He went straight from high school to the NBA. Sometimes it shows.

College and high school coaches do a disservice to their players by constantly stroking them while letting them develop bad playing habits. Players like Shaquille O'Neal, Shawn Kemp and Darryl Dawkins, who are blessed with a man's body while they're still children, have to work much harder than their coaches generally force them to do. When you get to the pros, everyone has a man's body. Everyone is as big, fast and tough as you are. That's when you need to rely on the fundamentals. The proper footwork. The discipline. The ability to outthink someone.

Luck also plays a part in determining greatness. A team's future can be determined by a Ping-Pong ball in the lottery or the flip of a coin.

Magic Johnson was the luckiest guy in the history of basketball to get drafted by the Los Angeles Lakers. The luxury of getting to play with Jabbar, instead of the New Orleans Jazz.

Teams get lucky as well. You can't predict how hard a player is willing to work, how much he is willing to sacrifice to push himself to the next level. It's not solely how good you are. Equally important is who you play with. John Wooden and Red Auerbach were masters of building teams with complementary skills. A team only needs one star player.

It is not by accident that the Lakers and Celtics have the most championships. Jerry West's and Red Auerbach's abilities at putting together organizations that make the proper decisions and evaluations regarding personnel separate them from the rest of the NBA.

It is getting tougher to pick players because of the incredible exposure that everyone gets in college. Advantages still exist, though, for the top talent evaluators. Some teams make mistakes by drafting according to need rather than talent. Take the best player available regardless of position.

A classic draft day mistake was made in 1985, when the Sacramento Kings whittled their choice to Arkansas center Joe Kleine or Louisiana Tech forward Karl Malone. The Kings already had Otis Thorpe at power forward, so they passed on Malone and paid the consequences. Sacramento wasn't the only team to misjudge Malone. They liked him, but they didn't think they needed him. They erred. Good basketball players always make room for themselves on a team. Malone would have done that, Thorpe or no Thorpe.

As great as Magic and Bird were, they were incredibly fortunate to play with teammates such as James Worthy, Norm Nixon, Michael Cooper, Jabbar and Wilkes, or Dennis Johnson, Robert Parish and McHale. The leadership, maturity and foresight in the front office is critical to total team success. Chick Hearn, Pat Riley, Bill Sharman and Jerry West were vitally important to the Lakers during their championship years. Auerbach did the same for the Celtics.

A few years ago, there was some talk of New Orleans possibly getting an NBA franchise. I considered an offer made to me by Dale Brown. If the franchise came to the city, Brown was going to be the head coach, general manager and president of the organization. He wanted me to be the player personnel director and also serve as an assistant coach.

I get offers all the time to be a coach, assistant coach, director of player personnel. I prefer my job in broadcasting.

One team with a horrible draft record is the Boston Celtics. Their recent first-round picks have been: 1981, Charles Bradley; 1982, Darren Tillis; 1983, Greg Kite; 1984, Michael Young; 1985, Sam Vincent; 1986, Len Bias; 1987, Reggie Lewis; 1988, Brian Shaw; 1989, Michael Smith; 1990, Dee Brown; 1991, Rick Fox; 1992, Jon Barry. They haven't reached the NBA finals since the 1987 season and haven't won a championship since 1986. As each year passed and the veterans grew older, the new Celtics couldn't or wouldn't take the steps necssary to fill the void.

The Celtics are victims of injury (Bird's back and McHale's ankles, which hastened their retirements), age (McHale's retirement, Parish) and misfortune (Bias's and Reggie Lewis's death). Other teams, like Houston, Portland, New York, Indiana, San Antonio, Atlanta and, until recently, Seattle, were victims of their own low standards. Underachieving teams that never quite reached their expected level.

The teams of the 1990s besides Chicago are going to be Charlotte, Orlando, Golden State and maybe Houston. San Antonio, because of the coaching skills of John Lucas, should be included on the list.

The SuperSonics, because of Shawn Kemp and coach George Karl, are on their way. The Knicks, because of Pat Riley, will always have a chance.

Riley is a phenomenal coach. He doesn't miss a trick and he's willing to adapt to changing times and personnel. At Los Angeles, he won championships with a finesse team. At New York, the material and the conference dictated otherwise. Riley did what was necessary. The common denominator in both of Pat Riley's teams has been how hard and consistently they play.

The Knicks have one of the best defenses in basketball today. They force the other team to try to beat them one on one. They don't give you the luxury of having open guys on your team because they don't needlessly or automatically double-team opponents who don't deserve it.

Riley's problem is that he inherited a team without a great offensive player. Ewing is a good player, but he's not a creative playmaker, he's not a good passer and he's not an especially gifted rebounder. His statistics aren't bad, but he doesn't sweep the boards like the great rebounders in the history of the game. Bird and Magic were great rebounders because they knew where the ball was going. Wilt and Russell were great rebounders, as is Barkley. Without that top scoring threat, the Knicks offense is in trouble because other good teams don't have to double-team Ewing, freeing up spot-up shooters.

Ewing came up totally empty in Games 5 and 6 of the 1993 Eastern Conference championship series against Chicago. It was the greatest opportunity of his life and he was not even a factor in the games. What a disappointment for him.

If there is a championship in the souls of the New York Knicks, Pat Riley will find it . . . or he'll find new players.

Despite their appearances in recent NBA finals, the Trail Blazers are another frustrating team to watch. Anyone who has ever won a championship knows that second-place finishes are or should be the most embarrassing and disappointing moments in their lives, the kind of day that just makes you want to crawl into a hole.

Players like Magic, Bird, Jordan, Wilt, Jabbar, Isiah Thomas and Russell accomplished what they were capable of accomplishing. Some guys don't have what it takes to get to the top. Yet, because of their personalities, their values, their desire and pride, they do better than you could reasonably expect them to. Bird was a perfect example of that.

There are many guys who appear to have everything it

takes to become a great player, but they never reach their potential. This frustrates me and drives me crazy. Lack of discipline, lack of organization and lack of commitment are the usual culprits.

The list of overachieving players is short. It doesn't seem to ever grow much longer.

CHAPTER 13

"Bill, your acceptance speech lasted longer
than your career."
—*Brian McIntyre, NBA, following Bill Walton's
induction speech in the Hall of Fame, 1993*

"When life looks like easy street, there's
danger at your door."
—*Jerry Garcia*

Basketball at all levels has never been more popular.
But basketball, like everything else, needs direction
as it looks to the future.

College basketball is a different game from professional
basketball and needs a different guiding scheme. College
administrators should convince people that the CBA is a
better alternative for marginal student athletes than
college.

College should not be a training ground for professional
basketball players. College should be a beacon for accomplished students, accomplished athletes and accomplished
people who are ready, willing and able to take the next step,
to become the future leaders of our society.

Lloyd Daniels, whom Jerry Tarkanian tried to recruit at
UNLV, had no business being in college. Lloyd Daniels
should have gone straight to the CBA.

The NBA, the CBA and the NCAA need to get together

and create a system that will address the needs of these kinds of athletes. Lloyd Daniels and players like him can turn their lives around once they make the commitment. Players who attend college for the sole purpose of using it as a stepping stone to the pros are abusing the educational process. The players suffer because they miss out on some of the more important things college offers—namely, a safe haven in which to grow and mature at their own pace.

Because non-qualified athletes are taking up seats at colleges, other, less gifted student/athletes have possibly been denied the oportunity to participate in the educational system. Those are the players who most often really want to be there and reap its benefits, who know what it could do for them in an educational, not an athletic sense. There are too many people on athletic scholarships who are always whining and complaining about how they can't wait to leave.

Some will argue that through the magic of osmosis, academically unqualified players will leave college as better people, however short their stay.

If they don't make the grades, get them out of there. There are too many people who want to go to school, who want to work hard and who want to earn a degree. Universities should have very strict academic standards at their schools. They have their own pride and self-respect to think of. Prop. 48 has markedly increased the academic performance levels of most athletes.

David Stern has done a fabulous job with the NBA by insisting that there be a higher standard of behavior than just staying out of jail.

Digger Phelps, when he was at Notre Dame, demanded that his players meet the general student body requirements of Notre Dame. All of his players earned their degrees. When people are expected to produce at higher levels, they generally respond.

Bob Knight has had similar results at Indiana. If a player encounters academic difficulties, he kicks the player off the team until the schoolwork is resolved.

Duke's Mike Krzyzewski demands that his players reach their academic, as well as athletic, potential.

If you accept poor performance and mediocrity, that's what you get. John Wooden always made you believe that if you didn't do your absolute best, you were going to fail. His players rarely lost.

Top recruiters can walk into a prospect's house and usually tell right away if that player can handle college academics. The warning signs are easy to spot: The TV will be on. Styrofoam junk-food containers strewn about. There won't be a single book, magazine or any written material in sight.

The decision to achieve academic success ultimately comes down to the players. These are young men, people who are on their own, making their own decisions. They still have to be taught, supervised and monitored, but they shouldn't be coddled. Coddling is for children.

Dale Brown is constantly throwing players off the LSU basketball team each year. He throws them off because of academic problems, because of social problems. In essence, he throws them off because they aren't willing to take responsibility for themselves.

The NCAA needs to define more clearly the relationship between college sports and television.

The networks want the best schedules possible, the best product without regard to what goes on during the rest of the student athlete's life. Television doesn't really care if a star player has to miss a class to play a game. It wants the star players on the court. The top players attract the viewers.

Television causes games to be scheduled every night of the week. That breeds a quasi-professionalism in college athletics. More than ever, players are living a professional athlete's lifestyle. The glorification of that professional lifestyle hurts the student athletes in their quest to develop a balanced life.

Professional athletes don't have a regular schedule. When you're in the middle of a season, you have no idea what week it is, what time of day it is, what city you're in. All you know is when the next game is. You gear everything in your life to that contest.

In college, there are other responsibilities: a regular schedule of classes, exams. When you add a playing schedule to the mix, and add TV's influence, something gets compromised: the player's regular routine, his studies, his classes.

Bob Knight is right on the money when he complains about the late starting times for evening TV games. The viewers might find the starting times convenient, but maybe someone ought to consider the convenience of the players for once.

The NCAA should insist that each school teach its athletes how to deal with the media.

John Wooden never required us to talk to reporters. So I didn't. I made a mistake.

I was scared to death to talk to them. Actually, I couldn't talk.

I thought the media was going to create an image of me regardless of my input. I didn't have time for that. I wanted to go to college. I wanted to be a student. I didn't have time for interviews. I wanted to go to lectures, to classes, movies, to be part of the entire campus environment.

I had a very limited amount of free time while at UCLA and I didn't want to spend it with notepads and microphones stuck in my face. When I did agree to an interview, it inevitably was a bad experience.

I wasn't wise to the media. That was my problem. It might have helped had there been someone available to teach me the importance of media relations. I had no clue about the relationshp between the media and sports until very late in my career.

I have a tremendous respect for the media. I certainly appreciate the job the media has done in creating a freer society in the United States.

I simply didn't understand, though, the media's responsibility as it relates to sports. I don't regret trying to be a college student. But I'm sure I would have had a better relationship with the media and probably enjoyed a fuller life if someone had taught me how to develop a working relationship with the media. I think college and pro teams do an incredible disservice to their players if they don't provide that help.

A media specialist or coach could explain how to give interviews, how to deal with reporters, how to accept the fact that these reporters are going to sometimes write things about you that you won't like or might not be true, how to develop a working relationship with the media, how to speak, how to answer a question, how to deal with reporters when they're causing you problems, how to say no, how to realize they have a job to do too.

When I played in Portland, the media always wanted to know "Where's Patty Hearst?" and "Why do you wear your hair long?"

How many ways can you say, "I've never met Patty Hearst" and "It's my hair."

If the importance of interviews and media relations had been fully explained to me, I would have done them in a more professional manner.

At UCLA, I would get many requests to appear at functions and awards banquets. Could I please fly to this dinner? Could I please attend this function and receive that award? I would invariably decline the requests, citing my responsibility to classes, homework, lectures, practices, games and anything else that would possibly keep me away. Besides being scared to death of people because of my speech impediment, I just didn't have time for any of this kind of stuff.

Every now and then, John Wooden would tell me, "Bill, we really need you to come to this one awards dinner." Or "Bill, we really need you to make this phone call to this reporter. This is important."

Once he said, "Bill, there are some people who want to give you an award. Can you please give me some dates and times when you can make it."

"Where?" I said.

"They'll come here to campus," John Wooden said. "Just give me a time."

It was in the spring quarter and the season was over. After checking my class schedule we settled on 3:15 P.M. on a certain day. I wrote down the time and date and was on my way.

"Now don't forget, Bill," Wooden said. "You need to be there because they'll want to give you a plaque."

"I'll be there," I said.

On the day of the award, I got out of my last afternoon class about five minutes late. I was wearing sandals, blue jeans and a work shirt. I had bike grease all over me and I was sweating from cranking down to make up the lost time.

I pulled up to the Founders Room at Pauley Pavilion—a nice anteroom where the chancellor hangs out during games—and the door was already open. Rather than park my bike, I just rode right on in.

I knew I was in trouble as soon as I came through the

door. I pedaled in and the room was full of guys in dark blue suits. Our athletic director, J. D. Morgan was there, as was John Wooden. He wasn't too pleased. He just shook his head in dismay and disappointment as I made my way to the front of the room.

"Oh, hi," I said. Deep down I was thinking, "Uh, this just isn't right."

Once inside, I was escorted to a chair and was immediately asked, "Well, Bill, what do you have to say about this?"

"Uh, what am I doing here?" I said.

That's the day I won the 1973 Sullivan Award, which is presented to the world's best amateur athlete. First presented in 1930, the award has been won by only one other basketball player, Bill Bradley.

At the time, I didn't have a clue what the Sullivan Award was. Now, I know. There were about a hundred reporters there, each one of them taking notes of my Sullivan Award ignorance.

The media ripped me unmercifully for not knowing about the award's importance. I was also roundly criticized for my appearance and for riding my bike into the room.

In today's world, none of that would have happened. There would have been massive preparation. I would have been told what I had won and been briefed on its importance. I would have been told about what to wear and been asked to prepare a brief acceptance speech.

Whenever John Wooden would ask me to attend an out-of-town awards banquet, I would tell him to send Greg Lee or Jamaal Wilkes. I felt uncomfortable with the individual attention.

"No, Bill, you've got to go," he would say. "You won the award."

"Well, I'm not going unless you go. I'm also not going if I have to say anything."

Coach Wooden would agree to my deal and he would always deliver a beautiful thank-you speech on my behalf. There was no way I could ever stand up and say anything to large crowds. I was terrified of public speaking. My greatest accomplishment in life is my newfound ability to speak.

Now I'm usually the first to get to the microphone. They can't get me to shut up. I'm making up for lost time. A lot of people wish I'd go back to the days when I couldn't speak, especially the losing coaches, the bad and undisciplined ballplayers and horrible referees.

Thank you, Marty Glickman.

The NCAA needs to convince players not to leave school early for the NBA.

I could have come out early. I could have joined the ABA, made a lot of money and even owned the franchise in Los Angeles. I didn't want to leave. In fact, I wish I could *still* be at UCLA. To me, that was the greatest thing in the world.

Spencer Haywood is the guy responsible for all of this. In 1968, while playing college basketball, he punched a referee and was suspended. He tried to go straight to the pros, but was told he couldn't do so. He sued and won, thus opening the door for players to go straight to the pros at any time.

The arguments concerning this issue are always the same: "Why should a player risk injury and a big NBA contract for his final year of eligibility?" and "What are you going to get out of your final year(s) at school?"

There hasn't yet been a franchise player who received an injury during his final collegiate season that prevented him from going on to the pros—although I recognize that it could happen.

If you do happen to get injured, you will need the education more than ever. There's more to life than making money in professional basketball. You're always going to be able to make money if you have skills. College is where you learn to develop skills. You can't go through life worrying about what might happen. You've got to make things happen for yourself.

I've got big problems with guys rushing off from college for the pros. It seems to be getting worse and worse.

To become eligible for the most recent NBA draft, Chris Webber left Michigan after his sophomore season. Anfernee Hardaway left Memphis State after two years of play (he didn't play his freshman season). Shawn Bradley left Brigham Young after just one year at the school.

Today, it's more a surprise when a top underclassman decides to stay in school, not leave it. Granted, the money is fantastic, but unless there are circumstances in the family that require immediate financial assistance, every underclassman should stay put.

There is tremendous pressure to give up your childhood, to forfeit your youth so that you can join the work force. You've got your whole life to work. Why trade the chance to experience college and all of its greatness to its full degree, earn an education, for an extra year or two of work?

The exodus of underclassmen into the pro ranks hurts everybody. It hurts the colleges, because whole programs can be decimated. It hurts the pros, because more and more players enter the league without a sense of perspective or the fundamental skills. They don't have the necessary foundations in an athletic sense, in an educational sense, in a cultural sense and in a social sense. There's no balance to their lives.

———

The NCAA should resist the idea of providing officially approved stipends or lump-sum payments to college players.

That's what the scholarship is for.

Within the scholarship itself, significant adjustments need to be made to create a more equitable system. In the process, colleges should give athletes a life with dignity and prevent them from seeking out or succumbing to the illegal payments offered by boosters and alumni.

There has to be a way to reflect the differences between going to college in the middle of nowhere and going to an urban college such as UCLA. There has to be some appropriate sliding scale that would take into account how much it actually costs to attend school in Pullman, Washington, or Lawrence, Kansas, as opposed to Los Angeles.

Cash payments for college players are wrong. Are we going to pay Glenn Robinson more than the rest of his Purdue teammates because he scores more points?

I grew up in the 1960s and 1970s. Our material desires were not very great. We were California kids. We weren't looking to drive sports cars or wear fancy clothes. We were happy living in the dorms, in the boardinghouses. We didn't need or want a fancy apartment.

A lot of that had to do with the era. It also had to do with our upbringing.

It's disgusting in college basketball when parents act as agents and pimps for their children. They broker deals during the recruiting process. Later, if the player is extraordinarily talented, they convince him to leave school early for the pro draft. That way, the player can support the parents.

By stooping to such tactics, by scheming to become financial parasites, the parents are failing to teach the most elementary of societal skills: honesty, integrity and ethics, self-reliance and the value of one's own work.

In 1974, when I signed my first professional contract, it was the highest-paying contract in the history of professional team sports. (Nowadays, Michael Jordan makes more money in ten minutes than I did during my entire rookie season.) I offered to buy my parents anything they wanted—

a new house, cars, travel . . . anything. They said no, thanks.

"We're doing fine," they'd say. "You keep what's yours. You've earned it."

Of course, not all situations are alike. Isiah Thomas, who was raised by his mother in one of the worst sections of Chicago, is probably the best example of someone who did something nice for a parent. To spend your money on someone who truly needs it is fine. There are few things worse than those parents, relatives or friends who think they're owed something just because someone they know signed a big professional sports contract.

The next collective-bargaining agreement between the players and management is critical to the long-term prosperity of the NBA. The adoption of the salary cap in the 1980s has made the players literally partners with management in the business of basketball. This partnership has forged a change in the players' sense of responsibility toward promoting their game and themselves. The importance of teamwork for ultimate success is nowhere more evident than in what the salary cap concept has done for the NBA. But for the first time since the mid-1960s, the NBA Players Association will enter the negotiations without Larry Fleisher, the single most important man in the history of professional basketball.

Fleisher, who died in 1989, guided the players union for twenty-eight years. Without ever having to call for a strike, he was able to increase player salaries from an average of $9,400 in 1967 to an average of well over $1 million in recent years.

It is Charles Grantham's turn now.

Grantham, now the executive director of the Players Association, will be the lead negotiator when discussions for a new collective-bargaining agreement begin. That agreement expires after the 1994 season.

In Grantham's hands is the future of many vital issues including increased pensions for ex-players and long-term health benefits for former players.

My body is partially destroyed because of the physical damage caused by a fourteen-year NBA career. Yet I'm not eligible for any sort of NBA medical insurance that will help me pay for the long-term permanent health problems I incurred playing in the NBA.

The league argues: "You no longer work for us. It's your problem now." With the money that's now available in the NBA, there should be a long-term health care plan for long-term former players.

Until I was eligible for coverage under my American Federation of Television and Radio Artists plan, I had to pay an incredible amount of money for a medical insurance plan. Insurers took one look at my medical history and fled. I was in no condition to give chase.

The only carrier who would provide coverage was Prudential, because of their affiliation with the NBA. The policy itself was set in stone, the premiums were unbelievably high and the deductibles were a joke. I had no other choice.

The issue of HIV testing needs to be resolved.

I was initially in favor of mandatory testing for HIV. In a simple world, I think that's what you would want.

This is no simple world, nor is HIV a simple problem that will just go away. In the NBA, many questions arise: How are you going to administer the tests? Who are you going to test? How often are you going to test? What will be the policy if a player tests positive? If a player tests positive, what happens to his contract?

HIV testing will be a very, very big issue, and it should be. One of the most pressing issues of our time deserves decisive, but well-reasoned action.

The league needs to improve the medical care of the players by eliminating the conflict of interest that sometimes exists between the team doctor and the club itself. "Team doctor" is one of the two greatest misnomers in sports. He is not the team's doctor, he's management's doctor. "Free agent" is the other great misnomer in sports.

A player gets hurt. The team management wants and needs him to play. The team management applies presure to the team doctor. The team doctor allows the team's best interests to override the player's best interests.

Doctors should be independent of the team, responsible to the players, and paid by the NBA Players Association.

The players have a right to more of the defined gross revenue.

A big issue in the upcoming collective-bargaining agreement will be the disbursement of merchandising dollars. Right now, that money belongs to the NBA and it's not included in the salary cap.

Players are guaranteed 53 percent of the defined gross revenue. At issue is the definition of "defined gross revenue." Some monies are excluded and some are included. One of the major exclusions is the right to the merchandising dollars, which was negotiated away by the union in exchange for assorted guaranteed dollars and information (pension figures, licensing figures, etc.).

The National Players Association bargained away merchandising income, which, at the time, was negligible. Now it's one of the most successful moneymaking ventures of the league, overshadowed only by the television rights fees.

The players are entitled to their share of the merchandising riches. The owners are going to want to keep it for themselves. Nobody ever bought a ticket to watch an NBA owner at a ballgame.

Still to be determined is the unity and commitment of the top NBA players in support of the union's efforts. In the past, that was never a problem. Hall of Famer Oscar Robertson served as the president of the Players Association and was the lead plaintiff in the union's antitrust lawsuit seeking free agency. He had the support of every player in the league.

Today's union president, Isiah Thomas, must create that same solid coalition. If he can, the union will have unity, which begets the strength, and the power to negotiate.

The game's most influential player, Michael Jordan, was not Isiah Thomas' best friend. Grantham must make sure Charles Barkley, Shaquille O'Neal, Patrick Ewing and the other visible stars of the league are all prominent and active members of the union.

A lot of the responsibility will fall on Isiah's shoulders. Will his being president help or hurt the union? Will he be able to inspire the membership the same way he inspired the Detroit Pistons during their two championship seasons? Can he work with players such as Barkley?

The NBA should arrange for the leasing of a fleet of planes to be used by each of the NBA's twenty-seven teams.

The most important advance since the 24-second shot clock is chartered airplane travel. When I was a player, there were few things worse than dealing with the travel demands of the NBA. Some teams fly charter. Some teams still fly commercial. Some teams fly the MGM Grand charter air service. Some fly charters that might be run by the CIA—the planes seem always to break down.

The commissioner should make the use of MGM Grand a league rule.

Charter air travel cuts the time in half and doubles the quality of basketball played. By flying MGM Grand, you alleviate the pain, the pressure, the delays, the discomfort of traveling. A fresh, well-rested player is a happy player. And a happy player plays better basketball, which is what the ticket buyer and network television want.

Ex-basketball players wake up at 5 A.M every morning the rest of their lives because they're used to those gawd-awful early-morning wake-up calls. Flying charter eliminates the first-flight-out syndrome regularly used by the NBA.

You're on the road and the game is over at 9:45 P.M. By the time you talk to the media, shower and dress, it's close to 10:30. By the time you get back to your hotel room and get something to eat, it's near midnight. But you can't sleep. You've trained to reach your peak physical and mental performance in the evening, between 7:30 P.M. and 10 P.M. You're still pumped up. You can't just go to bed and fall asleep. You toss and turn all night. If you're lucky you fall asleep by 2 or 3 o'clock in the morning.

At 5 A.M., okay, time to go. Welcome to the NBA.

You get up and it takes an hour to check out and travel to the airport. If you fly commercial, try getting a direct flight to Portland, or San Antonio, or Milwaukee, Indianapolis, or Charlotte.

Throughout my NBA career, we always flew commercial, with rare exceptions. We often arrived at the airport at 6 A.M., only to discover that our flight had been delayed because of weather or mechanical problems. We spent all day at the airport, doing nothing but killing time and eating horrible airport food. By the time we eventually arrived in the next city, the day was lost. There was no time for mental preparation. No opportunity to get a quality meal, fuel for the machine. No time to rest. In some extreme cases, the tipoff time had come and gone and we had to proceed straight from the airport, complete with police escort, to the game. Needless to say, we lost all those games, badly. The fans and the sport lost those days as well.

Charter flights take care of that. They provide a team with what little travel flexibility is available. The seats are bigger. The food is better. There are no fans, no autographs that drain you emotionally. Instead, you're resting and focusing on the upcoming game.

The NBA has done so much to improve the quality of play, particularly its rules regarding the schedule. Teams are no longer required to play three, four, or even five games on consecutive days. Nor do they have to play a Saturday night game followed immediately by a Sunday afternoon game, in different cities.

An immediate switch to charter flights would be another giant step in improving the game.

The NBA is in a veritable quandary because of the temptation to expand.

When the Charlotte Hornets and Miami Heat joined the league in time for the 1988–89 season, the other 25 NBA owners split the $32.5 million franchise fee paid by each of those two new teams. The same thing happened when the Minnesota Timberwolves and Orlando Magic—both franchises also paid $32.5 apiece—entered the league in 1989. If the league expands again, the franchise fee is expected to exceed $100 million.

The financial successes of those newest franchises has been remarkable. *Financial World* magazine's 1993 analysis showed that the Hornets were the seventh most valuable franchise in the NBA. The team, worth an estimated $77 million, has only been in existence since the 1988–89 season. Minnesota and Orlando finished an impressive twelfth and fifteenth, respectively.

The NBA must be careful not to be blinded by expansion money.

The player talent pool is already diluted. One of the best things from a purely basketball standpoint that could happen would be for David Stern to eliminate ten teams from the league. Just get rid of them.

Most of the teams in the NBA are without any decent reserve players. Some teams don't even have creditable starting lineups.

The quality of play is not as good as it should be. The number of good players has not expanded at the same rate as the number of teams in the league.

There are 324 active players on NBA rosters. If you got rid of the 120 worst players and reduced the number of teams by ten, the quality of play would skyrocket. Guys who were starters on bad teams would become role players on good teams. I'm not holding my breath.

The NBA is most fortunate to have David Stern as its commissioner. He regularly finds the correct balance between business and sports, between making money and preserving the integrity of the game.

The NBA is looking extremely hard at putting a franchise in Toronto. In due time, there is a need to go beyond the borders of the United States. Mexico City is a great opportunity as well.

It's the quality of the game and the people who play it that keeps the fans coming back.

CHAPTER 14

"We will get by, We will survive."
—*Jerry Garcia*

At 9:15 A.M. on Monday, February 8, 1993, the phone rang in my New York hotel room. Joe O'Brien, the executive director of the Naismith Memorial Basketball Hall of Fame, was on the line.

"Congratulations," he said, "you're among the elite of the basketball world. You've been elected to the Hall of Fame."

I felt a tremendous sense of relief and satisfaction. At last I could let my emotions run free. It was like releasing your hold on a blown-up balloon.

Every player wants to make it to the Hall of Fame. But I don't think players realize its importance until after their basketball careers are finished. By then, you understand what an honor it is to be considered among basketball's best.

This isn't someone slapping you on the back after a victory and saying, "Good game." This isn't getting credit for Larry Bird's ability to win championships, or sharing in the success created by the leadership of Maurice Lucas and Jack Ramsay, or accepting praise because of John Wooden's fabulous teaching methods.

This is an anonymous voice that is accountable to no one. A twenty-four-person Honors Committee comprised of Hall of Fame members, trustees and media representatives who assess your contribution to the game long after your career is complete (five years). I am ever so grateful and feel so proud that those committee members said, "Yes, this person had an impact on the history of basketball."

Up until the very moment O'Brien told me the news, I had serious doubts about earning the necessary number of votes for induction. When the ultimate control of your fate is in someone else's hands, you worry. I lay awake at night hoping and praying I would get there.

O'Brien asked if I could attend a Hall of Fame press conference in New York the next day. I told him that my weekend work with NBC was done but that I was leaving the city in a few hours to broadcast a Mavericks-Lakers game in Los Angeles.

"Bill, please," he said. "It's the Hall of Fame."

He was right. I called the Mavericks with the news, pleading for the day off. They agreed.

It was a bright, beautiful, sunny winter day. I sat down in front of my hotel-room window and stared out at the expansive beauty that is Central Park. It was almost three years to the day since my foot had given out for the final time. Three years to the day that I had to crawl across the pool deck to call my friend on the telephone so he could find my crutches.

I had come so far. As I sat there looking down on the park, I felt very proud. Proud and happy. I've been 6'11" ever since I was nineteen years old, but after O'Brien's call, I actually feel a couple of inches taller now.

My first call was to my mom and dad in San Diego. With

the three-hour time difference, it was only 6:18 there, but they didn't seem to mind.

Without their love and support, I would have never made it to the Hall of Fame. I thanked them for instilling in me the values necessary to become successful in life.

I then called each of the five Hall of Fame members who had had such an incredible impact on my college and professional playing career—John Wooden, Lenny Wilkens, Jack Ramsay, K. C. Jones and Red Auerbach—and thanked them for making me not only a better player but a better person.

My former Portland teammate Steve Jones made an interesting observation about my career. He said, "At this point, you look back on someone's life and hope that they understand their flaws and grow and become better people despite those flaws. You can say that about Bill. He's become a better person than he was twenty years ago. And maybe that's what the basketball gods had in mind for him. Maybe they said, 'We'll give you something, break you down a bit, and in the end you'll be like all the others.' "

I have learned patience and tolerance in my life. I've learned not to hold others to the standards I demand of myself. That wasn't the case when I played basketball. But my life's experiences have pushed me in that direction. The inability to answer the bell, the inability to avoid the injuries and the operations has forced me to change my outlook.

By 10 A.M. February 8, 1993, the results of the Hall of Fame balloting had been made public. The Class of 1993 would include Julius Erving, Dan Issel, Calvin Murphy, Walt Bellamy, Dick McGuire, Ann Meyers, Uljana Semanova and me. After the press release I started to receive thousands of wonderful congratulatory messages from friends around the world.

In typical Celtics fashion, a bottle of Dom Pérignon was

sent to my hotel. My agent, Art Kaminsky of Athletes &
Artists, sent along another.

Each day brought hundreds of heartfelt messages of congratulations. It was incredible and I was moved by the volume and sincerity. Some of the messages brought tears to
my eyes.

The nicest call came from Kevin McHale. He phoned the
day the announcement was made.

"Congratulations, Bill. Your election is richly deserved.
But I just want you to know that you would have never
made it to the Hall of Fame if you hadn't beaten me that
day at Hellenic College."

"Kevin," I said, "I don't belong in the Hall of Fame if I
couldn't beat you."

When you're a basketball player, and you're healthy, you
think you can do anything. Considering my many injuries
and my many missed games, I didn't even think about the
Hall of Fame during my playing days. All I wanted was for
the pain to leave my feet.

But once the ankle fusion alleviated a relative amount
of the pain, my life changed. I could concentrate on other
things: my family and my broadcasting career. And maybe
once in a while I could dream about the way things were
and the Hall of Fame.

It was Auerbach and the Celtics who officially nominated
me for consideration by the Hall of Fame Honors Committee. Both Auerbach and John Wooden wrote beautiful letters to the Hall of Fame on my behalf. Red's letter was two
pages long and detailed my contributions to the game. In
part, he wrote: "It takes a special individual to go from the
league's dominant player to a sixth man's role. Bill was the
type to put the team first and all individual goals second.

He still has a following in Boston, despite setbacks after that first season here. What he helped accomplish was our 16th title. He was great for us on and off the court."

Coach Wooden's four-paragraph handwritten letter to the Honors Committee was brief.

"Dear Friends,

"Although Alcindor is the most valuable player I ever had under my supervision because of the problems he caused opponents at each end of the court, Bill Walton probably was a better all-around player.

"As a matter of fact it is my honest belief that Bill Walton may have been the most fundamentally skilled of any center who played the game during my time.

"Some may have been better in certain areas, such as Bill Russell, Wilt Chamberlain, Nate Thurmond, etc., but I feel if all individual fundamentals on both offense and defense and all team concepts were graded on a one to ten basis by qualified coaches, I believe that Bill Walton would record the highest score.

"It would be a serious error in judgment by the selection committee if he failed to be voted into the Basketball Hall of Fame as soon as he becomes eligible for that honor."

———

Shortly after the Hall of Fame announced its list of inductees for 1993, I was asked to be part of the first *Wheel of Fortune* Sports Superstars Week, with the cash winnings going to our favorite charities. I had never seen the show, didn't know how the game was played, was not aware of Vanna, but was familiar with host Pat Sajak from previous events.

This wouldn't be my first game show appearance. In 1982, I advanced to the finals on *Tic Tac Dough*. An error in strategy cost me the coveted championship, which went to

Dick Butkus, the NFL Hall of Fame linebacker, who is an actor now.

During the taping of that final round of *Tic Tac Dough,* there were several technical problems which caused the director to shut down the set. Butkus and I were told to sit tight until the problems were solved.

As time dragged on, Butkus and I, both extremely bored, got very thirsty. We sent out for some beer and started pounding them down.

When the game resumed, everything was fine. Every question that host Wink Martindale asked, I answered. I was on fire, on a roll. The championship was mine for the taking.

But then I mistakenly chose the wrong square. I didn't pick in a straight line, which allowed Butkus to win the game.

Twelve years later, I was back on the game show circuit. Butkus was still there.

Because of the contestants' schedules, we taped five days' worth of *Wheel of Fortune* in a single day. My first-round opponents were NFL running back Herschel Walker and Olympic champion Jackie Joyner-Kersee.

I'm forty-one years old, but you would have thought I was a hundred and forty-one to hear Walker talk. During the pregame introductions with Sajak, Walker said he enjoyed watching me play when he was a kid.

"And I suppose you watched me in the days of black-and-white television, huh?" I said.

The game itself is cute. You spin a wheel to determine the dollar or prize amount, and then try to solve a puzzle by choosing the appropriate consonants and vowels. This game is apparently the No. 1 moneymaking program on television, which tells you a lot about ourselves.

I had a blast on the show. I beat Walker and Joyner-

Kersee and earned my two charities—the Ex-NBA Players Association and the Rex Foundation (an organization based in Marin County, California, that specializes in musical, educational, environmental and social programs)—a total of $27,470 during that first round. And for myself, I won a gourmet dining trip to Paris.

The top three winners advanced to the championship round. The finalists were NHL Hall of Famer Phil Esposito, who's now the president and general manager of the Tampa Bay Lightning; my old *Tic Tac Dough* nemesis, Butkus; and me.

Esposito solved the first puzzle to take the early lead. Still available for the taking, though, was a car and a Palm Springs vacation package worth $10,954.

The second puzzle category was "The Sixties." Butkus moved ahead on the clues for the six-word phrase, but lost his turn when he asked if there were any D's on the board. There weren't, so it went to Esposito.

Esposito immediately asked for a B. There was one. And then he made the critical mistake.

He asked for a D.

"No?" said Esposito, realizing that Butkus had already missed on his request for the same letter. "What a dum-dum I am."

Meanwhile, Butkus roared with laughter, enough so that Sajak walked over and said, "What we try to do is not laugh at the other players."

But Butkus couldn't help it. Esposito had opened the door with his ill-timed error.

It was my turn. I couldn't believe my good fortune.

"Is the car still available?" I said.

It was, said Sajak.

I spun the wheel and the marker signifying the car settled in front of me. All I had to do was get one letter and the car would be mine.

"An H," I said.

There were two. Butkus was going nuts.

I ran the table, as I should have. After getting the two H's, I decided to solve the puzzle. The answer that buried Butkus was: "Joe Namath Wins the Super Bowl."

Butkus lost on a football puzzle to a basketball player.

Next came a segment where I had to solve a one-word puzzle using six preselected consonants and three consonants and one vowel of my own choosing. By the time I made my picks, five of the word's seven letters flashed up.

It was easy: "Madonna."

Sajak flipped open the grand prize. It was a check for $25,000.

In all, I won $63,924 worth of cash and merchandise. A little more than $47,000 was earmarked for my two charities. Since I already have a car and can't really fit into a Geo Metro Storm, I donated the car to charity too.

The trips to Paris and Palm Springs, though, were mine.

I have received a tremendous amount of public recognition during my playing days, during my broadcast career and even more so during the days following my selection to the Hall of Fame. It all pales in comparison to my appearance on *Wheel of Fortune*.

I used to think I was recognizable person. I had come to grips with the fact that people would see me on the street and say, "That guy looks like Bill Walton. He must be a basketball player." But since that *Wheel of Fortune* appearance, things have gone through the roof. Everywhere I go now people say, "Hey, there's that guy from *Wheel of Fortune*."

The *Wheel of Fortune* championship round aired Friday, May 7, 1993. On Saturday and Sunday, I was in New York doing *NBA Showtime* for NBC. Late Sunday I flew to Springfield for the preinduction news conference and the enshrinement dinner to be held Monday.

What a roll. It would have been nice if I had had some time to sit and really reflect on what it meant to be inducted into the Hall of Fame, but my schedule wouldn't allow it. That's okay. My life is full again. I don't have time to think about what might have been. I'm always thinking now about what will be.

At the Hall of Fame press conference, I tried to explain why the Hall of Fame was so very important to me.

"My career," I said, "was one of frustration and disappointment, which makes today even more special, because everyone else here has the career numbers, the career statistics, career acomplishments to back up their being here. I really don't.

"I'm here and I'm not going to say no, thanks. I'm going to say thank you ever so much."

Mark Heisler, covering the induction ceremonies for the *Los Angeles Times,* put it this way: "Julius Erving made the basketball Hall of Fame on showmanship. Walt Bellamy made it on numbers. Bill Walton made it on love."

What a wonderful time I had at the dinner. My parents and Lori made the trip, as did several friends from Portland, Los Angeles and Alabama. McHale and Jerry Sichting were there too, which was extra special.

John Wooden was unable to attend, but he did appear via a prerecorded congratulatory videotape.

Before each inductee was introduced to the audience, a three-minute highlight film of that player's career was shown.

Issel, of course, was an overachieving star in both the ABA and NBA. He now coaches the Denver Nuggets, the team he played for for nine years. Issel and I had some great battles when I was with the Blazers.

Murphy was a remarkable guard for the Rockets, someone I had known since my days growing up in San Diego.

Bellamy was a prolific scorer during his fourteen-year professional career.

McGuire was a star for the New York Knicks in the 1950s.

Meyers, a UCLA All-American who was named the college player of the year in 1978, was a trendsetter in women's basketball. I knew her from the days I played with her brother, Dave.

Semanova, a 7-foot, 284-pound Latvian center for the U.S.S.R.'s women's dynasty in the 1970s, won two Olympic gold medals and never lost a game from 1958 to 1982. Not one. I thought our 88-game winning streak at UCLA was a big deal. Semanova's record makes our streak and accomplishments look pale by comparison.

Dr. J helped define the way the game is played today.

It was interesting and entertaining that Dr. J's highlight film at the Hall of Fame induction ceremony included lots of footage of him dunking on me. Quite embarrassing, but Julius told the audience that night, "I better watch what I say because I know Bill's up here last."

Jack Ramsay was kind enough to be my presenter. I played my best basketball for Jack and I was honored he agreed to join me for the ceremony.

The recipients were asked to limit their remarks to four minutes, but I had more than four minutes' worth of people to thank.

You only get up there once. I wasn't going to waste my only chance. Now that I've learned how to talk, you can't get me to stop. And we didn't have to go to a commercial break.

I made mention of Dr. J dunking on me.

"I'm sure it happened," I said, "but that's not quite the way I remember it."

I thanked my parents. My coaches. My teammates. And the fans. They had made my life special. I thanked them for their patience, for their support and for pushing me to places that I could never have reached by myself.

When I finally sat down fourteen minutes later, NBA vice president Brian McIntyre remarked that my acceptance speech was longer than my career.

Marty Glickman did a dangerous thing when he set my tongue free.

Unfortunately my four sons were missing from the evening's event. On a great, great day, it was sad for me that my children could not be there to share in the moment. But they had their responsibilities to attend school, which is more important than listening to me give a speech.

I wish John Wooden and Red Auerbach could have been there that night, but health problems prevented them from attending. Auerbach underwent angioplasty surgery to clear a blocked artery the same day I was inducted. As for John Wooden, the long cross-country plane trip would have been too much.

My game was a product of their dreams. I would have felt so proud and honored had they been able to attend. They gave their lives to basketball and I was one of the many beneficiaries of their expertise. I'll never be able to properly thank them.

Of all the thousands of players who have worn an NBA uniform, fewer than 60 have made it into the Hall of Fame. And while it is true that I averaged only 33 games and 13.3 points during my fourteen-year professional career, nobody cherished playing ball more than I did.

Last spring Jerry Garcia, Bob Weir, Phil Lesh and Vince Welnick of the Grateful Dead sang the national anthem at the San Francisco Giants' home opener at Candlestick Park. Jerry commented, "We're like bad architecture—or an old whore," he said. "If you stick around long enough, everyone gets respect eventually."

When I was with the Celtics we'd always tell each other, "Will you just go in there and *do* something."

Maybe I did. Now it's time to move on.

Aiko! Aiko! Jacamo fi na ney.